Edwin F. Taylor
Massachusetts Institute of Technology

John Archibald Wheeler
Princeton University

Spacetime Physics

W. H. Freeman and Company
San Francisco

Preface

The advances of the nineteenth century in mechanics, electromagnetism, and the properties of matter have been drawn together into a harmonious whole by the great modern unifying principles of relativity and the quantum. Teaching introductory physics courses unaided by the power of these simplifying concepts is like doing long division laboriously with Roman numerals, unaware of the advantages of Arabic symbols.

Developed for the first month of a freshman physics course, *Spacetime Physics* exemplifies today's readiness to place the simplifying discoveries of Einstein and others at the beginning of the study of physics rather than at the end. The book provides an elementary, yet sound and rigorous, introduction to relativity and brings closer the day when the student of physics will be as much at home with the geometry of spacetime as the student in an earlier century was with Euclidean geometry.

Preliminary drafts of this book have been used in freshman classes in several institutions, in intermediate classes, and in summer conference courses for college teachers. Calculus employed is minimal (the concept of velocity) and can easily be supplied by the instructor if it has not been covered in an earlier or a concurrent mathematics course. More than one hundred exercises—many of them solved in detail—analyze a wide variety of current experiments, probe the observational and philosophical foundations of relativity, and provide a rich menu of puzzles and paradoxes. A few of the advanced problems (marked with asterisks) require calculus and should prove challenging to upperclass students.

Chapter 1 develops the simplest and most essential properties of spacetime. Apparent paradoxes in spacetime geometry are seen to melt away on comparison with analogous "paradoxes" in the everyday Euclidean geometry of space. A close tie is established between the geometry of spacetime and the physics of freely moving objects. (The spaceman and spaceship on the front cover of the book symbolize the simplicity of physics in a freely falling, or inertial, frame of reference.)

Chapter 2 forgoes traditional—and premature—use of the Newtonian equation $F = ma$ and turns instead directly to the principle of action and reaction and the law of conservation of momentum. Momentum and energy, bursting the bounds of the Newtonian vision, reveal themselves as parts of a larger unity that also encompasses rest mass.

Chapter 3 discusses the limits of special relativity and the domain of general relativity. The book concludes with a panorama of physics as seen from the spacetime viewpoint—a path to the understanding of physics that is truly simple, because "that is how the machinery of the world really works."

Library of Congress Catalogue Card Number: 65-13566

International Standard Book Number: 0-7167-0314-9

987654

Contents

The Geometry of Spacetime

1

1. Parable of the Surveyors

Once upon a time there was a Daytime surveyor who measured off the king's lands. He took his directions of north and east from a magnetic compass needle. Eastward directions from the center of the town square he measured in meters (x in meters). Northward directions were sacred and were measured in a different unit, in miles (y in miles). His records were complete and accurate and were often consulted by the Daytimers. (See Fig. 1.)

Daytime surveyor uses magnetic north

Nighttimers used the services of another surveyor. His north and east directions were based on the North Star. He too measured distances eastward from the center of the town square in meters (x' in meters) and sacred distances north in miles (y' in miles). His records were complete and accurate. Every corner of a plot appeared in his book with its two coordinates, x' and y'.

Nighttime surveyor uses North Star north

One fall a student of surveying turned up with novel openmindedness. Contrary to all previous tradition he attended both of the rival schools operated by the two leaders of surveying. At the day school he learned from one expert his method of recording the location of the gates of the town and the corners of plots of land. At night school he learned the other method. As the days and nights passed the student puzzled more and more in an attempt to find some harmonious relationship between the rival ways of recording location. He carefully compared the records of the two surveyors on the locations of the town gates relative to the center of the town square:

Table 1. Two different sets of records for the same points.

Place	Daytime surveyor's axes oriented to magnetic north (x in meters; y in miles)		Nighttime surveyor's axes oriented to the North Star (x' in meters; y' in miles)	
Town square	0	0	0	0
Gate A	x_A	y_A	x'_A	y'_A
Gate B	x_B	y_B	x'_B	y'_B
Other gates	...	...	...	...

In defiance of tradition, the student took the daring and heretical step to convert northward measurements, previously expressed always in miles, into meters by multiplication with a constant conversion factor, k. He then discovered that the quantity $[(x_A)^2 + (ky_A)^2]^{1/2}$ based on Daytime measurements of the position of gate A had exactly the same numerical value as the quantity

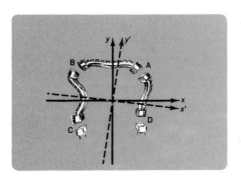

Fig. 1. The town and its gates, showing coordinate axes used by two different surveyors.

$[(x_A')^2 + (ky_A')^2]^{1/2}$ computed from the readings of the Nighttime surveyor for gate A. He tried the same comparison on the readings computed from the recorded positions of gate B, and found agreement here too. The student's excitement grew as he checked his scheme of comparison for all the other town gates and found everywhere agreement. He decided to give his discovery a name. He called the quantity

Discovery: invariance of distance

(1)
$$[(x)^2 + (ky)^2]^{1/2}$$

the *distance* of the point (x, y) from the center of town. He said that he had discovered the *principle of the invariance of distance;* that one gets exactly the same distances from the Daytime coordinates as from the Nighttime coordinates, despite the fact that the two sets of surveyors' numbers are quite different.

This story illustrates the naive state of physics before the discovery of *special relativity* by Einstein of Bern, Lorentz of Leiden, and Poincaré of Paris. How naive?

1. Surveyors in this mythical kingdom measured northward distances in a sacred unit, the mile, different from the unit used in measuring eastward distances. Similarly, people studying physics measured time in a sacred unit, the second, different from the unit used in measuring space. No one thought of using the same unit for both, or of what one could learn by squaring and combining space and time coordinates when both were measured in meters. The conversion factor between seconds and meters, namely the speed of light, $c = 2.997925 \times 10^8$ meters per second, was regarded as a sacred number. It was not recognized as a mere conversion factor like the factor of conversion between miles and meters—a factor that arose out of historical accidents alone, with no deeper physical significance.

2. In the parable the northbound coordinates, y and y', as recorded by the two surveyors did not differ very much because the two directions of north were separated only by the small angle of 10 degrees. At first our mythical student thought the small differences between y and y' were due to surveying error alone. Analogously, people have thought of the time between the explosion of two firecrackers as the same, by whomever observed. Only in 1905 did we learn that the time difference between the second event and the first, or "reference event," really has dif-

ferent values, t and t', for observers in different states of motion. Think of one observer standing quietly in the laboratory. The other observer zooms by in a high-speed rocket. The rocket comes in through the front entry, goes down the middle of the long corridor and out the back door. The first firecracker goes off in the corridor ("reference event") then the other ("event A"). Both observers agree that the reference event establishes the zero of time and the origin for distance measurements. The second explosion occurs, for example, 5 seconds later than the first, as measured by laboratory clocks, and 12 meters further down the corridor. Then its time coordinate is $t_A = 5$ seconds and its position coordinate is $x_A = 12$ meters. Other explosions and events also take place down the length of the corridor. The readings of the two observers can be arranged as in Table 2.

One observer uses laboratory frame

Another observer uses rocket frame

Table 2. Space and time coordinates of the same events as seen by two observers in relative motion. For simplicity the y and z coordinates are zero, and the rocket is moving in the x direction.

| Event | Coordinates as measured by observer who is | |
	standing (x in meters; t in seconds)	moving by in rocket (x' in meters; t' in seconds)
Reference event	0 0	0 0
Event A	x_A t_A	x'_A t'_A
Event B	x_B t_B	x'_B t'_B
Other events	. . . . . .	. . . . . .

3. The mythical student's discovery of the concept of distance is matched by the Einstein-Poincaré discovery in 1905 of the idea of *interval*. The interval as calculated from the one observer's measurements

(2) $$\text{interval} = [(ct_A)^2 - (x_A)^2]^{1/2}$$

Discovery: invariance of interval

agrees with the interval as calculated from the other observer's measurements

(3) $$\text{interval} = [(ct_A')^2 - (x_A')^2]^{1/2}$$

even though the *separate coordinates* employed in the two calculations *do not* agree. The two observers will find different space and time coordinates for events A, B, C, . . . relative to the same reference event, but when they calculate the Einstein *intervals* between these events, their results will agree. *The invariance of the interval*—its independence from the choice of the reference frame—forces one to recognize that time cannot be separated from space. Space and time are part of the single entity, *spacetime*. The geometry of spacetime is truly four-dimensional. In one way of speaking, the "direction of the time axis" depends upon the state of motion of the observer, just as the directions of the y axes employed by the surveyors depend upon their different standards of "north."

The rest of this chapter is an elaboration of the analogy between surveying in space and relating events to one another in spacetime. Table 3 is a preview of this elaboration. To recognize the unity of space and time one follows the procedure that makes a landscape take on meaning—he looks at it from several angles. This is the reason for comparing space and time coordinates of an event in two *different* reference frames in relative motion.

Table 3. Preview: Elaboration of the parable of the surveyors.

Parable of the surveyors: *geometry of space*	*Analogy to physics:* *geometry of spacetime*
The task of the surveyor is to locate the position of a point (gate A) using one of two coordinate systems that are rotated relative to one another.	The task of the physicist is to locate the position and time of an event (firecracker explosion A) using one of two reference frames which are in motion relative to one another.
The two coordinate systems: oriented to magnetic north and to North-Star north.	The two reference frames: the laboratory frame and the rocket frame.
For convenience all surveyors agree to make position measurements with respect to a common origin (the center of the town square).	For convenience all physicists agree to make position and time measurements with respect to a common reference event (explosion of the reference firecracker).
The analysis of the surveyors' results is simplified if x and y coordinates of a point are both measured in the same units, in meters.	The analysis of the physicists' results is simplified if the x and t coordinates of an event are both measured in the same units, in meters.
The *separate* coordinates x_A and y_A of gate A *do not* have the same values respectively in two coordinate systems that are rotated relative to one another.	The *separate* coordinates x_A and t_A of event A *do not* have the same values respectively in two reference frames that are in uniform motion relative to one another.
Invariance of distance. The *distance* $(x_A^2 + y_A^2)^{1/2}$ between gate A and the town square has the same value when calculated using measurements made with respect to either of two rotated coordinate systems (x_A and y_A both measured in meters).	*Invariance of the interval.* The *interval* $(t_A^2 - x_A^2)^{1/2}$ between event A and the reference event has the same value when calculated using measurements made with respect to either of two reference frames in relative motion (x_A and t_A both measured in meters).
Euclidean transformation. Using *Euclidean* geometry, the surveyor can solve the following problem: *Given* the Nighttime coordinates x_A' and y_A' of gate A and the relative inclination of respective coordinate axes, *find* the Daytime coordinates x_A and y_A of the same gate.	*Lorentz transformation.* Using *Lorentz* geometry, the physicist can solve the following problem: *Given* the rocket coordinates x_A' and t_A' of event A and the relative velocity between rocket and laboratory frames, *find* the laboratory coordinates x_A and t_A of the same event.

Measure time in meters

The parable of the surveyors cautions us to use the same unit to measure both distance and time. So use meters for both. Time can be measured in meters. When a mirror is mounted at each end of a stick one-half meter long, a flash of light may be bounced back and forth between these two mirrors. Such a device is a *clock*. This clock may be said to "tick" each time the light flash arrives back at the first mirror. Between ticks the light flash has traveled a round-trip distance of 1 meter. Therefore the unit of time between ticks of this clock is called *1 meter of light-travel time* or more simply *1 meter of time*. (Show that 1 second is approximately equal to 3×10^8 meters of light-travel time.)

One purpose of the physicist is to sort out simple relations between events. To do this here he might as well choose a particular reference frame with respect to which the laws of physics have a simple form. Now, the force of gravity acts on everything near the earth. Its presence complicates the laws of motion as we know them from common experience. In order to eliminate this and other complications, we will, in the next section, focus attention on a freely falling reference frame near the earth. In this reference frame no gravitational forces will be felt. Such a gravitation-free reference frame will be called an *inertial reference frame*. Special relativity deals with the classical laws of physics expressed with respect to an inertial reference frame.

Simplify: Pick freely falling laboratory

The principles of special relativity are remarkably simple. They are very much simpler than the axioms of Euclid or the principles of operating an automobile. Yet both Euclid and the automobile have been mastered—perhaps with insufficient surprise—by generations of ordinary people. Some of the best minds of the twentieth century struggled with the concepts of relativity, not because nature is obscure, but simply because man finds it difficult to outgrow established ways of looking at nature. For us the battle has already been won. The concepts of relativity can now be expressed simply enough to make it easy to think correctly—thus "making the bad difficult and the good easy."† The problem of understanding relativity is no longer one of *learning* but one of *intuition*—a practiced way of seeing. With this way of seeing, a remarkable number of otherwise incomprehensible experimental results are seen to be perfectly natural.‡

2. The Inertial Reference Frame

Less than a month after the surrender at Appomattox ended the American Civil War (1861–65), the French author Jules Verne began writing *A Trip from the Earth to the Moon* and *A Trip around the Moon*.§ Eminent American cannon designers, so the story goes, cast a great cannon in a pit dug in the earth of Florida with the cannon muzzle pointing skyward. From this cannon is fired a 10-ton projectile containing three men and several animals. As the projectile coasts outward in unpowered flight toward the moon after leaving the cannon, its passengers walk normally inside the projectile on the side

†Einstein, in a similar connection, in a letter to the architect Le Corbusier.

‡For a comprehensive set of references to introductory literature concerning the special theory of relativity, together with several reprints of articles, see *Special Relativity Theory*, Selected Reprints, published for the American Association of Physics Teachers by the American Institute of Physics, 335 East 45th Street, New York 17, New York, 1963.

§Paperback edition published by Dover Publications, New York. Hardcover edition published in the Great Illustrated Classics Series by Dodd, Mead and Company, New York, 1962.

IT WAS THE BODY OF SATELLITE.

Fig. 2. Illustration from an early edition of *A Trip around the Moon*. Satellite is the name of the unfortunate dog.

Passenger felt weight in Jules Verne's space ship

nearer the earth (Fig. 3, A). As the trip continues, the passengers find themselves pressed less and less against the floor of the space ship until finally, at the point where the earth and moon exert equal but opposite gravitational attraction for all objects, the passengers float free of the floor. Later, as the ship nears the moon, they walk around once again, but now against the side of the space ship nearer the moon. Early in the trip one of the dogs in the ship had died from injuries sustained at takeoff. The passengers had disposed of the remains of the dog through a scuttle in the side of the space ship, only to find that the corpse continues to float outside the window during the entire trip.

Paradox of passenger and dog

This story leads to a paradox of crucial importance to relativity. Verne thought it reasonable that the gravitational attraction of the earth would keep a passenger pressed against the earth side of the space ship during the early part of the trip. He also thought it reasonable that the dog should remain next to the ship, since both ship and dog independently follow the same path through space. But if the dog floats *outside* the space ship during the entire trip, why doesn't the passenger float around *inside* the space ship? If the ship were sawed in half would the passenger, now "outside," float free of the floor?

Passenger is weightless in real space ship

Our experience with actual space flights enables us to resolve this paradox. Jules Verne was in error about the motion of the passenger inside the space ship. Like the dog outside the ship, the passenger inside independently follows the same path through space as the space ship itself. Therefore he floats freely relative to the ship during the entire trip (Fig. 3,B). It is true that the gravitational field of the earth acts on the passenger. But it also acts on the space ship. In fact, with respect to the earth, the acceleration of the *spaceship* in the gravitational field of the earth is just *equal* to the acceleration of the

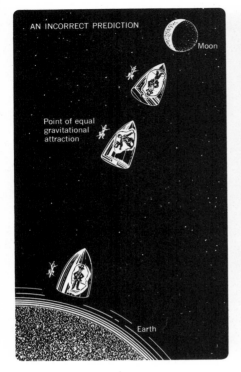

Fig.3, A. Jules Verne believed that a passenger in a free projectile would stand on the side of the projectile nearest to the earth or moon, whichever had greatest gravitational attraction—but that the dog would float along beside the projectile during the entire trip.

Fig 3, B. Correct prediction is that a passenger would float with respect to the projectile during entire trip. Verne was correct about the motion of the dog.

passenger in the gravitational field of the earth. Because of the equality of these accelerations there will be no *relative* acceleration between passenger and space ship. Thus the space ship serves as a reference frame ("inertial reference frame") relative to which the passenger does not experience an acceleration.

To say that the acceleration of the passenger relative to the space ship is zero is not to say that his velocity relative to it is necessarily also zero. He may have jumped from the floor or sprung from the side—in which case he will hurtle across the space and strike the opposite wall. However, when he has zero initial velocity relative to the ship the situation is particularly interesting, for he will also have zero velocity relative to it at all later times. He and the ship will follow identical paths through space. How remarkable that the passenger who cannot see the outside nevertheless moves on this deterministic orbit. Without a way to control his motion and even with his eyes closed he will not touch the wall. How could one do better at eliminating gravitational influences!

A modern space ship carrying a passenger is shot vertically from the earth, rises, and falls back toward the earth (Fig. 4). (The passenger of an elevator car experiences a close approximation to this fall when the elevator cable is cut!) Choose this freely falling space ship as the best possible reference frame in which to do physics. This reference frame is best because, among other

Concept of inertial reference frame

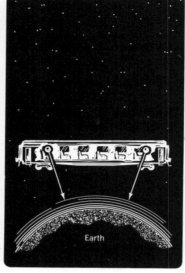

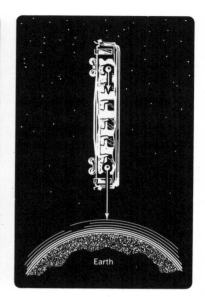

Fig. 4. Space ship in free fall near the earth.

Fig. 5. Railway coach in free fall in *horizontal* position near the earth.

Fig. 6. Railway coach in free fall in *vertical* position near the earth.

things, the laws of motion of a particle are simple in a falling space vehicle. A free particle at rest in the vehicle remains at rest in the vehicle. When the particle is given a gentle push, it moves across the vehicle in a straight line with constant speed. Further experiments show that *all* the laws of mechanics can be expressed simply with respect to a falling space ship. We call such a space ship that rises or falls freely—or more generally moves freely in space— an *inertial reference frame*.

Look at the freely falling space ship from the surface of the earth. There is a simple reason why the free particle at rest relative to the space ship remains at rest in the space ship. This reason is that, with respect to the surface of the earth, the particle and the space ship both fall with the same acceleration (Fig. 4). It is because of this equal acceleration that the *relative* positions of the particle and the space ship do not change if the particle is originally at rest in the space ship.

The definition of an inertial frame requires that *no gravitational forces will be felt in it*. If such a reference frame is to be a space ship near the earth, it cannot be a very large one because widely separated particles within it will be differently affected by the *nonuniform* gravitational field of the earth. For example, particles released side by side will each be attracted toward the center of the earth, so they will move closer together as observed from the falling space ship (Fig. 5). As another example, think of the two particles being released far apart vertically but directly above one another (Fig. 6). Their gravitational accelerations toward the earth will be in the same direction. However the particle nearer the earth will slowly leave the other one behind: the two particles will move farther apart as the space ship falls. In either of these instances the laws of mechanics will not be simple in a very large space ship: the large space ship will not be an inertial frame.

Earth's pull nonuniform: large space ship is not inertial frame

Now, we want the laws of mechanics to look simple in the space ship. Therefore we want to eliminate all relative accelerations produced by external causes—"eliminate" meaning to reduce these accelerations below the limit of detection so that they will not interfere with the more important accelerations we wish to study, such as those produced when two particles collide. This can be done by choosing a space ship that is sufficiently small. The smaller the space ship, the smaller will be the relative accelerations of objects at different points in the space ship. Let someone have instruments for the detection of relative accelerations with any given degree of sensitivity. No matter how fine that sensitivity, the space ship can always be made so small that these perturbing relative accelerations are too small to be detectable. Within these limits of sensitivity the space ship is then an *inertial reference frame*.

When is a space ship or any other vehicle small enough to be called an inertial reference frame? Or when is the relative acceleration of free particles at opposite ends of the vehicle too slight to be detected? Analyzing the conditions inside one vehicle will serve to illustrate these considerations. A railway coach 25 meters long is dropped in a *horizontal* position from a height of 250 meters onto the surface of the earth (Fig. 5). The time from release to impact is about 7 seconds, or about 21×10^8 meters of light-travel time. Let tiny ball bearings be released initially from rest—and in mid-air—at opposite ends of the coach. Then, during the time of fall, they will move *toward* each other a distance of 10^{-3} meters—the thickness of 9 pages of this book—because of the difference in *direction* of the earth's gravitational pull upon them (see Ex. 32). As another example, assume that the same railway coach is dropped in a *vertical* position, and that the lower end of the coach is initially 250 meters from the surface of the earth (Fig. 6). Again two tiny ball bearings are released from rest at opposite ends of the coach. In this case, during the time of fall, the ball bearings will move *apart* by a distance of 2×10^{-3} meters because of the greater gravitational acceleration of the one nearer the earth. In either of these examples let the measuring equipment in use in the coach be just short of the sensitivity required to detect the relative motion of the ball bearings. Then, with equipment of this degree of sensitivity, and with the limited time of observation, the railway coach—or, to use an earlier example, the freely falling space ship—serves as an inertial reference frame. When the sensitivity of the measuring equipment is increased, then the space ship will not serve as an inertial reference frame unless changes are made. Either the 25-meter domain in which observations are made must be shortened, or the time given to the observations must be decreased. Or, better, some appropriate combination of the space and time dimensions of the region under observation must be cut down. Or, as a final alternative, the whole apparatus must be shot by a rocket (part c of Ex. 32) up to a region of space where one cannot detect the "differential in the gravitational acceleration" between one side of the coach and another—to use one way of speaking. In another way of speaking, the accelerations of the particles *relative to the coach* must be too small to be perceived. These relative accelerations can be measured from inside the coach without observing anything external. Only when these relative accelerations are too small to be detected is there a reference frame with respect to which the laws of motion are simple—an *inertial reference frame*.

A reference frame is said to be inertial in a certain region of space and time when, throughout that region of spacetime, and within some specified accuracy, every test particle that is initially at rest remains at rest, and every test particle that is initially in motion continues that motion without change in speed or in

Example of space ship small enough to be inertial frame

Inertial reference frame defined

direction. An inertial reference frame is also called a *Lorentz reference frame.* In terms of this definition, inertial frames are necessarily always *local* ones, that is, inertial in a limited region of spacetime.

"Region of spacetime." What is the precise meaning of this term? The long narrow railway coach in the example served as a means to probe spacetime for a limited stretch of time and in one or another single direction in space. It can be oriented north-south, or east-west, or up-down. Whatever the orientation, the relative acceleration of the tiny ball bearings released at the two ends can be measured. For all three directions—and for all intermediate directions—let it be found by calculation that the relative drift of the two test particles is half the minimum detectable amount or less. Then throughout a cube of space 25 meters on an edge and for a lapse of time of 7 seconds, test particles moving every which way depart from straight-line motion by undetectable amounts.

Region of spacetime defined

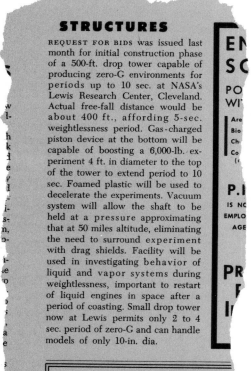

STRUCTURES

REQUEST FOR BIDS was issued last month for initial construction phase of a 500-ft. drop tower capable of producing zero-G environments for periods up to 10 sec. at NASA's Lewis Research Center, Cleveland. Actual free-fall distance would be about 400 ft., affording 5-sec. weightlessness period. Gas-charged piston device at the bottom will be capable of boosting a 6,000-lb. experiment 4 ft. in diameter to the top of the tower to extend period to 10 sec. Foamed plastic will be used to decelerate the experiments. Vacuum system will allow the shaft to be held at a pressure approximating that at 50 miles altitude, eliminating the need to surround experiment with drag shields. Facility will be used in investigating behavior of liquid and vapor systems during weightlessness, important to restart of liquid engines in space after a period of coasting. Small drop tower now at Lewis permits only 2 to 4 sec. period of zero-G and can handle models of only 10-in. dia.

SPACE SYS

Fig. 7. Modern inertial reference frame. From *Engineering Opportunities*, March 1964.

In other words, the reference frame is inertial in a region of spacetime with dimensions

(25 meters $\times$ 25 meters $\times$ 25 meters of space) $\times$ (21 $\times$ 10^8 meters of time)

For a discussion of spacetime regions larger than those of local inertial frames, see Chapter 3.

"Test particle." How small must a particle be to qualify as a test particle? It must have so little mass that, within some specified accuracy, its presence will not affect the motion of other nearby particles. In terms of Newtonian mechanics the gravitational attraction of the test particle for other particles must be negligible within the accuracy specified. As an example, consider a particle of mass 10 kilograms. A second and less massive particle placed one-tenth meter from it and initially at rest will, in less than three minutes, undergo a displacement of 10^{-3} meters. Thus the 10-kilogram object is not—in this sense—a test particle. A test particle *responds* to gravitational forces but it does not itself *produce* any significant gravitational force.

Test particle defined

It would be impossible to define an inertial reference frame if it were not for a remarkable feature of nature. Particles of different size, shape, and material in the same location all fall with the *same acceleration* toward the earth. If this were not so, an observer inside a falling space ship would notice a relative acceleration among different particles even when they are close together; at least some of the particles initially at rest would not remain at rest; that is, the space ship would not be an inertial reference frame according to the definition. How sure are we that particles in the *same* location but of *different* substances all fall toward the earth with the same acceleration? According to legend Galileo dropped balls made of different materials from the Leaning Tower of Pisa in order to verify this assumption.† In 1922 Baron Roland von Eötvös checked to an accuracy of five parts in 10^9 that the earth imparts the same acceleration to wood and to platinum. More recently Robert H. Dicke has pointed out that the sun is more suitable than the earth as source for the gravitational acceleration that one will measure (see Ex. 35). The alternation in direction of the sun's pull every 12 hours lends itself to fantastic amplification by resonance. Cylinders of aluminum and gold experience accelerations due to the sun (0.59×10^{-2} meters per second per second) that are the same to three parts in a hundred thousand million (3 in 10^{11}), according to R. H. Dicke and Peter G. Roll.‡ This is one of the most sensitive checks of a fundamental physical principle in all of physics: the identity of the acceleration produced by gravity in every kind of test particle.

Inertial frame is definable because all substances fall with same acceleration

It follows from this principle that a particle made of *any* material can be used as a test particle to determine whether a given reference frame is inertial. A reference frame that is inertial for one kind of test particle will be inertial for all kinds of test particles.

3. The Principle of Relativity

We describe the motion of test particles with reference to a particular reference frame in order to determine whether that frame is inertial. The same test particles and—if they collide—the same collisions may be described with reference to more than one inertial frame. The one reference frame might be carried by a space ship built like a hollow cylinder (Fig. 8,A), the other by a second craft of similar construction just enough smaller to zoom through in-

---

†On the question whether Galileo actually performed this experiment, see *Physics the Pioneer Science* by Lloyd W. Taylor, (Dover Publications, New York, 1959), Vol. 1, p. 25.

‡See the chapter on experimental relativity by Dicke in *Relativity, Groups, and Topology*, edited by C. and B. DeWitt, (Gordon and Breach, New York, 1964), pp. 173–177 or the book by Dicke *The Theoretical Significance of Experimental Relativity* (Gordon and Breach, New York, 1964).

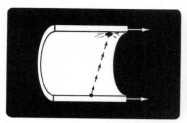
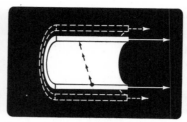
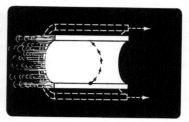

A. Typical test particle as seen from one inertial reference frame

B. Same test particle as seen from a second inertial reference frame moving with respect to the first one

C. Same test particle as seen from an accelerated—and therefore *noninertial*—reference frame

Fig. 8. Inertial reference frames versus accelerated reference frame.

Overlapping inertial frames move with uniform relative velocity

side as it catches up with the first and passes it (Fig. 8,B). There is a region of spacetime common to the interior of both vehicles during the time of passing. Flying across this region in one direction or another are numerous test particles. Every track will be straight as plotted with respect to the coordinates of one reference frame—and also with respect to the other frame—because both are *inertial* frames. This straightness in both frames is possible only because *one inertial reference frame has uniform velocity relative to any second and overlapping inertial reference frame.* In contrast, if the second rocket ship is powered so that it accelerates as it passes through the first ship (Fig. 8,C), test particles will follow curved paths—as observed from this second rocket. If the curvature of these paths is detectable with given equipment, then such an accelerated reference frame is a noninertial frame.

In each of two *inertial* frames in uniform relative motion, every test particle that is in motion continues that motion without change in speed or in direction, even though the direction and speed of a given particle will not look the same in both frames. Indeed, we have *defined* the inertial frame in such a way that the following law of mechanics (Newton's first law) is true in every inertial reference frame: "A free particle at rest remains at rest, and a free particle in motion continues that motion without change in speed or in direction." There are additional laws of mechanics. Each of these laws also holds true—according to experiment—in every inertial reference frame.

Relativity: laws of physics are same in every inertial frame

Do other laws of physics maintain their validity in every inertial frame? In designing electrical circuits for a jet plane must an electrical engineer use different circuit laws because the plane will be moving? Must different electromagnetic laws of radiation be used in designing a radio transmitter for a space probe because of the motion of the probe? If a small proton accelerator together with its targets and particle-detecting equipment is mounted on a railway flatcar, will the interpretation of collision experiments with protons require the use of different laws when the flatcar is moving uniformly than when the flatcar is at rest? As far as we know the answer to these three questions and others like them is "No." In spite of the most diligent search no one has ever found any violation of the following principle:

All the laws of physics are the same in every inertial reference frame.

We will call this statement the *principle of relativity*. The principle of relativity says that once the laws of physics have been derived in one inertial reference frame, they can be applied without modification in any other inertial reference frame. Both the *form* of the laws of physics and the *numerical values of the physical constants* that these laws contain are the same in every inertial reference frame. All inertial frames are equivalent in terms of *every* law of physics. Expressed in negative terms, the principle of relativity says that *the laws of physics cannot provide a way to distinguish one inertial frame from another*—any more than the surveyor's tape and level give a means to tell North Star north from magnetic north!

Notice what the principle of relativity does *not* say. It does not say that the time between events A and B will appear the same when measured from two different inertial reference frames. Neither does it say that spatial separation between the two events will be the same in the two frames. Ordinarily neither times nor distances will be the same in the two frames—any more than the northward and eastward components of the separation of gates A and B as read by the Daytime surveyor are identical to those recorded by the Nighttime surveyor. In consequence the momentum of a given particle will have a value in one frame that is different from its value in a second frame. Even the time rate-of-change of momentum will ordinarily differ between the two frames. And so will the force. Thus, when studying the motion of a charged particle, two observers in relative motion will not necessarily find the same values for the electric field or the magnetic field acting upon this charged particle. The total force, produced by the electric and magnetic fields together, will differ between the one inertial reference frame and the other.

What principle of relativity does NOT say!

The physics that is so different between one frame and the other is nevertheless the same in the two frames! Physical quantities differ in *value* between the two frames but fulfill identical *laws*. The time rate-of-change of momentum in one frame is equal to the total force as measured in that frame (Newton's second law). The time rate-of-change of momentum in the second frame is equal to the total force as measured in that second frame:

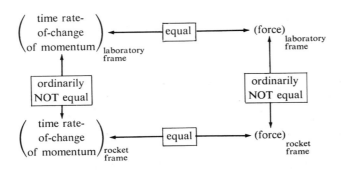

Not only the laws of mechanics but also the laws of electromagnetism and all other laws of physics hold true as well in one inertial reference frame as in any other inertial reference frame. This is what it means to say that "the laws of physics cannot provide a way to distinguish one inertial reference frame from another."

The laws of electromagnetism hold true as well in one inertial reference frame as in any other inertial reference frame. The numerical value of the speed of light, $c = 2.997925 \times 10^8$ meters per second, is one of the constants which appears in the laws of electromagnetism. According to the principle of relativity this experimental value must be the same in each of two inertial reference frames in uniform relative motion. Has experiment shown this to be true? The answer is yes, but the experiments to date are much less sensitive than they should be for so important a question. For the moment let us pull in our horns and concentrate on a simpler question which *can* be answered definitively. The laws of electromagnetism contain no expressions that depend upon direction. Therefore one expects to find the round-trip speed of a flash of light to be the same whether the flash travels north-south or east-west: the speed of light is *isotropic*. But now let these same flashes of light be observed from a uniformly moving rocket. With respect to this rocket, will the round-trip speed of light not be different for light moving out and back along different lines? The principle of relativity says *no*: the speed of light, which is isotropic in one inertial frame, is also isotropic in all other inertial frames that share the same spacetime region.

Michelson-Morley experiment: speed of light is isotropic in all inertial frames

How strange this result is! We know that the speed of sound in air is the same in all directions if the air is still. But let a stiff wind be blowing—or, to get the same result, move through the still air in an automobile. Then, with respect to the automobile, the "downstream speed of sound" is greater than the "upstream speed of sound." And a simple calculation shows that both these speeds are different from the speed of sound measured across the wind. The round-trip speed of sound measured with respect to the automobile will be different in different directions. The same result is true for every other form of wave motion we know about—except that of light! How can we be so sure that this result is *not* true for experiments with light? Our assurance is based on a series of refined experiments beginning with the classic experiment of A. A. Michelson and E. W. Morley performed after 1880.[†] They used the earth itself as a moving reference frame. (The earth is effectively an inertial frame for local experiments with light—see Ex. 31.) The earth moves at a speed of about 30 kilometers per second in its orbit about the sun. In essence, Michelson and Morley compared the round-trip speed of light along the line of the earth's motion with the speed of light perpendicular to this line. They repeated this experiment at different times of the year, when the earth was moving in different directions with respect to the fixed stars. No effect of the motion of the earth on the relative speed of light in the two perpendicular directions was observed. From the accuracy of their experiment they determined that the measured speed of light in the two perpendicular directions was the same to a sensitivity of one-sixth of the orbital speed of the earth (see Ex. 33). More recent experiments have reduced this uncertainty to three percent of the orbital speed of the earth.[‡] The Michelson-Morley experiment and its modern improvements tell us that in every inertial frame the round-trip speed of light is the same in every direction—the speed of light is *isotropic* in both laboratory and rocket frames as predicted by the principle of relativity. But the principle of relativity says more than this. Not only must the speed of light be isotropic in the laboratory frame—and also isotropic in the rocket frame—but also, if

[†]A. A. Michelson and E. W. Morley, American Journal of Science, **34**, 333 (1887).

[‡]T. S. Jaseja, A. Javan, J. Murray, and C. H. Townes, Physical Review, **133**, A1221 (1964).

Table 4. Modern tests to answer the question, "Does the round-trip speed of light differ between one reference frame and another?"

TWO REFERENCE FRAMES

ONE REFERENCE FRAME

The earth moving in one direction around the sun in, say, January.

ANOTHER REFERENCE FRAME

The earth moving in the opposite direction (with respect to the fixed stars) in July.

EXPERIMENTAL RESULTS

RESULT OF THE MICHELSON-MORLEY EXPERIMENTS

Original experiment

Observers in neither frame (may be the *same* observer on earth who repeats the experiment after waiting six months) can detect differences in the round-trip speed of light in any two perpendicular directions greater than one-sixth of the speed of the earth in its orbit.

The more modern experiment

Observers in neither frame can detect differences in the round-trip speed of light in any two perpendicular directions greater than three percent of the speed of the earth in its orbit.

RESULT OF THE KENNEDY-THORNDIKE EXPERIMENT

The round-trip speed of light is the same in one of the seasonal reference frames defined above as in the other reference frame with a sensitivity of about two meters per second.

INTERPRETATION OF THE EXPERIMENTS

THE MORE MODERN MICHELSON-MORLEY EXPERIMENT

The speed of the earth in its orbit about the sun is

30 kilometers per second = 1/10,000 of the speed of light

Thus the *difference* of the round-trip speed of light measured in two perpendicular directions is

less than 3/100 of 1/10,000 of the speed of light
which is less than 3/1,000,000 of the speed of light

Therefore the *principle of relativity* is supported by this modern experiment with a sensitivity of

three parts in a million

THE KENNEDY-THORNDIKE EXPERIMENT

The *difference* of the round-trip speed of light as measured in the two frames is
less than about 2 meters per second
which is less than 1/100,000,000 of the speed of light

Therefore the *principle of relativity* is supported by this experiment with a sensitivity of
one part in a hundred million

*Kennedy-Thorndike
experiment: speed of
light has same
numerical value in all
inertial frames*

this principle is correct, the *numerical value* of this isotropic speed, $c =$ 2.997925×10^8 meters per second, must be the same in the rocket frame as in the laboratory frame. Can this prediction also be verified by experiment? This verification was carried out by R. J. Kennedy and E. M. Thorndike about 50 years after Michelson and Morley did their experiment.[†] Like Michelson and Morley, Kennedy and Thorndike used the earth as a moving reference frame. They tried to detect any variation in the magnitude of the round-trip speed of light as the earth moved in different directions around the sun at different times of the year. From the accuracy of their negative results one can conclude that there is no difference as great as about two meters per second in the round-trip speed of light as between two reference frames with a relative velocity of 60 kilometers per second (twice the speed of the earth in its orbit; see Ex. 34). In the Kennedy-Thorndike experiment the standard of length is the interferometer base itself, a single block of fused quartz kept in a vacuum at a temperature constant to about a thousandth of a degree. The standard of time is provided by the characteristic vibration period associated with a particular green spectral line of a mercury atom. Keeping conditions constant for months constituted the most important single difficulty—and difference—of this Pasadena, California experiment as contrasted to the Cleveland, Ohio Michelson-Morley experiment, where the relevant comparisons (one direction as against another) could be made in the course of a single day. Table 4 summarizes the conclusions of the Michelson-Morley and the Kennedy-Thorndike experiments.

Although the sensitivity of neither of these experiments is as great as that of the Eötvös-Dicke experiment (three parts in a hundred thousand million), the results are nonetheless striking experimental support for the principle of relativity. Happily, there are plans to improve the sensitivity of the Kennedy-Thorndike experiment.[‡] This improvement in sensitivity is important. The measurement of time in meters of light-travel time has meaning only if light travels one meter in the same time in all frames. The equality of the speed of light in rocket and laboratory frames provides a simple way (Section 5) to compare clocks between the two frames. This comparison depends for its validity on the null result of the Kennedy-Thorndike experiment.

*Structure of spacetime
makes LINAC cost
$300,000,000*

In 1905 the principle of relativity was a shocking heresy, which offended the intuition and common-sense way of looking at nature of most physicists. It has taken a long time to become accustomed to the apparently absurd idea that one particular speed has the same value measured in two overlapping inertial frames in relative motion. The principle of relativity is used every day in many fields of physics where it is continually under severe tests. For example, the Stanford Linear Electron Accelerator (estimated cost: $300,000,000) has to be two miles long to push electrons up to a speed that is almost the speed of light (the difference from the speed of light is only 8 parts in 10^{11}). If the pre-Einstein Newtonian laws of mechanics were correct, then the accelerator

---

[†]R. J. Kennedy and E. M. Thorndike, Physical Review, **42,** 400 (1932).

[‡]See Jaseja, Javan, Murray, and Townes, Physical Review, **133,** A1221 (1964). For a careful analysis of the experimental foundations of special relativity see H. P. Robertson, "Postulate versus Observation in the Special Theory of Relativity," Reviews of Modern Physics, **21,** 378 (1949).

would need to be less than one inch long (Ex. 55) to produce electrons with the same speed!

4. The Coordinates of an Event

The inertial reference frame is to a student of physics what the north-south east-west grid of lines in a township is to a surveyor. The surveyor is concerned with position in space. The student of physics is concerned with location of an event in space and in *time*. The Daytime and Nighttime surveyors *could* have dispensed with north-south and east-west coordinates and simply measured the *distance* between any two gates; but at the start they did not even know there was any such quantity as "distance." In the same way in this chapter we could have gone about locating events in spacetime solely by measuring the *intervals* between one event and another, without any regard for "space" and "time" coordinates individually.† However, we have to start as physics did before 1905, without benefit of any concept of interval. This concept will force itself upon our attention as the concept of distance forced itself upon the surveyors. The two men measured north-south and east-west coordinates in two different coordinate systems. Only later did they see the connection ("invariance of the distance") between the very different numbers in their notebooks. Similarly, we will begin with space and time coordinates of events in the laboratory reference frame, and space and time coordinates of the same events in the rocket reference frame. Then there will be a firm basis for concluding that the interval between two events as determined from laboratory numbers is identical with the interval between the same two events as calculated from the very different rocket readings ("invariance of the interval").

Why use coordinates?

The fundamental concept in surveying is a *place*. The fundamental concept in physics is an *event*. An event is specified not only by a place but also by a time of happening. Some examples of events are: emission of particles or flashes of light (explosions), reflection or absorption of particles or light flashes, collisions, and near-collisions called *coincidences*.

Event defined

How can one determine the place and time at which an event occurs in a given inertial reference frame? Think of constructing a frame by assembling meter sticks into a cubical latticework similar to the "jungle gym" seen on playgrounds (Fig. 9). At every intersection of this latticework fix a clock. These clocks can be constructed in any way, but are *calibrated* in meters of light-travel time. In Section 1 we discussed how to obtain such a calibration by bouncing a flash of light back and forth between two mirrors one-half meter apart. This mirror clock is said to "tick" each time the light flash arrives back at the first mirror. Between ticks the light flash travels a round-trip distance of 1 meter: Call the unit of time between ticks *1 meter of light-travel time*, or more simply, *1 meter of time*. The speed of light in conventional units has the measured value $c = 2.997925 \times 10^8$ meters per second. Light will travel 1

Latticework of clocks

---

†Such a treatment is presented by Robert F. Marzke and John A. Wheeler in *Gravitation and Relativity*, edited by H.-Y. Chiu and W. F. Hoffmann, (W. A. Benjamin, New York, 1964).

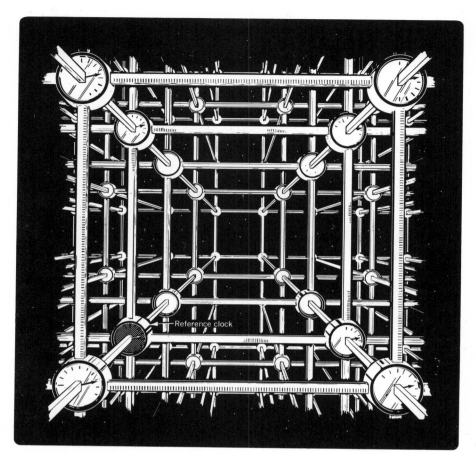

Fig. 9. Latticework of meter sticks and clocks.

meter in the time, 1 meter/c = 3.335640 × 10⁻⁹ seconds. Hence *1 meter of light-travel time is equal to 3.335640 × 10⁻⁹ seconds*—about 3.3 *nanoseconds* in the terminology of high-speed electronic circuits! We assume that *every* clock in the latticework, whatever its construction, has been calibrated in meters of light-travel time.

Synchronizing clocks in lattice

How are the different clocks in the lattice to be *synchronized* with one another? As follows: Pick one of the clocks in the lattice as the standard of time and take it to be the *origin* of an x, y, z coordinate system. Start this reference clock with its pointer at $t = 0$. At this instant let it send out a flash of light that spreads in all directions. Call this flash of light the *reference flash*. When the reference flash gets to a clock 5 meters away, we want that clock to read 5 meters of light-travel time. So an assistant *sets* that clock to 5 meters of time long before the experiment begins, *holds* it at 5 meters, and *releases* it only when the reference flash arrives. When assistants at all the clocks in the lattice have followed this procedure (each setting his clock to a time in meters equal to his own distance from the reference clock and starting it when the light flash arrives), the clocks in the lattice are said to be *synchronized*.

There are other possible ways to synchronize clocks. For example, an extra portable clock could be set to the reference clock at the origin and then carried around the lattice in order to set the rest of the clocks. However, this procedure involves a *moving* clock. We will see later that a moving clock runs at a different rate as measured by clocks in the lattice than do clocks that remain at rest in the lattice. The portable clock will not even agree with the first one when it is brought back next to it! (Clock paradox, Ex. 27). However, if we use a moving clock that travels at a speed that is a *very small fraction* of the speed of light, it is only slightly in error, and this second method of synchronization will give very nearly the same result as the first—and standard—method. Moreover the error can be made as small as desired by carrying the portable clock about sufficiently slowly.

The latticework of synchronized clocks can be used to determine the location and time at which any given event occurs. The *location* of the event will be taken to be the position of the clock nearest the event. The *time* of the event will be taken to be the time recorded on the lattice clock nearest the event. The *coordinates* of an event will then consist of four numbers: three numbers that specify the *spatial position* of the clock nearest the event and the *time* (in meters) when the event occured as recorded by that clock. The clocks, if they are installed by a foresighted experimenter, will be *recording* clocks. Each will be able to detect the occurrence of an event (passage of a light flash or particle). Each will punch onto a card the nature of the event, the time of the event and the location of the clock. The cards can then be collected from all the clocks and later analyzed, perhaps by automatic equipment.

Latticework used to measure the four coordinates of event

Why a lattice built of rods that are *one* meter long? When a clock in this lattice punches out a card, one will not know whether the event so recorded is 0.4 meters to the left of the clock, for instance, or 0.2 meters to the right. The location of the event will be uncertain by some substantial fraction of a meter. The time of the event will also be unknown within some appreciable fraction of a meter of light-travel time. This accuracy, however, is quite adequate for observing the passage of a rocket. It is extravagantly good for measurements on planetary orbits—it would even be reasonable to increase the lattice spacing from 1 meter to hundreds of meters. Neither 100 meters nor 1 meter is a lattice spacing suitable for studying the tracks of particles from a high-energy accelerator. There a centimeter or a millimeter would be more appropriate. The location and time of an event can be determined to whatever accuracy is desired by constructing a lattice with sufficiently small spacing.

Lattice spacing depends on scale of physics under study

In relativity we often speak about "the observer." Where is this observer? At one place or all over the place? *The word "observer" is a shorthand way of speaking about the whole collection of recording clocks* associated with one inertial frame of reference. No one real observer could easily do what we ask of the "ideal observer" in our analysis of relativity. So it is best to think of the observer as the man who goes around picking up the punched cards turned out by all the recording clocks in his employ. This is the sophisticated sense in which we will hereafter be using the phrase "the observer finds such and such."

Observer defined

The clocks reveal the motion of a particle through the lattice: each clock that the particle passes punches out the time of passage as well as the space coordinate of this event. How can the path of the particle be described in

Clock records reveal motion of particle through lattice

terms of numbers? By recording the coordinates of these events along this path. Differences between the coordinates of successive events reveal the velocity of the particle. The conventional units for speed, v, are meters per second. However, when time is measured in meters of light-travel time, then speed is expressed in meters of distance covered per meter of time. To avoid confusion, speed expressed in meters per meter will be represented by the Greek letter beta, β. A flash of light moves one meter of distance in one meter of light-travel time, or, $\beta_{\text{light}} = 1$. The speed of other particles in meters per meter represents a fraction of the speed of light. In other words $\beta = v/c$. Here and hereafter c represents the speed of light.

Verifying that lattice furnishes inertial frame

From the motion of test particles through the latticework of clocks—or rather from the records of coincidences punched out by the recording clocks—we can determine whether the latticework constitutes an inertial reference frame. *If* the records show (a) that—within some specified accuracy—a test particle moves consecutively past clocks that lie in a straight line, (b) that the speed β of the test particle calculated from the same records is constant—again, within some specified accuracy—and, (c) that the same results are true for as many test-particle paths as the most industrious observer cares to trace throughout the given region of space and time, *then* the lattice constitutes an inertial reference frame throughout that region of spacetime.

Laboratory and rocket frames; x axes coincide

Once again we have described the motion of test particles with respect to a particular reference frame in order to determine whether that frame is inertial. The same test particles and—if they collide—the same collisions may be described with reference to one inertial frame as well as another. Let two reference frames be two different latticeworks of meter sticks and clocks, one moving uniformly relative to the other, and in such a way that their x axes coincide. Call one of these frames the *laboratory frame* and the other—moving in the positive x direction relative to the laboratory frame—the *rocket frame* (Figs. 10 and 11). The rocket is *unpowered* and coasts along with constant velocity relative to the laboratory. Let the rocket and laboratory latticeworks be *overlapping* in the sense that there is a region of spacetime common to both frames (as described in Section 3 and Fig. 8). Test particles move through this common region of spacetime. From the motion of these test particles as recorded by his own clocks, an observer in each frame verifies that his frame is *inertial*.

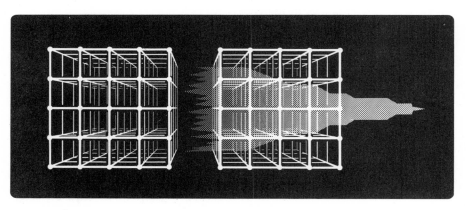

Fig. 10. Laboratory and rocket frames. The two latticeworks intermeshed a second ago.

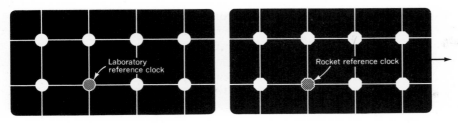

Laboratory frame   Rocket frame

Fig. 11. Laboratory and rocket frames, further schematized from Fig. 10. The central reference clock of each frame is shaded.

A firecracker explodes. The explosion is recorded by the clock in the laboratory lattice nearest to the explosion. It is recorded also by the clock in the rocket lattice nearest to the explosion. How do the coordinates of the recording laboratory clock compare with the coordinates of the recording rocket clock? One result can be derived immediately from the principle of relativity: the recording laboratory and rocket clocks will have the same y coordinates. To show this, let the recording rocket clock carry a wet paint brush that makes marks on the laboratory lattice as it moves past. Figure 12 shows this for the special case, $y = 1$ meter. The marks on the laboratory lattice serve to measure the laboratory y coordinate of the $y = 1$ rocket clock. These paint marks appear *on* the $y = 1$ laboratory clocks rather than *above* them or *below* them. For suppose that the paint marks appear on the lattice rods *below* the $y = 1$ laboratory clocks: Then *both* observers will agree that the $y = 1$ rocket clocks passed "inside" the $y = 1$ laboratory clocks. Permanent paint marks would verify this for all to see. Similarly, if the paint marks appear on the lattice rods *above* the $y = 1$ laboratory clocks, both observers will agree that the $y = 1$ rocket clocks passed "outside" the $y = 1$ laboratory clocks. In either case there would be a way to distinguish experimentally between the two frames. But no one has been able to distinguish between these two frames using any *other* experiment. The principle of relativity embodies the assumption that any such experimental distinction between inertial reference frames is impossible. Therefore we assume that no one could distinguish between the two frames using *this* experiment. It follows that the y coordinate of *any* event— such as the explosion that began this paragraph—will have the same y coordinate in the rocket frame as in the laboratory frame.

By a similar argument the z coordinate of an event is the same in the rocket frame as in the laboratory frame. Notice that both the y coordinate and the z coordinate of an event are measured in a direction *perpendicular* to the direc-

Laboratory and rocket observers record single event

y coordinate of event is same in lab and rocket frames

z coordinate of event is same in lab and rocket frames

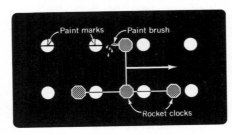

Fig. 12. Demonstration that y coordinate of an event is the same in laboratory and rocket frames.

tion of relative motion of the two frames. Equality of distance in each frame measured perpendicular to the direction of relative motion gives us a clean way to compare clocks in the two latticeworks. Let a flash of light bounce back and forth between a mirror mounted on the rocket reference clock and a mirror mounted on the $y = 1$ rocket clock directly above the reference clock. This flash will return to the origin every two meters of rocket light-travel time. We can trace the path of this flash of light in the laboratory frame up to the same y coordinate and back down again. Using the equality of the speed of light in the two frames we can calculate the laboratory time corresponding to the 2-meter round-trip time in the rocket frame. In the next section this study will lead to a demonstration of the invariance of the interval.

5. Invariance of the Interval

Looking for measure of separation AB that has same value in all inertial frames

Distance between two town gates is calculated from the difference between the x coordinates of the two gates and the difference between the y coordinates. How does one find the analogous physical quantity, the spacetime interval between two events? And between what two events shall this interval be evaluated?

Let *event A* be the *emission* of a flash of light. Let *event B* be the *reception* of this flash after its reflection from another object. All that matters in the end is the pair of events. Neither the light nor the object that reflects it is of any direct interest. Nevertheless, an analysis of the track of this pulse through spacetime reveals quickly and simply a quantity (the interval) that is associated with the two events and that has the same value in all inertial reference frames.

Event A: flash emission
Event B: flash reception

Event A: A spark plug fires. A flash of light flies up to reflector R in Fig. 13. Then the flash wings down. *Event B:* The flash is recorded. Now for the details (Figure 13).

The spark plug fires in the laboratory frame at the zero of time and at the origin of the x, y, z coordinate system (crosshatched). The rocket passes by with such timing that it records the spark as taking place also at *its* origin (likewise crosshatched) and at *its* zero of time. So much for the coordinates of the event of emission:

Details: lab and rocket coordinates of events A and B

$$x_{\text{emission}} = 0, \quad y_{\text{emission}} = 0, \quad t_{\text{emission}} = 0 \quad \text{(laboratory frame)}$$
$$x'_{\text{emission}} = 0, \quad y'_{\text{emission}} = 0, \quad t'_{\text{emission}} = 0 \quad \text{(rocket frame)}$$

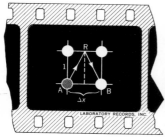
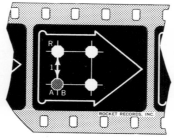
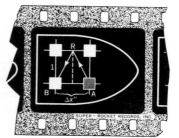

A. Light path as observed in laboratory frame

B. Light path as observed in rocket frame

C. Light path as observed in super-rocket frame

Fig. 13. Emission and reflection of the reference flash, and its reception at origin of rocket frame.

The reflector is mounted on the rocket clock 1 meter directly above the origin.

The reception of the flash occurs in the rocket frame at the same place as the emission. The light flash travels a round-trip path of 2 meters. This trip requires 2 meters of light-travel time. The coordinates of the event of reception in the rocket frame are therefore

$$x'_{\text{reception}} = 0, \qquad y'_{\text{reception}} = 0, \qquad t'_{\text{reception}} = 2 \text{ meters}$$

More relevant than an absolute coordinate is the difference in coordinates between the event of reception and the event of emission

$$\Delta x' = x'_{\text{reception}} - x'_{\text{emission}} = 0$$
$$\Delta y' = y'_{\text{reception}} - y'_{\text{emission}} = 0$$
$$\Delta t' = t'_{\text{reception}} - t'_{\text{emission}} = 2 \text{ meters}$$

In the *laboratory* frame the light flash is received, not at the origin, but at the distance Δx to the right of the origin. High rocket speed implies a large Δx; low rocket speed, a small Δx. (The distance is shown as 1 meter in the figure, but the following analysis is correct for any distance.) In the laboratory frame the flash travels the hypotenuse of two right triangles. Each has a base of $(\Delta x/2)$ and an altitude of 1 meter. The total length of the light path is

$$2[1 + (\Delta x/2)^2]^{1/2}$$

Recall that the speed of light is the same in the laboratory frame as in the rocket frame—the preposterous-but-true character of nature! Therefore the time difference between emission and reception in the laboratory frame is given by the identical formula

(4) $$\Delta t = t_{\text{reception}} - t_{\text{emission}} = 2[1 + (\Delta x/2)^2]^{1/2}$$

in meters of light-travel time.

Why is this time greater than 2 meters? Because the hypotenuse of a right triangle in Fig. 13,A, is greater than its altitude! There is no escape from the conclusion that *the time between emission and reception is not the same in the two reference frames.*

Time between A and B has different values for lab and rocket observers

Both time and space differences between the event of reception and the event of emission are summarized in Table 5.

Table 5. Difference in coordinates between the event of reception and the event of emission.

Laboratory frame	Rocket frame
$x_{\text{reception}} - x_{\text{emission}} = \Delta x$	$x'_{\text{reception}} - x'_{\text{emission}} = \Delta x' = 0$
$t_{\text{reception}} - t_{\text{emission}} = \Delta t = 2[1 + (\Delta x/2)^2]^{1/2}$	$t'_{\text{reception}} - t'_{\text{emission}} = \Delta t' = 2 \text{ meters}$

The time lapse is different in the two reference frames; and so is the space separation—just as the coordinates Δx and Δy of the separation between two town gates are different for the Daytime and Nighttime surveyors! However, for the surveyors there was a combination of coordinates—the square of the *distance* between gates—that was the same for both of them

$$(\text{distance})^2 = (\Delta x)^2 + (\Delta y)^2 = (\Delta x')^2 + (\Delta y')^2$$

Is there any similar combination of coordinates for two events that will have the same value in the laboratory and rocket frames? Answer: Yes! the square of the *interval*

Interval between A and B has same value for lab and rocket observers

$$(5) \qquad (\text{interval})^2 = (\Delta t)^2 - (\Delta x)^2 = (\Delta t')^2 - (\Delta x')^2 = (2 \text{ meters})^2$$

as one checks directly by substituting in the quantities listed in Table 5.

The rocket frame chosen in which to analyze these two events is a rather special one, in that both emission and reception occur at the same place in it. Figure 13,C, shows the path of the reflected light in a second rocket frame ("super-rocket frame") that is moving even faster relative to the laboratory frame than is the first rocket. In this second rocket frame the difference between the x coordinates for emission and reception (double primes on symbols) $x''_{\text{reception}} - x''_{\text{emission}} = \Delta x''$ is a *negative* quantity because the reception occurs on the negative x axis in this frame. Nevertheless, $(-\Delta x'')^2 = (\Delta x'')^2$ and we can still use the right triangles in Fig. 13,C, to show that the total length of the light path in this second rocket frame is given by the expression $2[1 + (\Delta x''/2)^2]^{1/2}$—which is the same in form as that for the laboratory frame. The speed of light must have the same value in the second rocket frame as in the first rocket frame. Therefore the time between emission and reception is given by

$$t''_{\text{reception}} - t''_{\text{emission}} = \Delta t'' = 2[1 + (\Delta x''/2)^2]^{1/2}$$

Interval AB has same value in all rocket frames!

Therefore

$$(\Delta t'')^2 - (\Delta x'')^2 = (2 \text{ meters})^2$$

also, and in summary

$$(6) \qquad (\Delta t)^2 - (\Delta x)^2 = (\Delta t')^2 - (\Delta x')^2 = (\Delta t'')^2 - (\Delta x'')^2 = (2 \text{ meters})^2$$

Now forget the outgoing light flash, the reflector, and the returning light flash. They were only tools. They helped to identify the quantity that has the same value in different frames of reference. From now on focus on the quantity itself, the interval. Disregard the details of the derivation.

What is the same in two inertial frames; what is nearly the same; and what is different

What has been learned? Two events, A and B, occur at the same point in the rocket frame ($\Delta x' = 0$) but at different times ($\Delta t' = 2$ meters). Viewed in the laboratory frame, those same two events are separated in space by a distance Δx—the faster the rocket happens to be moving, the greater the distance. This result is hardly surprising. One is even entitled to say, "What could be more obvious!" The surprise comes elsewhere. First, *the time Δt between the two events as recorded in the laboratory frame does not have the same value as it has in the rocket frame.* Second, the time between A and B as punched out by the two relevant recording laboratory clocks is *greater* than the time between the same two events as recorded by the indentical reference clock of the rocket: $\Delta t \geqslant \Delta t'$. Third, the factor of increase of the time (see Table 5)

$$\Delta t / \Delta t' = [1 + (\Delta x/2)^2]^{1/2}$$

is close to unity (that is, the increase itself is very small) if the distance Δx covered by the rocket between events A and B is small. However, if the rocket moves very fast, Δx is a very great quantity, and the factor of discrepancy between the two times is enormous. Fourth, despite this newly found difference in *time* as recorded in the two reference frames, and despite the long-known difference between the *space* separation of the events in the two reference frames ($\Delta x \neq \Delta x' = 0$), there is nevertheless a quantity that *is* the same in the laboratory frame as the 2 meters of elapsed light-travel time between A and B in the rocket frame. This quantity is the interval,

$$(\text{interval}) = [(\Delta t)^2 - (\Delta x)^2]^{1/2}$$

The rocket speed may be very high. Then Δx will be very large. But then Δt is also very large. Moreover, the magnitude of Δt is perfectly tailored to the size of Δx. In consequence, the special quantity $(\Delta t)^2 - (\Delta x)^2$ has the value $(2 \text{ meters})^2$, no matter how great Δx and Δt individually may be.

All of these relationships can be seen at a glance in Fig. 13,A. The hypotenuse of the first right triangle is $\Delta t/2$. Its base is $\Delta x/2$. To say that $(\Delta t)^2 - (\Delta x)^2$ has a standard value, and thus to state that $(\Delta t/2)^2 - (\Delta x/2)^2$ has a standard value, is to say that the altitude of this right triangle has a fixed magnitude (1 meter in the diagram) no matter how fast the rocket is going. What then was the keystone of the argument establishing the fact that $(\Delta t)^2 - (\Delta x)^2$ has the value $(2 \text{ meters})^2$, no matter how fast the rocket is moving? The keystone was the principle of relativity, according to which there is no difference in the laws of physics between one inertial reference frame and another. This principle was put to use here in two very different ways. First, it was used to reason that distances at right angles to the direction of relative motion are recorded as of equal magnitude in the laboratory frame and in the rocket frame. Otherwise one frame could be distinguished from the other as the one with the shorter perpendicular distances. Second, the principle of relativity was employed to deduce that the speed of light must be the same in the laboratory frame as in the rocket frame—a deduction supported by the Kennedy-Thorndike experiment. The speed being the same, the fact that the light-travel path in the laboratory frame (the hypotenuses of two triangles) is longer than the simple round-trip path in the rocket frame (the altitudes of the two triangles: up 1 meter and down again) directly implies a longer *time* in the laboratory frame than in the rocket frame.

In brief, in the one elementary triangle of Fig. 13,A, are displayed the four great ideas that underlie all of special relativity: invariance of perpendicular distance, invariance of the speed of light, dependence of space *and time* coordinates upon the frame of reference, and invariance of the interval.

If Fig. 13,A, thus epitomizes all of special relativity in a form easy to remember, the foregoing analysis of the figure nevertheless leads to what at first sight seems to be a preposterous conclusion. How can it possibly make sense for the lapse of time between two events to be longer in the laboratory than in the rocket? Has it not already been argued that "distances at right angles to the direction of relative motion" are equal, "otherwise one frame could be distinguished from the other as the one with the shorter perpendicular distances"? What about the difference between *time* lapses in the two frames? Does not this difference give a way to differentiate physics in one frame from

One diagram illustrates the four great ideas of special relativity

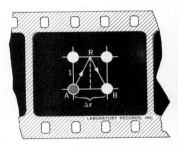

FIG. 13,A, PAGE 22

Is inequality of lab and rocket time lapses a paradox?

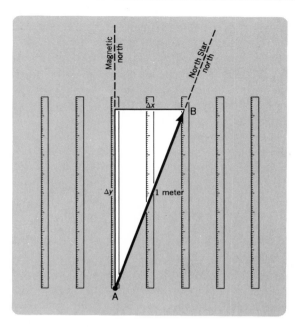

Fig. 14. The north-south separation of point B from point A (the "*northing* of B relative to A") depends upon the choice of the direction north.

*Relativity of time
(Lorentz) compared
with relativity of
"northing" (Euclid)*
physics in the other? Yet is not such a difference ruled out by the principle of relativity—the principle that one inertial reference frame is as good as another?

For answers to these questions, turn back to the parable of the surveyors. Consider point B in Fig. 14. It is one meter straight north of another point, A, according to the reckoning of the Nighttime surveyor and his North Star north. Now consider the location of point B according to the Daytime surveyor and his magnetic north. Is the y separation Δy between A and B (surveying terminology: the *northing* of B relative to A) also one meter in the Daytime frame? No, Δy is *less* than one meter! How can this be? Because the altitude (Δy) of a right triangle is shorter than the hypotenuse (1 meter). Does this mean that the rules of surveying in the Daytime coordinate system are different from those in the Nighttime coordinate system? Evidently not! Similarly, there is no flaw in the construction or functioning of the laboratory clocks that makes them give longer readings for the time lapse AB. The "discrepancy" between the laboratory clocks and the rocket clock is caused instead by the character of spacetime geometry itself. That is the way the world is built! The analogy between the Lorentz geometry of spacetime and the Euclidean geometry of the surveyors' world is expanded in Table 6 (pages 28 and 29).

6. The Spacetime Diagram; World Lines

*The spacetime
diagram: simple way
to display events*
A simple way to look at the events of emission and reception of the last section is to plot the position of the event on the horizontal axis and the time of the event on the vertical axis of a *spacetime diagram* (Fig. 15). The light is *emitted* from a spark plug attached to the reference clock of the first rocket. This plug fires at the instant when this clock passes the laboratory reference

clock. Both clocks then read zero. Therefore the event of emission is located at the origin of the spacetime diagram plotted by the rocket observer

$$x'_{\text{emission}} = 0, \qquad t'_{\text{emission}} = 0$$

It is also located at the origin of the spacetime diagram made by the laboratory observer

$$x_{\text{emission}} = 0, \qquad t_{\text{emission}} = 0$$

The further history of the relevant light ray looks different as plotted in the spacetime diagrams of the laboratory and the two rockets. In the first rocket the *reception* of the reflected flash occurs at $x' = 0$ and 2 meters of time later than the reference event

$$x'_{\text{reception}} = 0, \qquad t'_{\text{reception}} = 2 \text{ meters}$$

as already recorded in Table 5 and as seen more directly in Fig. 15,B. In the laboratory frame the event of reception is located to the right of the origin

$$x_{\text{reception}} = \text{a positive quantity}$$
$$t_{\text{reception}} = [(2 \text{ meters})^2 + x^2_{\text{reception}}]^{1/2}$$
$$= \text{a time } greater \text{ than 2 meters}$$

as shown in Fig. 15,A. In the second rocket frame (the second rocket is moving faster than the first!) the event of reception appears to the left of the origin (Fig. 15,C)

$$x''_{\text{reception}} = \text{a negative quantity}$$
$$t''_{\text{reception}} = [(2 \text{ meters})^2 + (x''_{\text{reception}})^2]^{1/2}$$
$$= \text{a time } greater \text{ than 2 meters} \quad \text{(again!)}$$

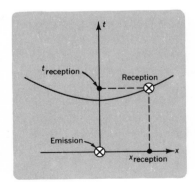 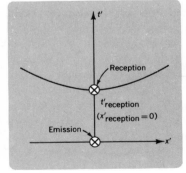 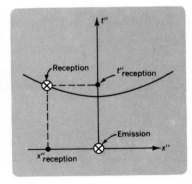

A. Laboratory spacetime diagram .   B. Rocket spacetime diagram   C. Super-rocket spacetime diagram

Fig. 15. Spacetime diagrams showing emission of the reference flash and its reception after reflection. The hyperbola drawn in each figure satisfies the equations (interval)$^2 = t^2 - x^2 = t'^2 - x'^2 = t''^2 - x''^2$

Table 6. Comparison of the difference in northing between points A and B in Daytime and Nighttime coordinate systems and the difference in time between events A and B in laboratory and in rocket reference frames.

Questions	Answers of a student of surveying concerning difference in northing between points A and B. (See Fig. 14.)	Answers of a student of spacetime physics concerning difference in time between events A and B. (See Fig. 13.)
In which frame of reference does the separation of B from A appear simplest?	Coordinate system of Night-time surveyor based on North-Star north.	Reference frame of rocket.
What is simplifying feature in this frame of reference?	Points have same x' coordinate; or $\Delta x' = 0$.	Events have same x' coordinate; or $\Delta x' = 0$.
Why does this feature simplify the measurement of the separation AB?	One meter stick oriented to North-Star north suffices (1) to verify that both points *do* have the same x' coordinate and (2) to measure directly the northing of B relative to A.	One recording clock attached to rocket frame suffices (1) to verify that both events *do* have the same x' coordinate and (2) to measure directly the time delay of B relative to A.
What is an alternative frame for analyzing the separation AB?	Coordinate system of Daytime surveyor based on magnetic north.	Reference frame of laboratory.
What complication is there in analyzing the separation in this alternative frame?	No single one of *his* meter sticks, oriented to magnetic north, can locate both A and B.	No single one of the recording laboratory clocks can register both A and B.
How is this difficulty met?	*Two* of these north-oriented meter sticks are needed, one located Δx meters to the right of the other.	*Two* of these laboratory clocks are needed, one located Δx meters to the right of the other.
What is the reading on the first of these measuring devices?	Point A at $y = 0$.	Event A at $t = 0$.
And the reading on the second of these measuring devices?	Point B located Δy meters north.	Event B delayed by Δt seconds.
Does the coordinate thus found for B directly measure its separation from A?	No! The northing Δy is less than the distance AB. More precisely, $$\Delta y = [(AB)^2 - (\Delta x)^2]^{1/2}.$$	No! The delay Δt is greater than the interval AB. More precisely, $$\Delta t = [(AB)^2 + (\Delta x)^2]^{1/2}.$$
Then how does one find the separation AB from measurements in this frame of reference?	From the formula for distance, $$(\text{distance})^2 = (\Delta x)^2 + (\Delta y)^2.$$ (Test by substituting in the expression for Δy from the entry above!)	From the formula for interval, $$(\text{interval})^2 = (\Delta t)^2 - (\Delta x)^2$$ (Test by substituting in the expression for Δt from the entry above!)

What is the distinction in the present examples between measurements made in the primed and the unprimed frames?	Δy is *less* than $\Delta y'$ ($=$ AB).	Δt is *greater* than $\Delta t'$ ($=$ AB).
Isn't there something preposterous about this result?	Meaning that identical meter sticks give nonidentical northings?	Meaning that identical clocks record nonidentical times?
Yes! Does not this discrepancy prove that there is some inner contradiction in the reasoning?	No! A single Nighttime meter stick suffices to establish the distance AB. But there is no *single* Daytime meter stick with which one establishes the (lesser) magnetic northing of B relative to A. Therefore no Daytime meter stick can be said to disagree with the Nighttime meter stick.	No! A single rocket clock records the interval AB. But there is no *single* laboratory clock with which one establishes the (greater) laboratory time delay of B relative to A. Therefore no laboratory clock can be said to disagree with the rocket clock.
Is there some fundamental difference between the primed and the unprimed frame of reference that is responsible for the one-sided difference between coordinate values?	For $\Delta y < \Delta y'$? No!	For $\Delta t > \Delta t'$? No!
Then what *is* responsible for this one-sidedness?	The point B happens to lie on the same North-Star north line as A, but *not* on the same magnetic north line as A.	Event B by chance occurs at the same point in the rocket frame as A, but *not* at the same point as A in the laboratory frame.
How can the identical character of the physics in the two frames of reference be readily illustrated?	Pick a point C that has the same x coordinate as A (C in the line of magnetic north relative to A)	Pick an event C that has the same x coordinate as A (C at the same *place* as A in the laboratory frame, but later in *time*).
For such a choice of C, what is the distinction between measurements made in the primed and the unprimed frames?	Δy ($=$ AC) is *greater* than $\Delta y'$.	Δt ($=$ AC) is *less* than $\Delta t'$.
How can the discussion be summarized?	There is no paradox about northward component of AB having different values in two coordinate systems; the discrepancy is not a fault of the meter sticks; not even a fault at all; the "discrepancy" is caused by the inner workings of Euclidean geometry.	There is no paradox about time lapse from A to B having different values in two reference frames; the discrepancy is not a fault of the clocks; not even a fault at all; the "discrepancy" is caused by the very structure of the geometry of the spacetime in which all physics takes place.

*Invariant interval
corresponds to
hyperbola on
spacetime diagram*

The different points marked "reception" in the different spacetime diagrams all refer to the *same event*. The event is the same but its coordinates in different frames are different. What do these different coordinates of the same event have in common? They all satisfy the equation

$$(\text{time separation})^2 - (\text{space separation})^2 = (\text{interval})^2 = \text{constant}$$

This is the equation of a *hyperbola*. Therefore, *an event which is plotted on the hyperbola $t^2 - x^2 = (constant)$ in the spacetime diagram of any laboratory or rocket frame will be plotted somewhere on a hyperbola with the same equation in the spacetime diagram of every other laboratory and rocket frame.*

Is there likewise a single curve that correlates the different coordinate values obtained by the Daytime and Nighttime surveyors for a single gate? The x and y coordinates of, say, gate A with respect to the town square depends on the choice of the north direction (Fig. 16). The Daytime and Nighttime plots of this gate are shown in Fig. 17, parts A and B. Think of a third and still different set of axes rotated even more than the Nighttime axes relative to the Daytime axes. For the surveyor who uses this third set of axes the x'' coordinate of gate A may be negative (Fig. 17,C).

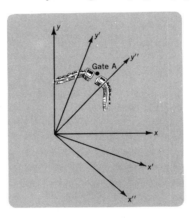

Fig. 16. Relative standards of north for Daytime, Nighttime, and a third surveyor respectively.

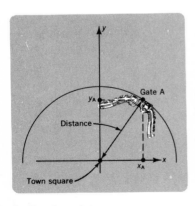

A. Daytime plot

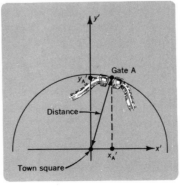

B. Nighttime plot

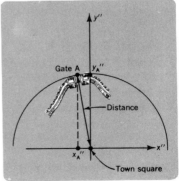

C. Plot by third surveyor

Fig. 17. Coordinates of Gate A as observed by Daytime, Nighttime, and a third surveyor respectively. The circle drawn in each figure satisfies the equations $(\text{distance})^2 = x^2 + y^2 = x'^2 + y'^2 = x''^2 + y''^2$

The different points marked "gate A" in the different plots all refer to the *same gate*. The gate is the same but its coordinates in different plots are different. What do these different coordinates of the same gate have in common? They all satisfy the equation

Invariant distance corresponds to circle on xy diagram

$$(x \text{ separation})^2 + (y \text{ separation})^2 = (\text{distance})^2 = \text{constant}$$

This is the equation of a *circle*. Therefore, *a point that is plotted on the circle* $x^2 + y^2 = (constant)$ *in the coordinate system of any surveyor will be plotted somewhere on a circle with the same equation in the coordinate system of every other surveyor.*

Here is the fundamental difference between textbook Euclidean geometry and the real Lorentz geometry of spacetime. In Euclidean geometry the *distance* between two points is an invariant, and as a result, for all surveyors gate A will lie somewhere in the *xy* plane on a *circle* centered on the town square. In Lorentz geometry the *interval* between events is an invariant, and as a result, for all laboratory and rocket observers a given event will lie somewhere on a *hyperbola* in the spacetime diagram when referred to the reference event.

In Euclidean geometry the length—or its square—is always a *positive* quantity

$$(\Delta x)^2 + (\Delta y)^2 = (\Delta x')^2 + (\Delta y')^2 \geqslant 0$$

In contrast, the squared interval of Lorentz geometry

$$(\Delta t)^2 - (\Delta x)^2 = (\Delta t')^2 - (\Delta x')^2$$

Three types of separation between two events: timelike lightlike spacelike

may be *positive*, *negative*, or *zero*, depending on whether the time or the space component predominates. Moreover, whichever of these three descriptions characterizes the interval in one reference frame also characterizes the interval in *any other* reference frame, because the interval has the same value in all frames. Accordingly we find that nature provides a fundamental way to classify the relation between two events. An interval between two events is called *timelike*, *lightlike*, or *spacelike* depending on whether the squared interval is positive, zero, or negative, respectively, as shown in Table 7.

Table 7. Classification of the relation between two events.

Description	Squared interval	Name
Time part of interval dominates over space part	positive	timelike interval
Time part of interval equals space part	zero	lightlike interval
Space part of interval dominates over time part	negative	spacelike interval

The value of the interval between two events is represented by different symbols depending on whether it is timelike or spacelike. The value of a timelike interval is given the Greek letter tau (τ) and is called the *invariant timelike distance* between two events or the *proper time* (or sometimes the *local time*) between the two events

Proper time and proper distance

(7)
$$\Delta\tau = [(\Delta t)^2 - (\Delta x)^2]^{1/2}$$

The value of a spacelike interval between two events is given the Greek letter sigma (σ) and is called the *invariant spacelike distance* or the *proper distance* between the two events

(8)
$$\Delta\sigma = [(\Delta x)^2 - (\Delta t)^2]^{1/2}$$

World line of particle

Figure 18 represents as a function of time the location of a particle which started along the x axis from the origin at $t = 0$. Such a plot of position versus time in a spacetime diagram is called the *world line* of the particle. Each lattice clock encountered by the particle punches out the time of coincidence. Thus the world line of the particle can be considered to be made up of these separate events of coincidence. No particle has ever been observed to travel faster than light. Therefore a particle will always travel *less* than one meter of distance in one meter of light-travel time. It follows that events along this world line will have a greater time separation than their separation in space: the world line of a particle will consist of events that are *timelike* with

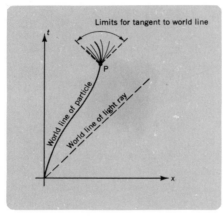

Fig. 18. Timelike world line of a particle.

respect to the initial event and to each other. In other words, *a particle must follow a timelike world line*. A timelike world line is characterized at every point P by a local tangent which lies between the world lines of light rays originating at that point. These light rays travel one meter of distance in one meter of light-travel time. Events along the world line of a light ray have equal space and time separations. Therefore the world line of a light ray consists of events that are *lightlike* with respect to the initial event and to each other. In other words *light rays follow lightlike world lines*.

Path in space has length

Distance is a central idea in all applications of Euclidean geometry. For instance, using a flexible tape measure it is easy to measure the distance s along a path that starts at the town square and winds out through gate A (Fig. 19,A). The distance Δs between any two nearby points on the path (for instance, those marked 3 and 4 in the figure) can also be *calculated* using the difference in coordinates Δx and Δy of the two points with respect to any coordinate system. Since distance is invariant, the distance between these two points will be the same when calculated in any coordinate system even though the separate coordinates Δx and Δy have different values in different coordinate systems. Elsewhere along the path the distance between another pair of nearby points will also be independent of the coordinate system used in evalu-

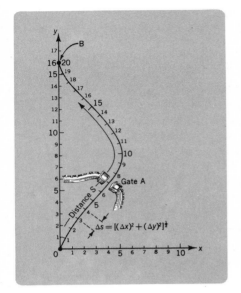

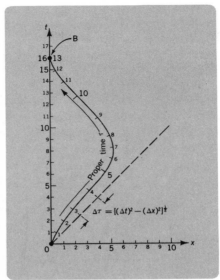

Fig. 19, A. Distance along a winding path which starts at the town square. Notice that the total *distance along the winding path* from point O to point B is *greater* than the *distance along the straight y axis* from point O to point B.

Fig. 19, B. Proper time along a curved world line in a spacetime diagram. Notice that the total *proper time along the curved world line* from event O to event B is *smaller* than the *proper time along the straight t axis* from event O to event B.

ating that distance. So too for the *sum* of the lengths of all the segments of the path! Thus different surveyors using different coordinate systems will all agree on the distance along a given path from a specified initial point O to a specified final point B.

It is possible to proceed from O to B along quite another path—for example, along the straight line OB in Fig. 19,A. The length of this alternative path is evidently different from that of the original path. This difference in length of different paths between O and B is a feature of Euclidean geometry so well known as to occasion hardly any comment and certainly no surprise. In Euclidean geometry a curved path between two specified points is *longer* than a straight path between the same two points. The existence of the difference of length between two paths violates no law. No one would claim that a tape measure fails to perform properly when laid along a curved path.

Length is shortest for direct path

Proper time is to a world line in Lorentz geometry what length is to a path in Euclidean geometry. The world line is started at an event O and ended at an event B. There are many different world lines that start at O and end at B. The lapse of proper time on each is well defined; but it differs between one world line and another. Is this surprising? Then it is appropriate to look more closely at how the proper time is defined and measured.

Consider a particle moving from O to B along the curved world line of Fig. 19,B. In this example, the particle travels along the x axis at a changing speed. Let the particle emit a flash of light every meter of time as recorded on a clock carried with it. The proper time $\Delta\tau$ between any two consecutive flashes (for instance, those marked 3 and 4 in the figure) can be *calculated* using the difference in coordinates Δx and Δt of the two events measured in a

Stretch of world line measured by proper time

particular inertial frame. Because the interval is invariant, the proper time between these two events will be the same when calculated in any inertial frame, even though the separate space and time coordinates Δx and Δt will have different values in different reference frames. Elsewhere along the world line the interval between another pair of consecutive flashes will also be independent of the reference frame which is used in evaluating that interval. So too for the *sum* of the proper-time intervals of all the flashes along the world line! Thus observers in different inertial reference frames will all agree on the proper time along a given world line from a specified initial event O to a specified final event B.

Proper time is longest for direct world line

It is possible to proceed from event O to event B along quite another world line—for example, along the straight world line OB in Fig. 19,B. The elapsed proper time along this alternative world line is different from the proper time along the original world line. In Lorentz geometry a curved world line between two specified events is *shorter* than the direct world line between the same two events—shorter as measured by the elapsed proper time along the world line. This contrast between Euclidean and Lorentz geometry is shown in Fig. 20. The *distance* between nearby points along a *curved path* is always equal to or *greater* than the y displacement between those two points. In contrast, the *proper time* between nearby events along a curved *world line* is always equal to or *less* than the corresponding time along the direct world line. The determination of proper time is a fundamental method of comparing different world lines between two events.

The change of slope of the world line from point to point in Fig. 19,B, and Fig. 20,B, means that the clock being carried along the world line changes velocity: it is *accelerated*. Different clocks will behave differently when accelerated unless these clocks are sufficiently small. As a rule a clock can withstand a great acceleration only if it is small

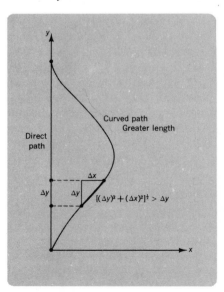

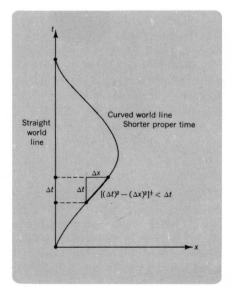

A. Euclidean geometry   B. Lorentz geometry

Fig. 20. Contrast between Euclidean and Lorentz geometry. In Lorentz geometry the *curved* world line is traversed in the *shorter* proper time.

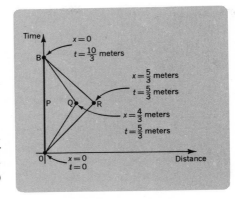

Fig. 21. Three alternative world lines connecting event O and event B. The sharp changes of speed at events Q and R have been drawn for the ideal limit of small (acceleration-proof) clocks.

and compact. The smaller the clock, the more acceleration it can withstand, and the sharper the curves on the world line can be. In all figures like Fig. 19,B, and Fig. 20,B, we assume the ideal limit of infinitesimally small clocks.

We are now free to analyze a motion in which the particle and the clock are subject to a great acceleration. In particular, consider a simple special case of the world line of Fig. 19,B. That world line gradually changed in slope as the particle speeded up and slowed down. Now make the period of speeding up shorter and shorter (great driving force!); also make the period of slowing down shorter and shorter. In this way the proportion of time spent in steady motion at high speed becomes greater and greater. Thus come eventually to the limiting case where the times of acceleration and deceleration are too short even to show up on the scale of the spacetime diagram (world line OQB in Fig. 21). In this simple limiting case the whole history of the motion is specified by (1) the initial event O, (2) the final event B, and (3) the coordinate x of the turnaround point Q, halfway in time between O and B. In this case it is particularly easy to see how the lapse of proper time between O and B depends upon the coordinate x of the halfway point—and thus to compare the three world lines OPB, OQB, and ORB.

Proper time from O to B compared for three world lines

Path OPB is the world line of a particle that does not move: $x = 0$ for all time. The proper time from O to B by way of P is evidently equal to the time as measured in the inertial reference system.

$$\tau_{\text{OPB}} = 10/3 \text{ meters of light-travel time}$$

In contrast, on the way from O to B by way of R, each stretch is lightlike: for each segment the space and time components of the displacement are equal, and

$$\tau_{\text{ORB}} = (\text{twice proper time on stretch OR}) = 2\,[(\text{time})^2 - (\text{distance})^2]^{1/2} = 0$$

Of course no clock can travel as fast as the speed of light. Therefore the world line ORB is not actually attainable. However, it is the ideal limit of world lines that actually *are* attainable. Or, in other words, one can find a speed sufficiently close to the speed of light, and yet *less* than the speed of light, so that a trip with this speed first one way then the other will bring an ideal clock back to $x = 0$ with a lapse of proper time as short as one pleases.

As distinguished from the limiting case ORB, the world line OQB demands an amount of proper time

$$\begin{aligned}
\tau_{\text{OQB}} &= (\text{twice proper time on stretch OQ}) \\
&= 2\,[(5/3)^2 - (4/3)^2]^{1/2} \\
&= 2\left[\frac{25-16}{9}\right]^{1/2} \\
&= 2 \text{ meters of light-travel time}
\end{aligned}$$

This is *less* proper time than the proper time $\tau_{OPB} = 3\ 1/3$ meters that characterized the "direct" world line OPB!

Evidently *proper* time in the real physical world of spacetime differs remarkably from the *distance* of textbook Euclidean geometry. Distance is shortest for the direct route: "A straight line is the shortest distance between two points." In contrast, the lapse of proper time is less for the traveler who travels away, accelerating to high speed, then reverses his course and comes back, than for the man who stays home! (See Ex. 27 and Ex. 49 on the clock paradox). In brief, proper time is the appropriate measure of time as it will be observed by a particle that travels along a world line, just as the graduations along a flexible tape provide the appropriate measure of distance covered by a traveler along a winding path.

7. Regions of Spacetime

Interval including y and z coordinates

Thus far in dealing with the interval between two events, A and B, we have had occasion to consider only the situation in which they have the same y and z coordinates. In this situation the separation in space between the two events is measured by the single quantity

$$\text{distance} = \Delta x$$

The interval is given by the expression

$$[(\Delta t)^2 - (\Delta x)^2]^{1/2}$$

However, the orientation of the x, y, and z coordinate axes is evidently a matter of arbitrary choice. With another orientation of the axes the component Δx of the separation between the two events will ordinarily have quite a different value. Yet the separation in space between the two events is quite independent of any choice of orientation, and is given by the expression

$$(\text{distance})^2 = (\Delta x)^2 + (\Delta y)^2 + (\Delta z)^2$$

In other words, this is the quantity that must replace $(\Delta x)^2$ in the full formula for the interval. Thus we have the complete expression for the interval between two events

$$\text{A} \quad \text{at} \quad (t, x, y, z)$$
and
$$\text{B} \quad \text{at} \quad (t + \Delta t, x + \Delta x, y + \Delta y, z + \Delta z)$$
in the form

(9) $$(\text{interval of proper time})^2 = (\text{time})^2 - (\text{distance})^2$$
$$= (\Delta t)^2 - (\Delta x)^2 - (\Delta y)^2 - (\Delta z)^2$$

when the interval is timelike; and when it is spacelike,

(10) $$(\text{interval of proper distance})^2 = (\text{distance})^2 - (\text{time})^2$$
$$= (\Delta x)^2 + (\Delta y)^2 + (\Delta z)^2 - (\Delta t)^2$$

How is one to understand the new kind of geometry described by an expression for "interval of proper distance" that contains three plus signs—as in ordinary Euclidean geometry—but also one minus sign? One can follow

Minkowski (1908) and introduce a new quantity w to measure time, a quantity defined by

$$w = (-1)^{1/2} t$$

or

(11) $$\Delta w = (-1)^{1/2} \Delta t$$

Then the expression for the interval of proper distance takes the form

$$\text{(interval of proper distance)}^2 = (\Delta x)^2 + (\Delta y)^2 + (\Delta z)^2 + (\Delta w)^2$$

The signs are now all positive. The geometry superficially appears to be that of Euclid—in four dimensions, of course, instead of three. Impressed by this formula, Minkowski wrote his famous words, "Henceforth space by itself, and time by itself, are doomed to fade away into mere shadows, and only a kind of union of the two will preserve an independent reality."† Today this union of space and time is called spacetime. Spacetime is the arena in which stars, atoms, and people live and move and have their being. Space is different for different observers. Time is different for different observers. Spacetime is the same for everyone.

Minkowski's insight is central to the understanding of the physical world. It focuses attention on those quantities, such as interval, which are the same in all frames of reference. It brings out the relative character of quantities, such as velocity, energy, time, distance, which depend upon the choice of frame of reference.

Today we have learned not to overstate Minkowski's argument. It is right to say that time and space are inseparable parts of a larger unity. It is wrong to say that time is identical in quality with space. Why is it wrong? Is not time measured in meters, just as distance is? Are not the x and y coordinates of the surveyor quantities of identical physical character? By analogy, are not the x and t coordinates of the spacetime diagram of the same nature as one another? How else could it be legitimate to treat these quantities on an equal footing, as in the formula $[(\Delta x)^2 + (\Delta y)^2 + (\Delta z)^2 - (\Delta t)^2]^{1/2}$ for a space-like interval? Equal footing, yes; same nature, no. There is a *minus* sign in this formula that no sleight of hand can ever conjure away. *This minus sign marks the difference in character between space and time.* It does not really remove this minus sign to introduce the imaginary number $\Delta w = (-1)^{1/2}\Delta t$. It would if w were a real quantity. But w is not real. No clock ever reads $(-1)^{1/2}$ seconds, or $(-1)^{1/2}$ meters. Real clocks show real time: $\Delta t = 7$ seconds, for example. Consequently the term $-(\Delta t)^2$ is always opposite in sign to the distance term $(\Delta x)^2 + (\Delta y)^2 + (\Delta z)^2$. No twisting or turning can ever make the two signs the same.

The difference in sign between the time term and the space terms in the expression for the interval gives Lorentz geometry a unique feature, which is new and quite different from anything in Euclidean geometry. In Euclidean geometry it is never possible for the distance AB between two points to be zero unless all three of the quantities Δx, Δy, and Δz are simultaneously zero. In contrast, the interval AB between two events can vanish even when the

---

†A. Einstein *et al.*, *The Principle of Relativity*, (Dover Publications, New York).

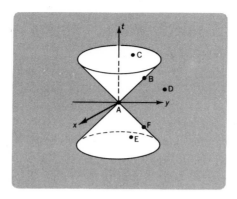

Fig. 22. Spacetime diagram showing x, y, and t coordinates of events for which $z = 0$.

separations Δx, Δy, Δz in space and Δt in time between B and A are individually quite large.

Case where interval vanishes

Under what condition does the interval AB vanish? *The interval vanishes when the time part of the separation between A and B is identical in magnitude to the space part of the separation*

$$(12) \qquad \Delta t = \pm[(\Delta x)^2 + (\Delta y)^2 + (\Delta z)^2]^{1/2}$$

What is the physical interpretation of this condition? The expression on the right is the distance between the two points. But light travels one meter of distance in one meter of light-travel time. Therefore the expression on the right also represents the time that is *needed* by light to travel the distance between A and B. On the other hand, Δt represents the time that is *available* to travel this distance. In other words, condition (12) is satisfied—and the interval AB vanishes—when a light flash starting at event A can arrive precisely in time for event B (or when a flash starting at B can arrive at A). *The interval between two events is zero when they can be connected by one light ray.*

It is interesting to map out in an appropriate diagram the location of *all* events B that can be connected with one given event A by a light ray. For simplicity let event A occur at the origin of the spacetime diagram. Let the coordinates x, y, z of event B be taken to have any values. Then the time coordinate of event B has either the value

$$(13) \qquad t_{\text{future}} = +(x^2 + y^2 + z^2)^{1/2}$$

or the value

$$(14) \qquad t_{\text{past}} = -(x^2 + y^2 + z^2)^{1/2}$$

Light cones: partitions in spacetime

It simplifies the graphical presentation of this formula to limit attention to events B whose z coordinate is zero. Then it is appropriate to construct a spacetime diagram with two spatial coordinates x and y and the time coordinate t, as shown in Fig. 22. Every event B in this diagram that is separated from A by a zero interval ("lightlike interval") lies either on the "future light cone" of A (plus sign in Eq. 13) or on the "past light cone" of A (minus sign in Eq. 14).

In Fig. 22 consider all those events that have time coordinates 7 meters later than the zero time of flash A. These events lie on a plane 7 meters above the *xy* plane, and parallel to the *xy* plane. Among these events those which lie on the future light cone of A are on a circle. This circle has a radius of 7 meters. This circle (circle in the present *x*, *y*, *t* diagram; a sphere in a full *x*, *y*, *z*, *t* diagram!) is the locus of the pulse of radiant energy which emerged from A. Observed at a later time, the pulse has expanded to a still larger radius. Thus the forward light cone tells the history of the expanding spherical pulse that started at A. Similarly the backward light cone tells the history of a converging pulse of radiation, so perfectly focused that it collapses at the origin at time zero.

The light cone is a unique feature of Lorentz geometry; there is no such feature in Euclidean geometry. Moreover, associated with the light cone, Lorentz geometry has a characteristic of the greatest importance for the structure of the physical world. It provides the following ordering of all events with respect to their causal relationship to any chosen event A (Fig. 22).

Spacetime classified into five regions relative to event A

1. Can a *particle* emitted at A affect what *is going* to happen at C? If so, C lies *in* the future light cone of A.
2. Can a *light ray* emitted at A affect what *is going* to happen at B? If so, B lies *on* the future light cone of A.
3. Can *no effect whatever* produced at A affect what happens at D? If so, D lies *outside* the light cone of A.
4. Can a *particle* emitted at E affect what *is happening* at A? If so, E lies *in* the past light cone of A.
5. Can a *light ray* emitted at F affect what *is happening* at A? If so, F lies *on* the past light cone of A.

Now, the light cone of event A—and the light cone of every other event—has an existence in spacetime quite apart from any coordinates that may be used to describe it. Therefore the possibilities mentioned in the five preceding questions, that one event will affect another event are independent of the reference frame in which this connection between events is observed. In this sense *the causal connection between two events is preserved in every reference frame.*

Figure 23 summarizes the relations between a selected event A and all other events of spacetime.

8. The Lorentz Transformation

At heights of 10 to 30 kilometers above the earth, cosmic rays are continually striking the nuclei of oxygen and nitrogen atoms and producing π-mesons, both charged and neutral. Follow one of the π^+-mesons on its way down (Fig. 24). In the reference frame attached to this particle ("rocket frame") the average life of the π^+-meson is 2.55×10^{-8} seconds. In this rocket frame let the coordinates of the event of birth be $x' = 0$, $t' = 0$ (Fig. 25,B). Let the coordinates of the event of explosion of the π-meson (into muon plus neutrino) be written

Coordinates more convenient than interval for describing trip of π-meson

$$x' = 0, \qquad t' = \tau_\pi$$

How do these events appear to the laboratory observer? As recorded by his clocks, how long does the π-meson live from birth to death? Or how much is

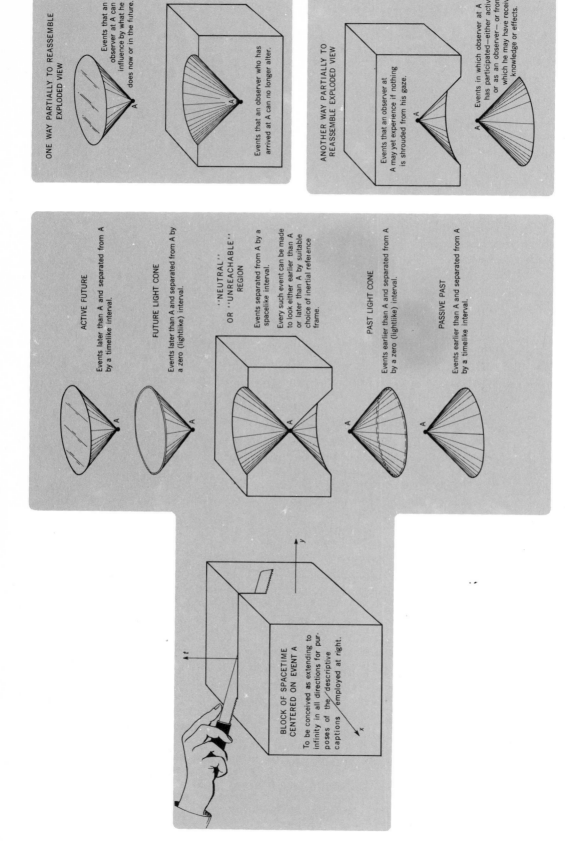

Fig. 23. Exploded view of the five regions into which the events of spacetime fall apart when classified with respect to a selected event A.

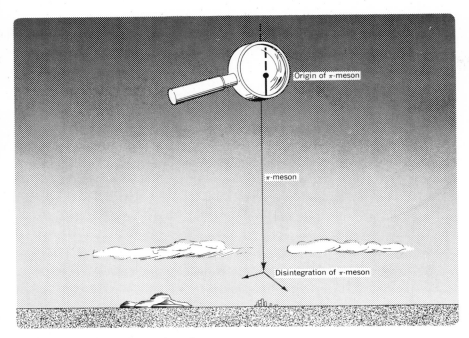

Fig. 24. Origin and disintegration of a π-meson.

the lapse of laboratory time t? And how far does it travel? Or how much is the laboratory distance x, measured downward through the upper atmosphere from the point of formation? In a word, given an event E separated from an origin O by known coordinates x', t' in the rocket frame, how can one predict the coordinates x, t of the same event relative to the same origin in the laboratory frame (Fig. 25,A)?

This is a new kind of question. Up to now we have limited attention to the invariant interval as a way to describe the separation between two events. This interval has a value independent of the choice of reference frame; thus

(15)   (spacelike interval)^2 = $-$(timelike interval)^2 = $x^2 - t^2 = (x')^2 - (t')^2$

Fig. 25. Coordinates of the origin (point O) and disintegration (point E) of a π-meson as plotted on a laboratory and on a rocket spacetime diagram.

A. Laboratory spacetime diagram   B. Rocket spacetime diagram

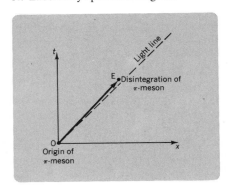

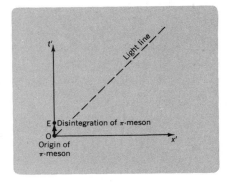

Coordinates of event
differ from frame to
frame

Now we focus attention on the coordinates themselves as indicators of the separation of the event E from the origin O. We do so recognizing in advance that these quantities depend upon the choice of frame of reference. In this respect the coordinates lack the universal standing that the invariant interval has as a measure of separation. But no matter. Physics has to get on with the world's work. One uses the method of describing separation that is best suited to the job in hand. On some occasions the useful fact to give about a torpedo boat is the 50-meter separation between bow and stern. On another occasion it may be much more important to know that the bow is 40 meters north of the stern and 30 meters east of it. In the present example it does not meet our needs to know that the point of disintegrative explosion of the π-meson is separated from the point of origin by an invariant interval τ of $\sim 10^{-8}$ second. We want to know the x and t coordinates individually for the separation.

Lorentz transformation
for coordinates

However much the (x, t) coordinates of the event E in the laboratory frame differ from the (x', t') coordinates of the same event in the rocket frame, these two sets of coordinates are related to each other by a well-defined and simple law. This law is summarized in the *Lorentz coordinate transformation*

$$(16) \qquad \begin{aligned} x &= (1 - \beta_r^2)^{-1/2}x' + \beta_r(1 - \beta_r^2)^{-1/2}t' \\ t &= \beta_r(1 - \beta_r^2)^{-1/2}x' + (1 - \beta_r^2)^{-1/2}t' \end{aligned}$$

where β_r is the speed of the rocket frame *relative* to the laboratory. Because of the existence of this law, the *coordinates* are said to provide a *covariant* description of the separation of events in spacetime, in contrast to the *invariant* measure of separation supplied by the *interval*. The portion "variant" of the adjective "covariant" indicates that the coordinates vary from one reference system to another. The prefix "co" implies a coordinated variation of the coordinates of all events according to the same law. Thus x' and t' differ from one event to another; and so do x and t; but the four coefficients

Covariant defined

$$(1 - \beta_r^2)^{-1/2} \qquad\qquad \beta_r(1 - \beta_r^2)^{-1/2}$$
$$\beta_r(1 - \beta_r^2)^{-1/2} \qquad\qquad (1 - \beta_r^2)^{-1/2}$$

that connect these two sets of coordinates have values that are independent of the event under consideration.

The derivation of the Lorentz transformation formula, its use, and its points of analogy to well known features of Euclidean geometry—seen in the parable of the surveyors—form the theme of this section.

Three ideas leading to
Lorentz transformation

The three ideas that go into deriving the Lorentz transformation can be stated at once: (1) The coefficients in the transformation are independent of the event under consideration ("covariant transformation"). (2) The coefficients in the transformation are such as to guarantee that a point that is at rest in the rocket frame moves in the laboratory frame with a speed β_r in the x direction. (3) The coefficients are also such as to guarantee that any interval has the same value in laboratory and rocket frames.

The principles (1,2,3) have a simple application to the disintegration of the π-meson. In the laboratory reference frame this event is separated from the event of birth by coordinates (x, t), now to be calculated in terms of the velocity β_r of the rocket frame attached to the π-meson. The *ratio* of x to t is directly given by the velocity

$$x/t = \beta_r$$

or

Derivation of Lorentz transformation: first details

$$x = \beta_r t$$

or

(17) $$x^2 = \beta_r^2 t^2$$

The timelike *interval* defined by x and t is given by the time between birth and death in the rocket frame (where the π-meson stays always at $x' = 0$)

$$t^2 - x^2 = t'^2 - x'^2 = t'^2 - 0 = \tau_\pi^2$$

Make use of Eq. 17 and insert $\beta^2 t^2$ in place of x^2 in this formula. Find

$$t^2 - \beta_r^2 t^2 = t'^2 = \tau_\pi^2$$

or

$$t^2 = t'^2/(1 - \beta_r^2) = \tau_\pi^2/(1 - \beta_r^2)$$

or

$$t = (1 - \beta_r^2)^{-1/2} t' = (1 - \beta_r^2)^{-1/2} \tau_\pi$$

(Example: $\beta_r = (12/13)$ of the speed of light; $1 - \beta^2 = 1 - (144/169) = 25/169$; $(1 - \beta_r^2)^{-1/2} = 13/5 = 2.6$; thus π-meson life as measured in laboratory is 2.6 times longer than "proper life;" that is, 2.6 times longer than the life measured in the reference frame attached to π-meson itself.) The distance traveled is given by the velocity multiplied by the time; thus,

$$x = \beta_r t = \beta_r (1 - \beta_r^2)^{-1/2} t'$$

π-meson problem solved

This calculation completes the original problem: to find the laboratory coordinates of the point of disintegration of the π-meson relative to its point of birth.

The problem of the π-meson was an introduction to a general problem: to find the laboratory coordinates of a given event from a knowledge of the rocket coordinates of that event. If we say that this objective is equivalent to deriving the equations of the Lorentz transformation, then we have come a certain way in deriving that transformation by the simplest of arguments. In effect, we have found two of the four coefficients in the equations of the Lorentz transformation

$$t = \quad (1 - \beta_r^2)^{-1/2} t' + A x'$$
$$x = \beta_r (1 - \beta_r^2)^{-1/2} t' + B x'$$

About the two remaining coefficients, which we temporarily call A and B, we know nothing for an elementary reason. The π-meson was always at the point $x' = 0$ in the rocket frame. Therefore the two coefficients A and B could have had any finite values whatever without affecting the numerical results of the calculation. To determine these coefficients we turn our attention from the special event of disintegration, E, to a more general event, one which occurs at a point with arbitrary x' and t'. Once again we demand that the interval have

Derivation of Lorentz transformation: final details

the same numerical value in laboratory and rocket frames. In other words, we demand fulfillment of the equality

$$t^2 - x^2 = t'^2 - x'^2$$

or

$$[(1 - \beta_r^2)^{-1/2}t' + Ax']^2 - [\beta_r(1 - \beta_r^2)^{-1/2}t' + Bx']^2 = t'^2 - x'^2$$

or

(18) $$t'^2 + 2(1 - \beta_r^2)^{-1/2}(A - \beta_r B)x't' + (A^2 - B^2)x'^2 = t'^2 - x'^2$$

It is impossible to satisfy this equation with a single choice of values for A and B for all conceivable choices of t' and x' unless these values for A and B are chosen in a very special way. The quantities A and B must, first, be such as to make the coefficient of $x't'$ on the left-hand side of (18) vanish as it does on the right; hence,

$$A = \beta_r B ;$$

and, second, be such as to make the coefficient of $-x'^2$ be the same on the left and right of (18); hence

$$B^2 - A^2 = 1$$

We have here two equations for the two unknowns, A and B, from which we find

$$A = \beta_r(1 - \beta_r^2)^{-1/2}$$

and

$$B = (1 - \beta_r^2)^{-1/2}$$

This calculation completes the derivation of the Lorentz transformation of Eqs. 16.

Significance of Lorentz transformation

The new point of view of covariance focuses on the components x, t of a spacetime interval (Eqs. 16), rather than on the magnitude of this interval (Eq. 15). Intervals have the character of a universal language; they are the same for observers in all reference frames. In contrast, the components of a spacetime separation as measured in one reference frame provide a very specialized language for speaking about the separation. This specialized language is similar in form to the specialized language used in another reference frame to describe the same separation. Both languages employ "space components" and "time components." This circumstance in and by itself is of no help in comparing information possessed by one set of observers with information possessed by the other set of observers. An English reader looking at a Turkish newspaper gets little comfort from knowing that Turkish, too, uses verbs and nouns! He requires more—a dictionary. In translating information about space and time components supplied by observers on another frame of reference, one requires a dictionary. This dictionary is provided by the Lorentz transformation of Eqs. 16.

Analogy: surveyors need Euclidean transformation

A similar dictionary is required for a problem even closer at hand. A Daytime surveyor using magnetic north requires a dictionary. Only by using one can he translate into his own language the north and east readings that are made by a Nighttime surveyor (who uses North-Star north). No such dictionary is required if the two discuss their findings in the universal language of distances.

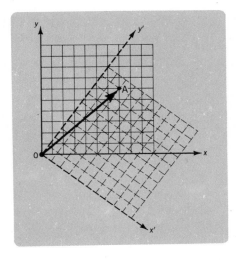

Fig. 26. The covariance approach to geometry deals with components, such as the components of the vector OA. (In contrast, the invariance approach to geometry deals with lengths, such as a length OA. Such a length has a value independent of any choice of frame of reference; in other words, it is the same whether determined by a surveyor who uses North-Star north or by a surveyor who uses magnetic north.)

The components in one frame are $(x, y) = (7, 6)$. The components in the other frame are $(x', y') = (2, 9)$, (numbers verifiable by reference to the diagram). These numbers evidently do not have the same values in the two frames of reference. Instead, they are connected by the "equations of a covariant transformation,"

$$x = (4/5) x' + (3/5) y' \qquad\qquad y = -(3/5) x' + (4/5) y'$$

or, in the example of the vector OA,

$$7 = (4/5) 2 + (3/5) 9 \qquad\qquad 6 = -(3/5) 2 + (4/5) 9$$

The special numerical values of the *coefficients* in the transformation equations as written above go with the special *rotation* illustrated in the diagram.

Evidently there is a striking contrast between the approach that focuses on invariants (distances, the universal language) and the method of description that deals with components (northward and eastward separations, different values found by the two surveyors). This contrast between invariant quantities and covariant quantities is illustrated in Fig. 26.

The student in the parable of the surveyors did only half a job, it now appears. He showed each surveyor how to translate his findings into the universal language of distance

$$(\text{distance})^2 = (\Delta x)^2 + (\Delta y)^2 = (\Delta x')^2 + (\Delta y')^2$$

However, he did not produce a dictionary that would interpret between discussions in the specialized Daytime and Nighttime languages of *components*. His achievement was useful as far as it went. But on occasion the Daytime surveyor wants to know, not merely a distance OA, but also the actual components $(\Delta x, \Delta y)$ of the separation OA. Moreover, circumstances may prevent him from directly measuring these components himself. In this event he has at his disposal only measurements of the components $(\Delta x', \Delta y')$ of the separation OA made by his colleague, the Nighttime surveyor. How is he to translate from the available numbers $(\Delta x', \Delta y')$ to the desired numbers $(\Delta x, \Delta y)$? Where is the dictionary? And what must one know in order to be able to construct the dictionary? Answer: Just as one has to know the *relative velocity* β_r of two reference frames to construct the Lorentz transformation from $(\Delta x', \Delta t')$ to $(\Delta x, \Delta t)$, so one must know the *slope* S_r of the line Oy' *relative* to the line Oy in order to translate from $(\Delta x', \Delta y')$ to $(\Delta x, \Delta y)$. In the example shown in Fig. 26, the slope of Oy' relative to Oy is $S_r = 3/4$. That is, for every 4 units of advance upwards along the y axis, one must travel 3 units to the right in order to arrive at the y' axis. In terms of the slope S_r the "transformation formula for rotation" is

Euclidean transformation for rotated coordinates

$$(19) \qquad \begin{aligned} \Delta x &= (1 + S_r^2)^{-1/2} \Delta x' + S_r(1 + S_r^2)^{-1/2} \Delta y' \\ \Delta y &= -S_r(1 + S_r^2)^{-1/2} \Delta x' + (1 + S_r^2)^{-1/2} \Delta y' \end{aligned}$$

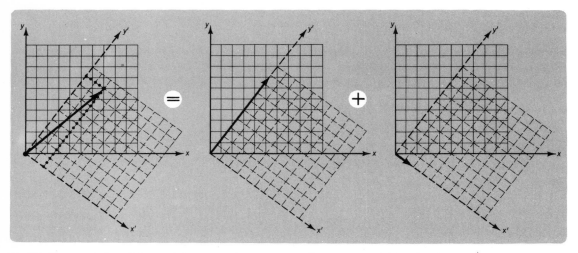

Fig. 27. Representation of the general vector as the vector sum of two vectors, which point along the y' and x' axes, respectively—a step in deriving the rotational transformation of Eqs. 19 as described in the text.

Derivation of Euclidean transformation

Proof:

1. Every arbitrary vector $(\Delta x', \Delta y')$ can be regarded (Fig. 27) as the sum of a vector $(\Delta x', 0)$ along the x' axis plus a vector $(0, \Delta y')$ along the y' axis. It is enough to establish the correctness of Eqs. 19 for these two types of vectors individually in order to confirm the correctness of Eqs. 19 in general.

2. A vector that points along the y' axis and that has length $\Delta y'$ has components along the x and y axes that stand to each other in the ratio S_r (definition of slope!); thus

$$\Delta x/\Delta y = S_r$$

or

$$(\Delta x)^2/(\Delta y)^2 = S_r^2$$

or

$$(\Delta x)^2 = S_r^2(\Delta y)^2$$

3. The distance from the origin to the tip of the vector has the same value in the two reference frames

$$(\Delta x)^2 + (\Delta y)^2 = (\Delta x')^2 + (\Delta y')^2$$

or

$$S_r^2(\Delta y)^2 + (\Delta y)^2 = 0 + (\Delta y')^2$$

or

$$(\Delta y)^2 = (1 + S_r^2)^{-1} (\Delta y')^2$$

or

$$\Delta y = (1 + S_r^2)^{-1/2} \Delta y'$$

and

$$\Delta x = S_r\Delta y = S_r(1 + S_r^2)^{-1/2} \Delta y'$$

Comparing these results with Eqs. 19 for a rotational transformation, we see that we have checked the two coefficients of $\Delta y'$.

4. Similarly, consider a vector that points exclusively along the x' axis, with components $(\Delta x', 0)$. Its components along the y and x axes stand to each other in the ratio

$$\Delta y/\Delta x = -S_r$$

This information plus the invariance of the distance

$$(\Delta x)^2 + (\Delta y)^2 = (\Delta x')^2 + 0$$

lead by the same type of reasoning to the result

$$\Delta x = (1 + S_r^2)^{-1/2}\Delta x'$$
$$\Delta y = -S_r(1 + S_r^2)^{-1/2}\Delta x'$$

These expressions confirm the remaining two coefficients in Eqs. 19 for a Euclidean transformation.

In summary, the covariant transformation in Euclidean geometry from $(\Delta x', \Delta y')$ to $(\Delta x, \Delta y)$ is clearly analogous to the transformation from $(\Delta x', \Delta t')$ to $(\Delta x, \Delta t)$ in the Lorentz geometry of the real physical world. The *slope* S_r of the axis of one coordinate system relative to the corresponding axis of the other system is analogous to the velocity β_r of one inertial reference frame relative to the other. The ratios between the two sides of a right triangle and its hypotenuse in Euclidean geometry

Relative slope S_r (Euclid) compared with relative velocity β_r (Lorentz)

$$\frac{1}{(1 + S_r^2)^{1/2}} \quad \text{and} \quad \frac{S_r}{(1 + S_r^2)^{1\,2}}$$

are replaced in Lorentz geometry by the expressions

$$\frac{1}{(1 - \beta_r^2)^{1/2}} \quad \text{and} \quad \frac{\beta_r}{(1 - \beta_r^2)^{1/2}}$$

The minus sign in the expression $(1 - \beta_r^2)^{1/2}$ contrasts with the plus sign in $(1 + S_r^2)^{1/2}$. The negative sign originates from the minus sign in the expression for the interval in Lorentz geometry.

9. The Velocity Parameter

Have we finished? We have determined how to go from a knowledge of the components of a separation in one reference frame to a calculation of the components of the separation in another reference frame. In brief, we have written down the covariant law of connection of components both for a Lorentz transformation ("transformation in x, t plane") and for a rotation ("transformation in x, y plane"). In one, the formulas contain the parameter β_r (the relative velocity); in the other, the parameter S_r (the relative slope). However, neither of these parameters provides the simplest way to describe the relation between two coordinate systems. It is desirable to replace both β_r and S_r by more natural parameters. We can find better means to describe a velocity and a rotation! *Angle* is the best measure of rotation. Similarly, a certain *velocity parameter* θ, yet to be defined, is the most convenient measure of velocity. The usefulness and meaning of this velocity parameter in describing

Additivity of angles suggests looking for additive velocity parameter

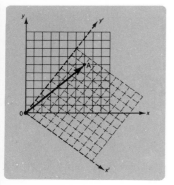

FIG. 26, PAGE 45

velocities will best be appreciated by asking here: Why is an angle a more convenient parameter than a slope for measuring a rotation?

And the answer is: Because *angles are additive and slopes are not.* What does this statement mean? Refer to Fig. 26. The vector OA is inclined to the y' axis. This inclination may be described by the slope S' (the number of units of distance in the x' direction per unit of distance in the y' direction). In the example this slope is

$$S' = 2/9$$

In contrast, the vector OA is inclined to the y axis by a slope

$$S = 7/6$$

Further, the y' axis is inclined to the y axis by a slope

$$S_r = 3/4$$

Question: Is the following law of addition of slope correct?

$$\begin{pmatrix} \text{slope of OA} \\ \text{relative to} \\ y \text{ axis} \end{pmatrix} \overset{?}{=} \begin{pmatrix} \text{slope of OA} \\ \text{relative to} \\ y' \text{ axis} \end{pmatrix} + \begin{pmatrix} \text{slope of } y' \text{ axis} \\ \text{relative to} \\ y \text{ axis} \end{pmatrix}$$

Slopes in Euclidean geometry are not additive

Test ("experimental mathematics"):

$$(7/6) \overset{?}{=} (2/9) + (3/4)$$
$$(42/36) \overset{?}{=} (8/36) + (27/36)$$
$$42 \overset{?}{=} 8 + 27 = 35 \qquad \text{No!}$$

Conclusion: Slopes are not additive! Question: If slopes are not additive and S is not equal to the sum of S' and S_r, what then is the correct way to deduce the slope S from S' and S_r? Answer:

$$\begin{pmatrix} \text{slope of OA} \\ \text{relative to} \\ y \text{ axis} \end{pmatrix} = S = \Delta x/\Delta y \qquad \text{(by definition of slope)}$$

$$= \frac{(1 + S_r{}^2)^{-1/2}\Delta x' + S_r(1 + S_r{}^2)^{-1/2}\Delta y'}{-S_r(1 + S_r{}^2)^{-1/2}\Delta x' + (1 + S_r{}^2)^{-1/2}\Delta y'} \quad \text{(from Eqs. 19)}$$

$$= \frac{\Delta x' + S_r\Delta y'}{-S_r\Delta x' + \Delta y'} \qquad \begin{array}{l}\text{(by eliminating } (1 + S_r{}^2)^{-1/2} \text{ from} \\ \text{numerator and denominator)}\end{array}$$

$$= \frac{(\Delta x'/\Delta y') + S_r}{-S_r(\Delta x'/\Delta y') + 1} \qquad \begin{array}{l}\text{(by dividing numerator and} \\ \text{denominator by } \Delta y')\end{array}$$

Thus finally,

(20) $$S = \frac{S' + S_r}{1 - S'S_r}$$

In other words, two slopes S' and S_r can be treated as additive only when the product $S' S_r$ in the denominator can be neglected in comparison with unity.

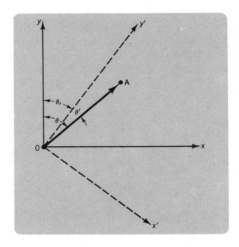

Fig. 28. The *angle* is a convenient way to measure inclination between y axis and y' axis—convenient because angles satisfy a simple law of addition: $\theta = \theta' + \theta_r$.

Since slopes are not additive and are thus not the convenient way to measure the inclination of two coordinate systems, what then is a more suitable way to measure this inclination? Answer: The *angle* between the y and y' axes. Why? Because angle does satisfy a simple law of addition (Fig. 28).

Angles ARE additive

$$\begin{pmatrix} \text{angle of OA} \\ \text{relative to} \\ y \text{ axis} \end{pmatrix} = \begin{pmatrix} \text{angle of OA} \\ \text{relative to} \\ y' \text{ axis} \end{pmatrix} + \begin{pmatrix} \text{angle of } y' \text{ axis} \\ \text{relative to} \\ y \text{ axis} \end{pmatrix}$$

or

(21) $$\theta = \theta' + \theta_r$$

The existence of this relation makes the angle the simple measure of inclination.

What is the relation between this new measure of inclination and the old measure, the slope S_r of the y' axis relative to the y axis? Answer:

(22) $S_r = \tan \theta_r$ (from the definition of tangent in trigonometry; see Fig. 29)

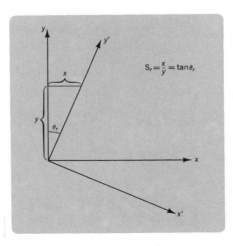

Fig. 29. Relation between relative slope S_r of corresponding axes of two Euclidean coordinate systems and the angle θ_r between these axes.

Euclidean law of addition of slopes

Question: How does one understand the law of addition of slopes when one recognizes that a slope is the tangent of an angle? Answer:

$$\tan\theta = \tan(\theta' + \theta_r) \qquad \text{(additivity of angles)}$$

(23)
$$= \frac{\tan\theta' + \tan\theta_r}{1 - \tan\theta'\tan\theta_r} \qquad \text{(trigonometry)}$$

or

$$S = \frac{S' + S_r}{1 - S'S_r} \qquad \text{(tangents measure slopes)}$$

Comparison of the complicated law of addition of tangents, or slopes, and the simple law of addition of angles, $\theta = \theta' + \theta_r$, confirms that angles provide the simplest measure of rotations.

What is the simplest measure of velocity? Not velocity itself. Velocity itself does not satisfy a simple law of addition. What is the law of addition of velocities? Let a bullet be fired forward at a velocity β' in the rocket frame of reference (Fig. 30).

Law of addition of velocities

$$\beta' = \frac{\left(\begin{array}{c}\text{number of meters of advance}\\\text{in the } x' \text{ direction for each}\end{array}\right)}{\left(\begin{array}{c}\text{meter of advance in the read-}\\\text{ings } t' \text{ of the rocket clocks}\end{array}\right)} = (\Delta x'/\Delta t')$$

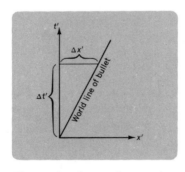

Fig. 30. World line of a bullet plotted in the rocket spacetime diagram. The bullet is fired forward with a velocity $\beta' = \Delta x'/\Delta t'$ in the rocket frame.

The rocket is moving at the velocity β_r relative to the laboratory. What is the velocity β of the *bullet* relative to the laboratory—as measured with the laboratory latticework of clocks? Answer: The velocity is

$$\beta = \frac{\left(\begin{array}{c}\text{number of meters of advance}\\\text{in the } x \text{ direction for each}\end{array}\right)}{\left(\begin{array}{c}\text{meter of advance in the read-}\\\text{ings } t \text{ of the laboratory clocks}\end{array}\right)} = (\Delta x/\Delta t)$$

$$= \frac{(1 - \beta_r^2)^{-1/2}\Delta x' + \beta_r(1 - \beta_r^2)^{-1/2}\Delta t'}{\beta_r(1 - \beta_r^2)^{-1/2}\Delta x' + (1 - \beta_r^2)^{-1/2}\Delta t'} \qquad \begin{array}{l}\text{(Lorentz transfor-}\\\text{mation, Eqs. 16)}\end{array}$$

$$= \frac{\Delta x' + \beta_r\Delta t'}{\beta_r\Delta x' + \Delta t'} \qquad \begin{array}{l}\text{(by eliminating } (1 - \beta_r^2)^{-1/2} \text{ from}\\\text{numerator and denominator)}\end{array}$$

$$= \frac{(\Delta x'/\Delta t') + \beta_r}{\beta_r(\Delta x'/\Delta t') + 1} \qquad \begin{array}{l}\text{(by dividing numerator and}\\\text{denominator by } \Delta t')\end{array}$$

Thus finally,

(24)
$$\beta = \frac{\beta' + \beta_r}{1 + \beta'\beta_r}$$

(law of addition of velocities)

In other words, velocities are not additive. *Limiting case, for low velocities only:* The two velocities β' and β_r can be treated as additive (to a certain level of accuracy) when the product $\beta'\beta_r$ in the denominator is negligibly small compared to unity (to that same level of accuracy, whether this level of accuracy is 1 part in 10 or 1 part in 10^6). *Example of lack of additivity of velocities:* The rocket is already going at 3/4 of the speed of light when it fires a bullet. The bullet itself moves at 3/4 of the speed of light relative to the rocket. What is the speed of the bullet relative to the laboratory? Answer: Not $(3/4) + (3/4) = 1.5$ times the speed of light, but instead

$$\beta = \frac{(3/4) + (3/4)}{1 + (3/4)(3/4)} = \frac{(3/2)}{(25/16)} = \frac{24}{25} = 0.96$$

(meters of laboratory distance per meter of travel time of light in the laboratory). Thus the relativistic law of addition of velocities (24) ensures that no object can ever be propelled at a speed as great as the speed of light.

Considering that velocities themselves are not additive, we propose to find a new measure of velocity, a "velocity parameter" θ, which *is* additive; thus,

$$\begin{pmatrix} \text{velocity parameter} \\ \text{of bullet relative} \\ \text{to laboratory} \end{pmatrix} = \begin{pmatrix} \text{velocity parameter} \\ \text{of bullet relative} \\ \text{to rocket} \end{pmatrix} + \begin{pmatrix} \text{velocity parameter} \\ \text{of rocket relative} \\ \text{to laboratory} \end{pmatrix}$$

Velocity parameter: defined to be additive!

or

(25)
$$\theta = \theta' + \theta_r$$

This parameter θ will be quite different in meaning from the angle that describes rotations. The velocity parameter cannot be represented as a simple angle in any diagram, and for a very good reason. Distances between points on a piece of paper are governed by the laws of Euclidean geometry. In contrast, the intervals between the events of the physical world are controlled by the Lorentz geometry of spacetime. But the impossibility of freezing moving bullets and ticking clocks onto a piece of paper does not deprive these lively objects of one iota of their reality. And the further impossibility of depicting the additivity of the velocity parameter θ on a page does not discourage us, but merely invites us to look at the real world of fast particles and high-energy physics to see the law of addition of velocity parameters in action. This law of addition of velocity parameters, $\theta = \theta' + \theta_r$, is every bit as real as the law of addition of angles of rotation.

What is the connection between velocity β and velocity parameter θ? The appropriate formula is analogous to the formula for slope in terms of angle (slope = tangent of angle). It has the form

Velocity is hyperbolic tangent of velocity parameter

(26)
$$\beta = \tanh \theta$$

Here "tanh" is read "hyperbolic tangent." The hyperbolic tangent function, as well as the hyperbolic sine and cosine functions, $\sinh \theta$ and $\cosh \theta$ (with

$\tanh \theta = \sinh \theta / \cosh \theta$), forms a standard part of mathematics. Tables of all three functions are given in every comprehensive compilation of tables. Formal definitions of these functions are presented in Table 8. Nevertheless, we need no knowledge of these tables and this mathematical literature. All that we want to know about the function $\tanh \theta$ can—naturally enough—be found from its very definition. Two properties define it: (*a*) It must correctly describe the law of addition of velocities. Out of the relation

$$\beta = \frac{\beta' + \beta_r}{1 + \beta'\beta_r}$$

and the demand $\theta = \theta' + \theta_r$ we read the law of addition

(27) $\tanh (\theta' + \theta_r) = \tanh \theta = \dfrac{\tanh \theta' + \tanh \theta_r}{1 + \tanh \theta' \tanh \theta_r}$ (from equation of definition 26)

(*b*) For low velocities the velocity parameter θ must reduce to the usual measure of velocity, β. This requirement means that $\tanh \theta$ must become arbitrarily close to θ itself for small θ. We recall that the ordinary tangent of an ordinary angle reduces to the angle itself for small angles, provided that the angle is measured in radians. When the angle is measured in degrees, there is a correction factor, $\pi/180°$. Similarly, the velocity parameter can here be measured in a variety of units, analogous to degrees and minutes, but the simplest unit is that in which $\tanh \theta \xrightarrow[\text{small } \theta]{} \theta$. We can call this unit the hyperbolic radian (dimensionless).

How can the connection between velocity parameter and velocity be found from the principles of (*a*) additivity and (*b*) $\tanh \theta = \theta$ for small velocity parameters?

Answer: (1) Start with a velocity parameter θ small enough so that $\tanh \theta$ can be identified with θ to some appropriate level of accuracy. Thus, write

$$\tanh 0.01 = 0.01$$

as the first entry in the desired table of hyperbolic tangents.

Constructing table of hyperbolic tangents

(2) Get the next entry by using the law of addition (27); thus,

(28) $\tanh 0.02 = \tanh (0.01 + 0.01) = \dfrac{\tanh 0.01 + \tanh 0.01}{1 + (\tanh 0.01)(\tanh 0.01)}$

$= \dfrac{0.01 + 0.01}{1 + 0.0001}$

(3) At this point a decision has to be made about the accuracy of the number work. Why not take $\tanh 0.02$ to have the value 0.02 just as we took $\tanh 0.01$ to have the value 0.01? Because there is a correction term of 0.0001 in the denominator of (28). Its presence implies that 0.02 will depart from the correct value of $\tanh 0.02$ by roughly 1 part of 10^4. We here and now decide that we will calculate all tanh values correct to one part in 10^4. We will therefore want to include the 0.0001 correction in the denominator. But if we have to make such a correction in evaluating $\tanh 0.02$, why did we not make such a correction in evaluating $\tanh 0.01$? Because that correction would have been still smaller. In other words, the difference between $\tanh 0.01$ and 0.01 can be

neglected when one is concerned to have his results correct to "only" one part in 10^4. To this accuracy we thus finally have

$$\tanh 0.02 = \frac{0.020000}{1.0001} = 0.019998$$

(4) Now ask for the value of tanh 0.04

$$\tanh 0.04 = \tanh (0.02 + 0.02) = \frac{\tanh 0.02 + \tanh 0.02}{1 + (\tanh 0.02)(\tanh 0.02)}$$

$$= \frac{2 \times 0.019998}{1 + (0.019998)^2} = 0.039980$$

The correction term in the denominator now affects the numerical value of the result by about 4 parts in 10^4. Nevertheless the result is good to about 1 part in 10^4. The result has been obtained by using a correct formula (Eq. 27) to combine hyperbolic tangent values, which were themselves correct to 1 part in 10^4.

(5) We construct further entries in the hyperbolic tangent table by the same type of combinatorial procedure. Thus, from a knowledge of tanh 0.04 and tanh 0.01 we can calculate tanh 0.05 = tanh (0.04 + 0.01). We go on to get tanh 0.1, tanh 0.2, and tanh 0.4; then tanh 0.5 = tanh (0.4 + 0.1). Similarly we calculate tanh 1, tanh 2, and any other values we want. In this way we find the results summarized in Fig. 31.

Two features of the velocity parameter stand out at once from Fig. 31, quite apart from any details of the numbers. First, the slope of the curve of tanh θ versus θ goes to unity at small θ—another way of saying that the velocity, $\beta = \tanh \theta$, and the velocity parameter θ approach equality at small θ. Second, the velocity parameter θ goes to indefinitely large positive (or negative) values as the velocity, $\beta = \tanh \theta$, itself approaches plus (or minus) unity. In other

Contrast between velocity parameter and ordinary angle

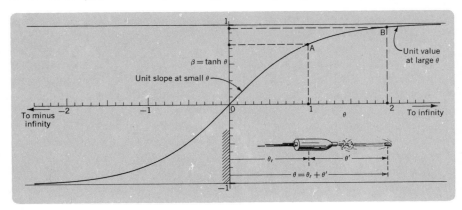

Fig. 31. Relation between velocity parameter θ and the velocity $\beta = \tanh \theta$ as determined directly from the law of addition

$$\tanh (\theta_1 + \theta_2) = \frac{\tanh \theta_1 + \tanh \theta_2}{1 + \tanh \theta_1 \tanh \theta_2}$$

as described in the text. Example: A bullet is fired at a speed $\beta' = 0.75$ from a rocket traveling at a speed $\beta_r = 0.75$. Find the speed β of the bullet relative to the laboratory. The velocity is not additive but the velocity parameter is. From the graph (point A) read off $\theta' = \theta_r = 0.973$. Add: $\theta = \theta' + \theta_r = 1.946$. For this value of the velocity parameter read off from the graph (point B) the result $\beta = 0.96$. The same result is obtained in the text in another way (p. 51).

words any values for the velocity parameter are conceivable, extending over the entire range from $\theta = -\infty$ to $\theta = +\infty$. The contrast between "hyperbolic angles" or velocity parameters, with this infinite extent of variation, and ordinary angles is evident. An ordinary angle leads to nothing new after it has increased through the finite range from 0 to 2π radians.

Velocity parameter and invariant speed of light

Velocity parameters and the law of addition of velocities—what connection have these ideas with the elementary physical observations that forced on physics the spacetime point of view? The most direct connection possible: From the observations—and from what was known even in 1905 about electromagnetic waves—Einstein was led to conclude that the speed of light is the same in all inertial reference frames. In other words—to translate into the language of idealized experiments—a photon shot with the speed of light from a fast rocket travels relative to the laboratory with a speed that is *also* equal to that of light. In the language of velocity parameters, the rocket has a finite parameter θ_r; but the photon ($\beta' = 1$) has an infinite velocity parameter ($\theta' = \infty$; Fig. 31, upper right, asymptotic limit). Add a finite number to infinity and end up with infinity for the sum $\theta = \theta' + \theta_r$. Thus the speed of the photon in the laboratory frame, $\beta = \tanh \theta = \tanh \infty = 1$, again agrees with the speed of light. We have come full circle, back to the starting idea of relativity: that the speed of light has the same value in all frames of reference.

Simplicity of velocity parameter

We conclude that the velocity parameter with its simple law of addition, $\theta = \theta' + \theta_r$, is the natural way to measure velocities. Then why does one not have a direct intuitive grasp of this measure of velocity? Why is not the hyperbolic angle as familiar to every school child as the ordinary angle? The answer is simple. Everyday experience deals with angles of all sizes, large and small. Therefore no one would be so naive as to add slope $S' = 1$ (angle of 45°) to slope $S_r = 1$ (another angle of 45°) and expect to get slope $S = S' + S_r = 2$ (angle of 63° 26'. Wrong!). One knows that the correct way is to add two angles (sum: 45° + 45° = 90°; slope $S = \infty$). But everyday experience does not deal with velocities close to the speed of light. Motor cars, real rockets, and real bullets travel with speeds that are extremely small compared to the speed of light. Therefore it is not surprising that it took a long time to recognize the truth about spacetime physics. But now, at last, the difference that exists in nature between the law of combination of velocities (the complicated Eq. 24) and the law of combination of velocity parameters (the simple Eq. 21: $\theta = \theta' + \theta_r$) is understood. Moreover, previously perplexing observations—such as the equality of the speed of light in all reference frames—become simple to describe when one adopts the concept of the velocity parameter. In addition, this parameter—and everything that goes with it in the spacetime description of physics—are necessities. There is no substitute for these ideas for anyone who wants to look upon the structure of the physical world as that four-dimensional world really is. More and more this necessity becomes clear as electronuclear machines and high velocity particles become part of the fabric of modern civilization.

There is no way around it! The velocity parameter provides the simple way to measure speed, as the ordinary angle provides the simple way to measure inclination. Having accepted this conclusion, what profit can we draw from it in the form of a simpler way to describe a Lorentz transformation?

Ask first, by way of orientation, the analogous question about the Euclidean geometry of the xy plane. Does the formula (Eqs. 19) for calculating one set of coordinates in terms of the other

$$\Delta x = \quad (1 + S_r^2)^{-1/2}\, \Delta x' + S_r(1 + S_r^2)^{-1/2}\, \Delta y'$$
$$\Delta y = -S_r(1 + S_r^2)^{-1/2}\, \Delta x' + \quad (1 + S_r^2)^{-1/2}\, \Delta y'$$

Simplify Euclidean transformation using angle

reduce in complexity when one expresses the relative slope S_r of the y and y' axes in terms of the ordinary angle θ_r? Answer: The coefficients in the rotational transformation become

$$(1 + S_r^2)^{-1/2} = (1 + \tan^2 \theta_r)^{-1/2} = \left(\frac{\cos^2 \theta_r + \sin^2 \theta_r}{\cos^2 \theta_r}\right)^{-1/2} = \left(\frac{1}{\cos^2 \theta_r}\right)^{-1/2} = \cos \theta_r$$

and

$$S_r(1 + S_r^2)^{-1/2} = \tan \theta_r \cos \theta_r = \frac{\sin \theta_r}{\cos \theta_r} \cos \theta_r = \sin \theta_r$$

Therefore the transformation equation itself takes the form

(29)
$$\Delta x = \quad \Delta x' \cos \theta_r + \Delta y' \sin \theta_r$$
$$\Delta y = -\Delta x' \sin \theta_r + \Delta y' \cos \theta_r$$

and we conclude: The relation between old and new coordinates takes its simplest form when the coefficients in the covariant transformation are expressed as "trigonometric," or "circular," functions of the angle of rotation.

Now turn to the Lorentz transformation written in terms of the relative velocity

$$\Delta x = \quad (1 - \beta_r^2)^{-1/2}\, \Delta x' + \beta_r(1 - \beta_r^2)^{-1/2}\, \Delta t'$$
$$\Delta t = \beta_r(1 - \beta_r^2)^{-1/2}\, \Delta x' + \quad (1 - \beta_r^2)^{-1/2}\, \Delta t'$$

Simplify Lorentz transformation using velocity parameter

How does this pair of equations look when expressed in terms of the improved measure of velocity, θ_r? Answer: Recall the connection between the velocity β_r and the velocity parameter

$$\beta_r = \tanh \theta_r$$

Note that the coefficients in the Lorentz transformation depend upon β_r, and by that very token are fixed by our choice of θ_r. These coefficients have the form

(30)
$$(1 - \beta_r^2)^{-1/2} = (1 - \tanh^2 \theta_r)^{-1/2}$$

and

(31)
$$\beta_r(1 - \beta_r^2)^{-1/2} = \tanh \theta_r\, (1 - \tanh^2 \theta_r)^{-1/2}$$

These expressions have a rather complicated appearance. Nevertheless, they are well defined. For any given value of θ_r we know how to find the value of $\tanh \theta_r$ (Fig. 31 and corresponding text). From this value of $\tanh \theta_r$ we can evaluate (30) and (31) with any desired accuracy for any given value of the velocity parameter. These two functions of θ_r have such importance that they have received names of their own in the literature on hyperbolic functions. To give the functions in question their standard names in no way decreases our ability to find the values of these functions at any time we please through our own efforts and without reference to any treatises or tables. Therefore we accept and use the standard names hereafter:

$$(1 - \tanh^2\theta_r)^{-1/2} = \cosh\theta_r = \left(\begin{array}{c}\text{hyperbolic} \\ \text{cosine of } \theta_r\end{array}\right)\left.\right)\begin{array}{l}\text{names;} \\ \text{nothing}\end{array}$$

$$\tanh\theta_r\,(1 - \tanh^2\theta_r)^{-1/2} = \sinh\theta_r = \left(\begin{array}{c}\text{hyperbolic} \\ \text{sine of } \theta_r\end{array}\right)\left.\right)\begin{array}{l}\text{but} \\ \text{names!}\end{array}$$

Using this nomenclature, we find that the equations of the Lorentz transformation take the following form

*Lorentz transformation
using velocity
parameter*

(32)
$$\Delta x = \Delta x' \cosh\theta_r + \Delta t' \sinh\theta_r$$
$$\Delta t = \Delta x' \sinh\theta_r + \Delta t' \cosh\theta_r$$

and we conclude: The relation between old and new coordinates takes its simplest form when the coefficients in the transformation are expressed as hyperbolic functions of the velocity parameter θ_r of the relative motion. Moreover, expressed in terms of hyperbolic sines and cosines, the Lorentz transformation takes a form that corresponds even more closely than before to the standard trigonometric form (29) for a rotational transformation.

What can one do to grasp and feel the properties of the hyperbolic functions that appear in the Lorentz transformation? The two most interesting and important properties of these functions follow immediately from the definitions (Eqs. 30 and 31). First, the ratio of the two hyperbolic functions has the value

(33)
$$\sinh\theta_r/\cosh\theta_r = \tanh\theta_r$$

in complete analogy to the corresponding relation for circular functions. Second, the difference between the squares of the two hyperbolic functions is

(34) $$\cosh^2\theta_r - \sinh^2\theta_r = \frac{1}{(1 - \tanh^2\theta_r)} - \frac{\tanh^2\theta_r}{(1 - \tanh^2\theta_r)} = \frac{1 - \tanh^2\theta_r}{1 - \tanh^2\theta_r} = 1$$

Contrast this formula with the analogous relation for trigonometric functions

(35) $$\cos^2(\text{angle}) + \sin^2(\text{angle}) = 1$$

*Circular functions
compared with
hyperbolic functions*

Equations 34 and 35 admit a simple geometrical interpretation. Plot sin (angle) as the horizontal coordinate and cos (angle) as the vertical coordinate in Fig. 32. Then Eq. 35 is the equation of a circle of unit radius—whence the often used term "circular functions" for the sine and the cosine. In contrast, (34) is the equation of a hyperbola (Fig. 33)—hence the word "hyperbolic functions." The positive sign in the expression $\cos^2 + \sin^2 = 1$ has its origin in the way x components and y components of a vector are combined to obtain the square of the length of that vector. And why the minus sign in $\cosh^2\theta - \sinh^2\theta = 1$? Because the square of a spacetime interval is given by the square of the separation in time *diminished* by the square of the separation in space.

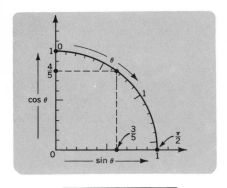

$$\cos^2 \theta + \sin^2 \theta = 1.$$

Fig. 32. Circle representing $\cos \theta$ versus $\sin \theta$ for circular functions. Example: $(3/5)^2 + (4/5)^2 = 1$.

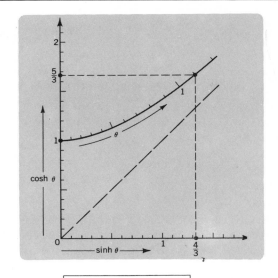

$$\cosh^2 \theta - \sinh^2 \theta = 1.$$

Fig. 33. Hyperbola representing $\cosh \theta$ versus $\sinh \theta$ for hyperbolic functions. Example: $(5/3)^2 - (4/3)^2 = 1$.

The distinction between the plus sign in $\cos^2 + \sin^2 = 1$ and the minus sign in $\cosh^2 \theta - \sinh^2 \theta = 1$ has to do with the contrast between the length in Euclidean geometry and the interval in Lorentz geometry. Look at this point more closely for the two kinds of geometry in turn. In Euclidean geometry reconfirm that the *covariant* transformation of *coordinates* (Eqs. 29)—now expressed in terms of circular functions rather than slope—guarantees the principle of *invariance of length*. For this purpose calculate (length)$^2 = (\Delta x)^2 + (\Delta y)^2$ from (Eqs. 29) and find

Confirmation: Euclidean transformation preserves distance invariant

$$\begin{aligned}
(\text{length})^2 &= (\Delta x)^2 + (\Delta y)^2 \\
&= (\Delta x' \cos \theta_r + \Delta y' \sin \theta_r)^2 + (-\Delta x' \sin \theta_r + \Delta y' \cos \theta_r)^2 \\
&= (\Delta x')^2 \cos^2 \theta_r + \cancel{2(\Delta x')(\Delta y') \cos \theta_r \sin \theta_r} + (\Delta y')^2 \sin^2 \theta_r \\
&\quad + (\Delta x')^2 \sin^2 \theta_r - \cancel{2(\Delta x')(\Delta y') \sin \theta_r \cos \theta_r} + (\Delta y')^2 \cos^2 \theta_r \\
&= [(\Delta x')^2 + (\Delta y')^2] (\cos^2 \theta_r + \sin^2 \theta_r) \\
&= (\Delta x')^2 + (\Delta y')^2
\end{aligned}$$

confirming the invariance of the expression for length. Note the importance of the relation

$$\cos^2 \theta_r + \sin^2 \theta_r = 1$$

in connecting the ideas of covariance (transformation of coordinates associated with different orientation of two coordinate systems) and invariance (length the same in both systems).

The connection between covariance and invariance in Lorentz geometry rests equally clearly on the relation

Confirmation: Lorentz transformation preserves interval invariant

$$\cosh^2 \theta_r - \sinh^2 \theta_r = 1$$

This one sees on calculating any interval whether spacelike or timelike

$$\left(\begin{array}{c}\text{interval of}\\ \text{proper distance}\end{array}\right)^2 = -\left(\begin{array}{c}\text{interval of}\\ \text{proper time}\end{array}\right)^2$$

$$= (\text{space separation})^2 - (\text{time separation})^2$$

$$= (\Delta x)^2 - (\Delta t)^2$$

$$= (\Delta x' \cosh \theta_r + \Delta t' \sinh \theta_r)^2 - (\Delta x' \sinh \theta_r + \Delta t' \cosh \theta_r)^2$$

$$= (\Delta x')^2 \cosh^2 \theta_r + \cancel{2(\Delta x')(\Delta t') \cosh \theta_r \sinh \theta_r} + (\Delta t')^2 \sinh^2 \theta_r$$
$$\quad - [(\Delta x')^2 \sinh^2 \theta_r + \cancel{2(\Delta x')(\Delta t') \sinh \theta_r \cosh \theta_r} + (\Delta t')^2 \cosh^2 \theta_r]$$

$$= [(\Delta x')^2 - (\Delta t')^2] (\cosh^2 \theta_r - \sinh^2 \theta_r)$$

$$= (\Delta x')^2 - (\Delta t')^2$$

Here one sees reconfirmed in the simplest way possible that a Lorentz transformation preserves the invariance of the expression for the interval.

The Lorentz transformation—we have now confirmed in all detail—translates from the specialized language of rocket coordinates (x', t') to the specialized language of laboratory coordinates (x, t). Moreover, the scheme of translation is consistent at every point with the universal language of intervals (consistency of covariant description of spacetime physics with invariant description of spacetime physics). However, we need still more: The typical Turkish-English dictionary is bound together with an English-Turkish dictionary—where is the second "relativity dictionary?" How can we go backwards from a knowledge of x and t to a knowledge of x' and t'? If one dictionary is provided by the formulas

Inverse Lorentz transformation

(36)
$$x = x' \cosh \theta_r + t' \sinh \theta_r$$
$$t = x' \sinh \theta_r + t' \cosh \theta_r$$

what are the formulas for translation backwards from laboratory records to rocket records? *Answer:* The Lorentz transformation "inverse" to Eqs. 36 is

(37)
$$x' = x \cosh \theta_r - t \sinh \theta_r$$
$$t' = -x \sinh \theta_r + t \cosh \theta_r$$

Proof: Substitute these expressions for x' and t' into Eqs. 36 and verify that identities result (an English word translated into Turkish and then back into English comes out as the original word provided that the one dictionary is the true inverse of the other!).

In the following table, formal definitions of the hyperbolic functions and some of the relations that they satisfy are presented in parallel with similar definitions and relations for circular functions. In this table e is the base of the natural logarithms and has the numerical value 2.718281 .... The symbol i stands for the square root of minus one, so that $i^2 = -1$. The usual rules for addition and multiplication of exponents apply to exponents containing i. The angle θ is expressed in circular or hyperbolic radians (*not* degrees). The ex-expression 4!, for instance, means *four factorial*: $4 \times 3 \times 2 \times 1$. To understand these relations derive lines 7 to 13 from the definitions in lines 1 to 6 on each side of the table and show qualitatively how the graphs of Figs. 32 and 33 follow from these relations. Note especially the differences in *sign* between the two sides of the table.

Table 8. Circular and hyperbolic functions.

Circular functions	*Hyperbolic functions*

DEFINITIONS

1. $\sin \theta = \dfrac{e^{i\theta} - e^{-i\theta}}{2i}$

1. $\sinh \theta = \dfrac{e^{\theta} - e^{-\theta}}{2}$

2. $\cos \theta = \dfrac{e^{i\theta} + e^{-i\theta}}{2}$

2. $\cosh \theta = \dfrac{e^{\theta} + e^{-\theta}}{2}$

3. $\tan \theta = \dfrac{\sin \theta}{\cos \theta}$

3. $\tanh \theta = \dfrac{\sinh \theta}{\cosh \theta}$

4. $\sin \theta = \theta - \dfrac{\theta^3}{3!} + \dfrac{\theta^5}{5!} - \dfrac{\theta^7}{7!} + \cdots$

4. $\sinh \theta = \theta + \dfrac{\theta^3}{3!} + \dfrac{\theta^5}{5!} + \dfrac{\theta^7}{7!} + \cdots$

5. $\cos \theta = 1 - \dfrac{\theta^2}{2!} + \dfrac{\theta^4}{4!} - \dfrac{\theta^6}{6!} + \cdots$

5. $\cosh \theta = 1 + \dfrac{\theta^2}{2!} + \dfrac{\theta^4}{4!} + \dfrac{\theta^6}{6!} + \cdots$

6. $\tan \theta = \theta + \dfrac{\theta^3}{3} + \dfrac{2}{15}\theta^5 + \cdots$

6. $\tanh \theta = \theta - \dfrac{\theta^3}{3} + \dfrac{2}{15}\theta^5 - \cdots$

RELATIONS

7. $\sin(-\theta) = -\sin\theta$

7. $\sinh(-\theta) = -\sinh\theta$

8. $\cos(-\theta) = \cos\theta$

8. $\cosh(-\theta) = \cosh\theta$

9. $\tan(-\theta) = -\tan\theta$

9. $\tanh(-\theta) = -\tanh\theta$

10. $\boxed{\cos^2\theta + \sin^2\theta = 1}$

10. $\boxed{\cosh^2\theta - \sinh^2\theta = 1}$

11. $\sin(\theta_1 + \theta_2) =$
$\sin\theta_1 \cos\theta_2 + \cos\theta_1 \sin\theta_2$

11. $\sinh(\theta_1 + \theta_2) =$
$\sinh\theta_1 \cosh\theta_2 + \cosh\theta_1 \sinh\theta_2$

12. $\cos(\theta_1 + \theta_2) =$
$\cos\theta_1 \cos\theta_2 - \sin\theta_1 \sin\theta_2$

12. $\cosh(\theta_1 + \theta_2) =$
$\cosh\theta_1 \cosh\theta_2 + \sinh\theta_1 \sinh\theta_2$

13. $\tan(\theta_1 + \theta_2) = \dfrac{\tan\theta_1 + \tan\theta_2}{1 - \tan\theta_1 \tan\theta_2}$

13. $\tanh(\theta_1 + \theta_2) = \dfrac{\tanh\theta_1 + \tanh\theta_2}{1 + \tanh\theta_1 \tanh\theta_2}$

POOR MAN'S QUICK RECIPES

For small θ $\sin\theta \approx \theta$
             $\tan\theta \approx \theta$

For small θ $\sinh\theta \approx \theta$
             $\tanh\theta \approx \theta$

Example: $\theta = 0.1$

     Poor man's recipe $\sin\theta \approx 0.1$
                        $\tan\theta \approx 0.1$

     Accurate values $\sin\theta = 0.0998$
                        $\tan\theta = 0.1003$

Example: $\theta = 0.1$

     Poor man's recipe $\sinh\theta \approx 0.1$
                        $\tanh\theta \approx 0.1$

     Accurate values $\sinh\theta = 0.1002$
                        $\tanh\theta = 0.0997$

For large θ $\sinh\theta \approx e^{\theta}/2$
             $\cosh\theta \approx e^{\theta}/2$

Example: $\theta = 3$ $e^{\theta} \approx 20$

     Poor man's recipe $\sinh\theta \approx 10$
                        $\cosh\theta \approx 10$

     Accurate values $\sinh\theta = 10.018$
                        $\cosh\theta = 10.068$

INTRODUCTION TO THE EXERCISES OF CHAPTER 1

Important areas of current research can be analyzed very simply using the theory of relativity. This analysis depends heavily upon a physical intuition, which develops with experience. Such experience cannot be obtained in the laboratory—simple experiments in relativity are difficult and expensive because the speed of light is so great. As alternatives to simple experiments, the following exercises involve a wide range of physical consequences of the properties of spacetime. These properties of spacetime recur here over and over again in different contexts:

> paradoxes
> puzzles
> derivations
> technological applications
> estimates
> precise calculations
> philosophical difficulties

The text of the chapter has presented all formal tools necessary to answer these exercises, but intuition—a practiced way of seeing—is best developed without hurry. For this reason it will prove useful to continue to do more and more of these exercises in relativity after one has moved on to material outside this book. Those who wish to cover the essential material in the least possible time may limit themselves to the exercises whose titles are set in boldface type in the list beginning below.

The mathematical manipulations in the exercises are very brief: only a few answers will take more than five lines to write down. On the other hand, the exercises will require some "rumination time." Unstarred exercises should require the least time; those marked with a single asterisk are more difficult; those marked with double asterisks are suitable for graduate students in physics.

WHEELER'S FIRST MORAL PRINCIPLE. *Never make a calculation until you know the answer.* Make an estimate before every calculation, try a simple physical argument (symmetry! invariance! conservation!) before every derivation, guess the answer to every puzzle. Courage: no one else needs to know what the guess is. Therefore make it quickly, by instinct. A right guess reinforces this instinct. A wrong guess brings the refreshment of surprise. In either case life as a spacetime expert, however long, is more fun!

A. THE SPACETIME INTERVAL (Text sections 5, 6, 7)

1. Space and time—a worked example
2. Practical synchronization of clocks
3. Relations between events
4. Simultaneity
5. Temporal order of events
*6. The expanding universe
7. Proper time in communication
8. Data-collecting and decision-making

B. THE LORENTZ TRANSFORMATION (Text sections 8 and 9)

9. **Lorentz contraction**—a worked example
10. **Time dilation**
11. **Relative synchronization of clocks**
12. Euclidean analogies
13. Lorentz contraction II
14. Time dilation II
15. Lorentz transformation equations with time in seconds
*16. Derivation of the Lorentz transformation equations
*17. Proper distance and proper time
*18. The place where both agree

A. THE SPACETIME INTERVAL (Text Sections 5, 6, 7)

1. Space and time—a worked example

Two events occur at the same place in the laboratory frame of reference and are separated in time by 3 seconds. (a) What is the spatial distance between these two events in a rocket frame in which the events are separated in time by 5 seconds? (b) What is the relative speed β_r of the rocket and laboratory frames?

Solution: (a) The spacetime *interval* between these two events has the same value measured in either frame of reference

$$(\Delta t)^2 - (\Delta x)^2 = (\Delta t')^2 - (\Delta x')^2$$

From the statement of the problem

$\Delta x = 0$

$\Delta t = 3$ (seconds) $\times\, c$ (meters/second)
$\qquad\qquad = 9 \times 10^8$ meters

$\Delta x' =$ to be found

$\Delta t' = 5$ (seconds) $\times\, c$ (meters/second)
$\qquad\qquad = 15 \times 10^8$ meters

Substitute these values into the expression for the interval

$$81 \times 10^{16} - 0 = 225 \times 10^{16} - (\Delta x')^2$$

From this equation find

$$(\Delta x')^2 = 144 \times 10^{16} \text{ meters}^2$$

or

$$\Delta x' = 12 \times 10^8 \text{ meters}$$

(b) In the *laboratory* frame the two events occur *at the same place*. In the *rocket* frame this laboratory "place" has moved 12×10^8 meters in 5 seconds—or in 15×10^8 meters of light-travel time. Therefore the relative speed of the two frames is

$$\Delta x'/\Delta t' = (12 \times 10^8)/(15 \times 10^8) = 4/5$$

2. Practical synchronization of clocks

You are an observer stationed near a clock with spatial coordinates $x = 6$ meters, $y = 8$ meters, and $z = 0$ meters in the laboratory frame. You wish to synchronize your clock with the one at the origin using the reference flash. Describe in detail and with numbers how to proceed.

3. Relations between events

Events A, B, and C are plotted in the laboratory spacetime diagram of Fig. 34. Answer the following questions for the pair of events A and B.

(a) Is the *interval* between the two events timelike, lightlike, or spacelike?

(b) What is the *proper time* (or *proper distance*) between the two events?

(c) Is it *possible* that one of the events *caused* the other event?

Answer the same questions for the pair of events A and C.

Answer the same questions for the pair of events C and B.

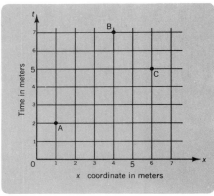

Fig. 34. What are the relations among the events A, B, and C?

4. Simultaneity

"A hits B and simultaneously one hundred million miles away C hits D." Explain in a sentence or two how special relativity teaches us to restate or qualify this statement.

5. Temporal order of events

"Event G occurred before event H." Prove that the *temporal order* of two events in the laboratory frame is the same as in all rocket frames if and only if the two events have either a timelike or a lightlike separation.

6.* The expanding universe

(a) A giant bomb explodes in otherwise empty space. What is the nature of the motion of one frag-

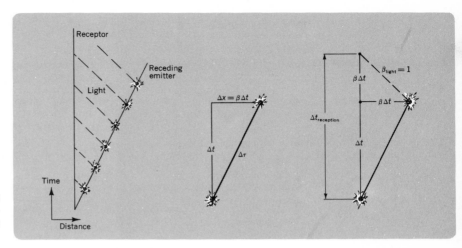

Fig. 35. Calculation of the time $\Delta t_{\text{reception}}$ between arrival at observer of consecutive flashes from receding emitter.

ment relative to another? And how can this relative motion be detected? *Discussion:* Imagine each fragment equipped with a beacon that gives off flashes of light at regular, known intervals $\Delta \tau$ of time as measured in its own frame of reference (proper time!). Knowing this interval between flashes, what method of detection can an observer on one fragment employ to determine the velocity β —relative to him—of any other fragment? Assume that he uses, in making this determination, (1) the known proper time $\Delta \tau$ between flashes and (2) *the time $\Delta t_{\text{reception}}$ between the arrival of consecutive flashes at his position.* (*Note:* This is *not* equal to the time Δt in his frame between the emission of the two flashes from the receding emitter; see Fig. 35.) Derive a formula for β in terms of $\Delta \tau$ and $\Delta t_{\text{reception}}$. How will the measured recession *velocity* depend upon the *distance* from one's own fragment to the fragment at which one is looking? (*Note:* In any given time in any given frame, fragments evidently travel *distances* in that frame from the point of explosion that are in direct proportion to their velocities in that frame!)

(b) How can observation of the light from stars be used to verify that the *universe is expanding*? *Discussion:* Atoms in hot stars give off light of different frequencies characteristic of these atoms ("spectral lines"). The *observed period* of the light in each spectral line from starlight can be measured on earth. From the *pattern* of spectral lines the kind of atom emitting the light can be identified. The same kind of atom can then be excited in the laboratory to emit light while at rest and the *proper period* of the light in any spectral line can be measured. Use the results of part (a) to describe how the *observed period* of light in one spectral line from starlight can be compared to the

proper period of light in the same spectral line from atoms at rest in the laboratory to give the *velocity of recession* of the star that emits the light. This observed change in period due to the velocity of the source is called the *Doppler shift.* (For a more detailed treatment see Ex. 75 of Chap. 2 and the exercises which follow it.) *If* the universe began in a gigantic explosion, how must the observed velocities of recession of different stars at different distances compare with one another? Slowing down during expansion—by gravitational attraction or otherwise—is to be neglected here but is considered in more complete treatments (Ex. 80).

7. Proper time in communication

A flash of light is emitted from the sun and is absorbed on the moon. "The proper time between the emission of this flash and its absorption is equal to zero." True or false? Is the proper time between the two events (emission and absorption) equal to zero if the flash is reflected back and forth between mirrors on the moon before being absorbed? (Careful!) A flash of light is emitted on earth and travels *through air* directly to another spot on the earth, where it is absorbed. (The speed of light in air is slightly less than c.) Is the proper time between the emission of this flash and its absorption equal to zero?

8. Data-collecting and decision-making

We have used a latticework of recording clocks to describe events. The position of an event is the position of the clock nearest to the event, and the time of an event is the time recorded on that clock. Physics deals with the study of the *relations* between events. If the data-analysis center is located at the origin of the latticework of clocks, what is the lag time (in that frame) between data available for analysis at this center and data already recorded on clocks at a distance R from that center? The clock at $x = 6 \times 10^9$ meters, $y = 8 \times 10^9$ meters, and $z = 0$ meters records the passage of a meteor at 41×10^9 meters of time.

The clock at $x = 3 \times 10^9$ meters, $y = 4 \times 10^9$ meters, and $z = 0$ meters records the passage of the same meteor at 47×10^9 meters of time. The observers in the data-analysis center require 3 seconds to take evasive action. If the data above are sent to them by light flash and are displayed instantly upon arrival, will they have time to protect themselves?

B. THE LORENTZ TRANSFORMATION (Text Sections 8 and 9)

9. Lorentz contraction—a worked example

A meter stick is attached to a rocket. The meter stick is observed from the laboratory frame of reference (laboratory framework of rods and clocks). In what way will the findings of the laboratory observer about the length of the meter stick contrast with those predicted by pre-relativity physics? We break this broad question down into four parts:

(a) How can this question about *length* be translated into a question about the separation of two *events?* Remarks: Each end of the meter stick traces out a world line through spacetime. But one world line is an infinite succession of events. So how is one going to pick out, in a reasonable way, exactly two events that will give the desired information about the apparent length of the meter stick?

> *Solution:* Select the following two events for attention. A: One end of the meter stick flashes past a laboratory clock just as that clock reads noontime. B: The other end of the meter stick flashes past another laboratory clock when it too reads noontime. *Discussion:* One must measure the location of both ends of the moving meter stick at the same time in the laboratory frame. Otherwise there would not be a well defined pair of laboratory points between which to carry out the length measurement. The two events are thus simultaneous in the laboratory frame of reference ($\Delta t = 0$). They may or may not be simultaneous in the rocket frame ($\Delta t'$ may or may not be zero). No matter! The meter stick is at rest in the rocket frame. In that frame the two ends may be located at leisure.

(b) When the meter stick points along the x axis (direction of motion) of the rocket so that the separation of the two ends in the rocket frame is $\Delta x' = 1$ meter, what length is observed in the laboratory frame?

Solution: The length is the separation in space of the two events A and B in the laboratory frame

$$(38) \qquad \Delta x = \Delta x'/\cosh \theta_r = \Delta x'(1 - \beta_r^2)^{1/2}$$

This length is less than one meter. The shortening is called the *Lorentz contraction.* Discussion: The Lorentz transformation (Eqs. 37) connects separations in the laboratory frame with separations in the rocket frame by the equations

$$(39) \qquad \begin{aligned} \Delta x' &= \quad \Delta x \cosh \theta_r - \Delta t \sinh \theta_r \\ \Delta t' &= -\Delta x \sinh \theta_r + \Delta t \cosh \theta_r \\ \Delta y' &= \Delta y \\ \Delta z' &= \Delta z \end{aligned}$$

The two events are simultaneous in the laboratory frame ($\Delta t = 0$). Therefore $\Delta x' = \Delta x \cosh \theta_r$, from which the answer follows. Note that $\Delta t'$ is not equal to zero; that is, the events A and B are not simultaneous as recorded in the rocket frame. This difference in time between events at the two ends of the meter stick raises no questions in the minds of the rocket workers as to the length of the meter stick. To them it is at rest and it is one meter long. Neither are they troubled that the laboratory observers record the length as shortened ("Lorentz contracted"). "Why not?" they say. "The laboratory observers marked down the positions of the two ends of the meter stick at times, t_A' and t_B', that we know to be different. How could they help but get a length different from 1 meter?"

(c) When the meter stick points along the y axis (perpendicular to the direction of motion) of the rocket frame, so that the separation of the two ends in the rocket frame is $\Delta y' = 1$ meter, what length is observed in the laboratory frame?

Solution: The length is the separation in space of the two events A and B in the laboratory frame

$$\Delta y = \Delta y'$$

This length is 1 meter. There is no shortening of dimensions perpendicular to the direction of motion. Discussion: Note that the two events are now simultaneous not only in the laboratory frame ($\Delta t = 0$), but also in the rocket frame ($\Delta t' = 0$; see Eqs. 39). Thus it is not surprising to the rocket workers that the laboratory observers should agree with them about the length of the meter stick.

(d) Reconsider the conclusion of part b. How can one possibly accept the result that a rocket meter stick appears to be shorter than one meter to laboratory observers? If this conclusion were true, would we not have a way to distinguish the physics in the rocket frame (where meter sticks have their standard length) from the physics in the laboratory (where the same meter sticks are recorded as shortened)? And if so, does not the reasoning of relativity destroy the very foundation principle of relativity? This principle states that one cannot distinguish between one inertial frame and another by any difference between the physics in the two frames. Have we not found a most striking difference between the physics in the two frames?

Solution: Yes, there is a difference between the x dimensions recorded in the two frames; but there is no difference between the *physics* in the two frames. A meter stick that is at rest relative to the rocket and that points along the direction of motion, is recorded as shorter than 1 meter in the laboratory. However, a meter stick that is at rest in the *laboratory* and that is parallel to the direction of motion is recorded as also shortened by the *rocket* workers. Objection: What preposterous story is this! I will stick to simple logic and defy all this relativity nonsense. You say that a rocket meter stick may be recorded in the laboratory as a half meter. Then you must agree that a length of a half meter in the laboratory is recorded as a full meter in the rocket frame. So rocket dimensions are longer than laboratory dimensions—along the direction of motion. Physics is as different as it could well be between the two frames. I would have no trouble at all telling whether I was in the laboratory frame or the rocket frame. Principle of relativity! What delusion! Reply: Perhaps all of us find Einstein and Lorentz disturbing at a first encounter because we have had so little experience with objects moving at really high velocities. Perhaps you will feel happier with the principle of relativity if you see

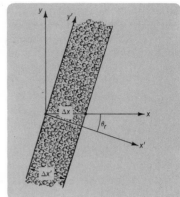

Fig. 36. A pasture extends for a greater distance in the x direction than in the x' direction.

its analog in Euclidean geometry. Of course there are some differences between the formula $(\Delta L)^2 = (\Delta x)^2 + (\Delta y)^2$ in Euclidean geometry and $(\Delta \tau)^2 = (\Delta t)^2 - (\Delta x)^2$ in Lorentz geometry. However, the question whether distances are different in two frames clearly worries you more than the question whether the distance in the new frame is less than in the old frame (Lorentz contraction in Lorentz geometry) or greater (length increase in Euclidean geometry). So look at Fig. 36. A pasture that extends for the distance $\Delta x'$ in the x' direction evidently extends for a greater distance in the x direction

$$(40) \qquad \Delta x = \Delta x'/\cos \theta_r$$

On the other hand, look now at Fig. 37 (see Ex. 48 for space and time analogs of Figs. 36 and 37). Here there is another field, which extends for the distance Δx in the x direction. However, its extension in the x' direction is greater

$$(41) \qquad \Delta x' = \Delta x/\cos \theta_r$$

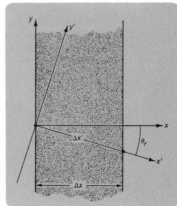

Fig. 37. Another field extends for a greater distance in the x' direction than in the x direction.

Surely you accept these results. You do not even worry about any inconsistency between formulas 40 and 41. You know as well as anyone that the Δx's in the two formulas refer to *different measurements* on *different fields*. So perhaps you will be willing to believe that the length of a meter stick that is at rest relative to a rocket will be recorded as less than a meter in the laboratory, whereas a meter stick that is at rest in the laboratory will be less than a meter to the recorders on the rocket. Response: I now agree that there is no logical inconsistency in what you have been telling me. But perhaps you will go a step further and really prove to me what you have just now said about a laboratory meter stick being recorded as less than a meter in the rocket frame. Answer: Solve the Lorentz transformation equations (Eqs. 39) for the coordinates in the laboratory frame in terms of the coordinates in the rocket frame; or merely interchange the role of the primed and unprimed coordinates in those equation, and reverse the sign of the velocity; or look up Eqs. 36, inverse to Eqs. 39; in any case, write down the relations

$$(42) \quad \begin{aligned} \Delta x &= \Delta x' \cosh \theta_r + \Delta t' \sinh \theta_r \\ \Delta t &= \Delta x' \sinh \theta_r + \Delta t' \cosh \theta_r \\ \Delta y &= \Delta y' \\ \Delta z &= \Delta z' \end{aligned}$$

Our new meter stick is at rest in the laboratory frame. It is moving as viewed from the rocket frame. Consequently a determination of its length in the rocket frame requires us to have in the rocket frame two fiducial points: the locations of the two ends of the meter stick at the same rocket time. Thus $\Delta t' = 0$. From the first of Eqs. 42 we find immediately

$$(43) \quad \Delta x' = \Delta x/\cosh \theta_r = \Delta x(1 - \beta^2)^{1/2}$$

The length recorded in the rocket frame is less than one meter when the meter stick is at rest in the laboratory—as was to be shown.

10. Time dilation

A clock is carried by a rocket (Fig. 38). The clock is observed from the laboratory frame of reference (laboratory latticework of rods and clocks). In what way will the findings of the laboratory observer about the time readings of the traveling clock contrast with those predicted by pre-relativity physics? Break this question down into four parts.

(a) How can this question about time lapse be translated into a question about the separation of two *events?*

(b) Let the rocket clock read one meter of light-travel time between the two events chosen in part a, so that the lapse of time recorded in the rocket frame is $\Delta t' = 1$ meter. Show that the time lapse observed in the laboratory frame is given by the expression

$$(44) \quad \Delta t = \Delta t' \cosh \theta_r = \Delta t'/(1 - \beta^2)^{1/2}$$

This time lapse is *more* than one meter of light-travel time. Such lengthening is called *time dilation* ("to dilate" means "to stretch").

(c) How can one possibly accept the conclusion of part b that one meter of rocket time appears longer than one meter to laboratory observers? Does not this result give one a way to distinguish the physics in the rocket frame (where clocks run at their standard rate) from the physics in the laboratory frame (where the same clocks are recorded as running slow)? Therefore does not this reasoning violate the *principle of relativity* (Sect. 3) on which rests the whole theory of relativity?

(d) Go one step further and show that one meter of time as recorded by a clock carried in the laboratory frame ($\Delta t = 1$ meter) is recorded as more than one meter of time by observers in the rocket frame, according to the formula

$$(45) \quad \Delta t' = \Delta t \cosh \theta_r = \Delta t/(1 - \beta^2)^{1/2}$$

In what way does this result verify the symmetry between laboratory and rocket frames required by the principle of relativity?

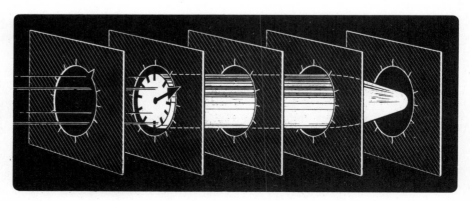

Fig. 38. A method for comparing several laboratory clocks with one rocket clock.

11. Relative synchronization of clocks

(a) Show that if two events occur simultaneously *and at the same place* in the laboratory frame they will occur simultaneously in all rocket frames. Show that if two events occur simultaneously in the laboratory frame but *not at the same position* on the *x* axis of the laboratory frame, they will *not* be simultaneous as observed in any moving rocket frame. The fact that observers in relative motion do not always agree whether two events are simultaneous is called the *relativity of simultaneity*.

(b) Two events occur simultaneously and at the same *x* coordinate in the laboratory frame, but are separated by the *y* and *z* coordinates Δy and Δz. Show that these two events are also simultaneous in the rocket frame.

(c) Use the Lorentz transformation equation to show that at $t = 0$ in the laboratory frame the clocks along the positive *x* axis in the rocket frame appear to be set behind those in the laboratory frame, with clocks farther from the origin set farther behind; and that clocks along the negative *x* axis in the rocket frame appear to be set ahead of those in the laboratory frame, with clocks farther from the origin set farther ahead, according to the equation

$$(46) \qquad t' = -x \sinh \theta_r = -x \beta_r/(1 - \beta_r^2)^{1/2}$$

(d) Use the inverse Lorentz transformation equation to show that at $t' = 0$ in the rocket frame the clocks along the positive *x* axis in the laboratory frame appear to be set ahead of those in the rocket frame, with clocks farther from the origin set farther ahead; and that clocks along the negative *x* axis in the laboratory frame appear to be set behind those in the rocket frame, with clocks farther from the origin set farther behind, according to the equation

$$(47) \qquad t = +x' \sinh \theta_r = +x' \beta_r/(1 - \beta_r^2)^{1/2}$$

The fact that neither of two observers in relative motion agrees that the reference event and the reading of zero time on all clocks of the *other* frame occur simultaneously is called the *relative synchronization of clocks*.

(e) The difference in sign between the equations in parts c and d seems to imply an asymmetry between frames that might be used to tell them apart—which would violate the principle of relativity. Show that if an observer in *either* frame chooses his positive *x* axis to lie in the direction of motion of the other frame, then physical measurements on the synchronization of clocks will give results in the two frames which are

indistinguishable. In other words, the two frames themselves are indistinguishable using this method. The difference in sign between the above equations is due to an arbitrary—and asymmetric—choice of a *common* direction for both positive *x* axes.

(f) The foregoing results are sometimes summarized by stating that a "rocket observer sees the laboratory clocks to be out of synchronism with one another." Explain what is wrong with this way of stating the matter. Show that a single rocket observer is not enough to make the required measurements. What is a sharp, clean, legalistically correct, and clear (even if considerably longer!) way to state the same result?

12. Euclidean analogies

(a) A straight rod lies in the *xy* plane of a Euclidean coordinate system. Draw a diagram showing the rod in the *xy* plane; label the projections of this rod on the *x*, *y* and *x'*, *y'* axes. Spell out an explicit analogy between the *x* components of the length of this rod as measured in two rotated Euclidean coordinate systems and the different lengths of a moving rod observed in the laboratory frame and in the rocket frame in which the rod is at rest.

(b) Spell out an explicit analogy between time dilation and the *y* components of length of the rod of part a as observed in two rotated Euclidean coordinate systems. What are the Euclidean and Lorentz invariants?

(c) Spell out an explicit analogy between the relative synchronization of clocks and the case of two rotated Euclidean coordinate systems in which points on the positive *x* axis of *one* coordinate system have, say, a negative *y* coordinate in the *other* coordinate system (more negative for points farther from the common origin).

13. Lorentz contraction II

A meter stick lies along the *x'* axis and at rest in the rocket frame. Show that an observer in the laboratory frame will conclude that the meter stick has undergone Lorentz contraction if he measures how long it takes the meter stick to pass one of his clocks and multiplies this result by the relative velocity of the two frames.

14. Time dilation II

Two events occur at the same place but at different times in the rocket frame. Show that an observer in the laboratory frame will conclude that the time between the two events has been dilated if he measures the distance between them in the laboratory frame and divides this distance by the relative velocity of the two frames.

15. Lorentz transformation equations with time in seconds

If time is expressed in seconds (written with a subscript: t_{sec}) and if v_r represents the relative speed between laboratory and rocket frames expressed in meters per second, show that the Lorentz transformation equations become

$$x' = x \cosh \theta_r - ct_{sec} \sinh \theta_r = \frac{x - v_r t_{sec}}{(1 - v_r^2/c^2)^{1/2}}$$
(48)

$$t'_{sec} = -(x/c) \sinh \theta_r + t_{sec} \cosh \theta_r = \frac{t_{sec} - (v_r/c^2)x}{(1 - v_r^2/c^2)^{1/2}}$$

where

$$v_r/c = \tanh \theta_r$$

Write down the *inverse* Lorentz transformation equations using the same notation.

16.* Derivation of the Lorentz transformation equations

Derive the transformation equations of Lorentz along new lines (due to Einstein) as follows. Let the rocket move uniformly with velocity β_r in the x direction of the laboratory. The coordinates x', y', z', t' of any event, such as an explosion, in the rocket reference frame have a one-to-one relation with the coordinates x, y, z, t of the same event measured in the laboratory frame. Moreover, $y = y'$ and $z = z'$ (perpendicular distances are the same). As for the relation between x, t and x', t', assume a *linear* relationship

$$x = ax' + bt'$$
$$t = ex' + ft'$$

with four coefficients a, b, e, f that (1) are unknown, (2) are independent of x, t and x', t', and (3) depend only upon the relative velocity β_r of the two frames of reference.

Find the *ratios* b/a, e/a, f/a as functions of velocity β_r using the following three arguments and these arguments alone: (1) A flash of light that starts at $x = 0$, $t = 0$ ($x' = 0$, $t' = 0$) moves to the *right* at the velocity of light ($x = t$; $x' = t'$) in *both* frames of reference. (2) A flash of light that starts at $x = 0$, $t = 0$ ($x' = 0$, $t' = 0$) moves to the *left* at the velocity of light ($x = -t$; $x' = -t'$) in *both* frames of reference. (3) The point $x' = 0$ has the velocity β_r in the laboratory frame.

Now use as the fourth piece of information, the invariance of the interval (Section 5): (4) $t^2 - x^2 = (t')^2 - (x')^2$ to find the constant a itself and thus all four coefficients a, b, e, f. Do the results obtained in this way agree with *Lorentz's* values for the transformation coefficients?

17.* Proper distance and proper time

(a) Two events P and Q have a spacelike separation. Show that a rocket frame can be found in which the two events occur at the *same time*. Also show that in this rocket frame the distance between the two events is equal to the proper distance σ between them. (One method: assume that such a rocket frame exists and then use the Lorentz transformation equations to show that the relative velocity of this rocket frame is less than the speed of light ($\beta_r < 1$), thus justifying the assumption made.)

(b) Two events P and R have a timelike separation. Show that a rocket frame can be found in which the two events occur at the *same place*. Also show that in this rocket frame the time between the two events is equal to the proper time τ between them.

18.* The place where both agree

At any instant there is just one plane in which both the laboratory and the rocket clocks agree. Show that the velocity of this plane in the laboratory frame is equal to $\tanh (\theta_r/2)$, where θ_r is the relative velocity parameter between laboratory and rocket frames.

19.* Transformation of angles

A meter stick lies at rest in the rocket frame and makes an angle ϕ' with the x' axis. What angle ϕ does the same meter stick make with the x axis of the laboratory frame? What is the *length* of the meter stick as observed in the laboratory frame? Next *assume* that the directions of electric-field lines around a point charge transform in the same way as the directions of meter sticks that lie along these lines. Draw qualitatively the electric-field lines due to an isolated positive point charge at rest in the rocket frame as seen in (a) the rocket frame and (b) the laboratory frame. What conclusions follow concerning the forces exerted, in the laboratory frame, on stationary test charges that surround a charge moving in that frame?

20.* Transformation of y velocity

A particle moves with uniform speed $\beta^{v'} = \Delta y'/\Delta t'$ along the y' axis of the rocket frame. Transform the components of y and t displacements using the Lorentz transformation equations. Show that the x component and the y component of the velocity of this particle in the laboratory frame are given by the expressions

(49)
$$\beta^x = \tanh \theta_r$$
$$\beta^y = \beta^{y'}/\cosh \theta_r$$

21.** Transformation of velocity directions

A particle moves with a velocity β' in the $x'y'$ plane of the rocket frame in a direction that makes an angle ϕ' with the x' axis. Find the angle that the velocity vector of this particle makes with the x axis of the laboratory frame. (Hint: Transform displacements rather than velocities.) Why does this angle differ from that found in Ex. 19? Contrast the two results when the relative velocity between the rocket and laboratory frames is very great.

22.** The headlight effect

A flash of light is emitted at an angle ϕ' with respect to the x' axis of the rocket frame. Show that the angle ϕ that the direction of this flash makes with respect to the x axis of the laboratory frame is given by the equation

(50)
$$\cos \phi = \frac{\cos \phi' + \beta_r}{1 + \beta_r \cos \phi'}$$

Show that your answer to the previous exercise gives the same result when the velocity β' is given the value one. Now consider a particle at rest in the rocket frame that emits light uniformly in all directions. Consider the 50 percent of this light that goes into the *forward* hemisphere in the rocket frame. Also, assume that the rocket moves very fast relative to the laboratory. Show that in the laboratory frame this light is concentrated in a *narrow forward cone* whose axis lies in the direction of motion of the particle. This effect is called the *headlight effect*.

C. PUZZLES AND PARADOXES

23. Einstein's train paradox— a worked example

Three men (A, O, and B) are riding on a train at a velocity β_r close to the value one. A is in front, O is at the middle, and B is at the rear (Fig. 39). A fourth man O′ is standing beside the rails. At the very instant O passes O′ it happens that two flash-bulb signals coming from A and B reach O and O′. Who emitted the signal first? Using *only* the fact that the speed of light is finite and independent of the source velocity, show that O and O′ give different answers to this question. Having answered this qualitative question, evaluate the quantitative difference between the times of emission of the flashes from A and B as observed in the frame of reference of the train (Δt_{BA}) and the frame of reference of O′ ($\Delta t_{BA}'$), either by the Lorentz transformation or by other means.

Solution: Observers A and B are *at rest* with respect to observer O. They are also equidistant from observer O, as he can verify with a meter stick at his leisure. Therefore flashes from A and B require *equal times* to arrive at O. Flashes from A and B are observed to arrive at O at the same time. *Observer O concludes, therefore, that observers A and B **emitted** their flashes at the same time:* $\Delta t_{BA} = 0$.

Observer O′ standing beside the rails draws an entirely different conclusion. He reasons as follows: "The two flashes arrived when the middle of the train (observer O) was passing me. Therefore the two flashes must both have been emitted *before* the middle of the train reached me. Before the middle of the train reached me, observer A was *nearer to me* than was observer B. Thus

Fig. 39. Did rider A or rider B emit his flash first?

light from B had farther to travel to reach me—and therefore *took a longer time* to reach me—than did light from A. But both flashes *arrived* at the same time. Therefore *observer B must have emitted his flash **before** observer A emitted his flash.*" ($\Delta t'_{BA} = t'_B - t'_A < 0$) In summary, observer O' beside the tracks concludes that B emitted his flash *before* A emitted his flash, while observer O riding on the train concludes that A and B emitted their flashes *at the same time.*

What is the observed difference of times between the emissions, A and B, of these flashes? In the unprimed train frame the flashes are emitted simultaneously, so $\Delta t = 0$. The separation between the emissions is $\Delta x = \Delta x_{BA} = x_B - x_A = L$ where L is the length of the train. Therefore in the primed frame (which moves to the *right* relative to the unprimed train frame, as is conventional in the primed-unprimed notation) the time between emissions can be found from the Lorentz transformation equation

$$\Delta t' = -\Delta x \sinh \theta_r + \Delta t \cosh \theta_r$$
$$\Delta t' = -L \sinh \theta_r = -L\beta_r/(1 - \beta_r^2)^{1/2}$$

The minus sign shows that observer B (who is on the positive x' axis) emitted his flash at an *earlier*—a more negative—rocket time than observer A emitted his flash.

24. Einstein puzzler

When Einstein was a boy, he mulled over the following puzzler: A runner looks at himself in a mirror that he holds at arm's length in front of him. If he runs with nearly the speed of light, will he be able to see himself in the mirror? Analyze this question in terms of relativity.

25.* The pole and barn paradox

A worried student writes, "Relativity must be *wrong*. Consider a 20-meter pole carried so fast in the direction of its length that it appears to be only 10 meters long in the laboratory frame of reference. Therefore at some instant the pole can be entirely enclosed in a barn 10 meters long (Fig. 40). However, look at the same situation from the frame of reference of the runner. To him the *barn* appears to be contracted to half its length. How can a 20-meter pole fit into a 5-meter barn? Does not this unbelievable conclusion prove that relativity contains somewhere a fundamental logical inconsistency?"

Write a reply to the worried student explaining

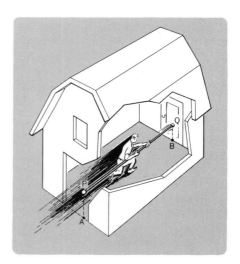

Fig. 40. Fast runner with "20-meter pole" enclosed in "10-meter barn." In the next instant he will burst through the back door, which is made of paper.

clearly and carefully how the pole and barn are treated by relativity without contradiction. (Clear up the paradox by making two carefully labeled space-time diagrams, one an xt diagram, the other an $x't'$ diagram. Take the "event" Q coinciding with A to be at the origin of both diagrams. In both plot the world lines of A, B, P, and Q. Pay attention to the *scale* of both diagrams. Label both diagrams with the times (in meters) at which Q coincides with B. Do the same for the times at which P coincides with B. Calculate these times, using the equations of the Lorentz transformation or some other method.)

26.** Space war

Two rockets of equal rest length are passing "head on" at relativistic speeds. Observer O has a gun in the

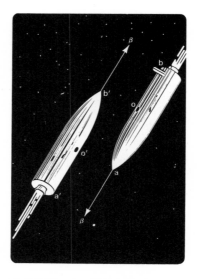

Fig. 41. Two rocket ships passing at high speed.

tail of his rocket pointing perpendicular to the direction of relative motion. He fires the gun when points a and a' coincide:

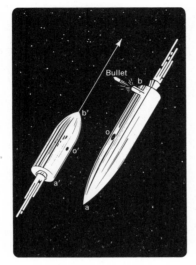

Fig. 42. In frame of *o* one expects a bullet fired when *a* coincides with *a'* to *miss* other ship.

In the frame of O the other rocket ship is Lorentz contracted. Therefore O expects his bullet to miss the other rocket. But in the frame of the other observer, O', it is the rocket ship of O that appears to be Lorentz contracted. Therefore when points a and a' coincide, observer O' sees

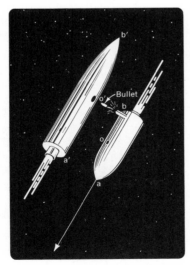

Fig. 43. In frame of *o'* one expects a bullet fired when *a* coincides with *a'* to *hit* other ship.

Does the bullet actually hit or miss? Discuss your answer: Pinpoint the looseness of the language used to state the problem, also the error in one diagram.

27.* The clock paradox†
Version I; other versions in Exs. 49, 51, and 81

On their twenty-first birthday, Peter leaves his twin Paul behind on the earth and goes off in the *x* direction for seven years of *his* time (2.2×10^8 seconds or 6.6×10^{16} meters of time) at $(24/25) = 0.96$ the speed of light, then reverses direction and in another seven years of his time returns at the same speed. (a) What is Peter's age on his return? (b) Make a spacetime diagram showing the motion of Peter. Indicate on it the *x* and *t* coordinates of the turn-around point and of the point of reunion. For simplicity idealize the earth as an inertial frame, adopt this inertial frame in the construction of the diagram, and take the origin to be the event of departure. (c) How old is Paul at the moment of reunion?

28.* Things that move faster than light‡

The Lorentz transformation equations have no meaning if the relative velocity of the two frames is greater than the velocity of light. This is taken to imply that mass, energy, and information (messages) cannot be moved from place to place faster than the speed of light. Check this implication in the following examples.

(a) The scissors paradox. A very long straight rod, which is inclined at an angle ϕ with the *x* axis, moves downward with uniform speed β^y (Fig. 44). Find the speed β_A of the point of intersection A of the lower edge of the stick with the *x* axis. Can this speed be greater than the speed of light? Can it be used to transmit a *message* from the origin to someone far out on the *x* axis?

(b) Suppose that the same rod is initially at rest with the point of intersection A at the origin. The region of the rod which is centered on the origin is struck by the downward blow of a hammer. The point of intersection moves to the right. Can this motion of the point of intersection be used to transmit a message faster than the speed of light?

†For reprints of several articles on the clock paradox, together with references to many more articles, see *Special Relativity Theory*, Selected Reprints, published for the American Association of Physics Teachers by the American Institute of Physics, 335 East 45th Street, New York 17, New York, 1963.

‡See Milton A. Rothman, "Things that go Faster than Light," Scientific American **203**, 142 (July, 1960).

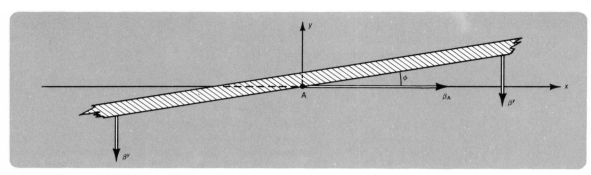

Fig. 44. Can the point of intersection A move with a speed greater than the speed of light?

(c) A very powerful searchlight is rotated rapidly in such a way that its beam sweeps out a flat plane. Observers A and B are on the plane and each the same distance from the searchlight but not near to each other. How far from the searchlight must A and B be in order that the searchlight beam will sweep from A to B faster than a light signal could travel from A to B? Before they took their positions, the two observers were given the following instructions:

To A: "When you see the searchlight beam, fire a bullet at B."

To B: "When you see the searchlight beam, duck because A has fired a bullet at you."

Under these circumstances, has not a warning gone from A to B with a speed faster than that of light?

(d) The manufacturers of some oscilloscopes claim writing speeds in excess of the speed of light. Is this possible?

D. BACKGROUND

29. Synchronization by a traveling clock—a worked example

Mr. Engelsberg does not approve of our method of synchronizing clocks by light flashes (Sect. 4). "I can synchronize my clocks in any way I choose," he says. Is he right? Mr. Engelsberg wishes to synchronize two identical clocks, named Big Ben and Little Ben, which are separated by one million miles (a little more than 1.5×10^9 meters) and which have zero relative velocity. He uses a third clock, identical in construction to the first two, that travels with constant velocity between them. As his moving clock passes Big Ben, it is set to read the same time as Big Ben. When the moving clock passes Little Ben, that outpost clock is set to read the same time as the traveling clock. "Now Big Ben and Little Ben are synchronized," says Mr.

Engelsberg. Is he right? How much out of synchronism are Big and Little Ben as measured by a lattice-work of clocks—at rest relative to them both—that has been synchronized in the conventional manner using light flashes? Evaluate this lack of synchronism when the traveling clock that Mr. Engelsberg uses moves at one hundred thousand miles per hour (4.5×10^4 meters per second). Is there any earthly reason—aside from matters of personal preference—why we all should not adopt the method of synchronization used by Mr. Engelsberg?

Solution: Start with the numerical part of the solution. A latticework of clocks at rest with respect to Big Ben and Little Ben—a latticework whose clocks are synchronized by the standard method using light flashes—can be used to make observations of the traveling clock. Relative to this latticework the traveling clock moves at $v = 4.5 \times 10^4$ meters per second, or $\beta = v/c =$

$$\frac{4.5 \times 10^4 \text{ meters per second}}{3 \times 10^8 \text{ meters per second}} = 1.5 \times 10^{-4} \text{ meters}$$

of distance per meter of light-travel time. At this rate it covers the distance between Big Ben and Little Ben in a time, $\Delta t = 10^{13}$ meters of light-travel time. Comparison of readings of the lattice clocks with the traveling clock as it passes these in turn will show the phenomenon of *time dilation* (Ex. 10). With respect to the lattice clocks the traveling clock will run slow by a factor $(1 - \beta^2)^{1/2}$. Therefore, the time, $\Delta t'$, of travel between Big Ben and Little Ben as recorded on the *traveling clock* is

$$\Delta t' = \Delta t (1 - \beta^2)^{1/2}$$
$$= \Delta t (1 - 2.25 \times 10^{-8})^{1/2}$$

Use the binomial expansion

$$(1 - \delta)^{1/2} = 1 - (\delta/2) - (1/8)\delta^2 - \cdots \approx 1 - \delta/2$$
$$\text{(for small } \delta)$$

to give an approximate answer

$$\Delta t' \approx \Delta t - (1/2)\, 2.25 \times 10^{-8}\, \Delta t$$

or

(51) $\Delta t' - \Delta t = -1.12 \times 10^{-8} \times 10^{13}$
$= -1.12 \times 10^{5}$ meters $= -0.4 \times 10^{-3}$ seconds

Set Little Ben by the traveling clock and then compare its reading with nearby clocks of the lattice. Little Ben will then read *earlier* than the lattice clocks by 0.4 millisecond.

There is a more direct way to find the lapse of time $\Delta t'$ recorded by the traveling clock on its way from Big Ben to Little Ben. The route is straight. The lapse of traveling-clock time along this world line is therefore equal to the proper length of the world line itself between the two events; that is, equal to the *interval* between the passages past Big and Little Ben:

$$\Delta t' = \Delta(\text{proper time}) = (\text{interval})$$
$$= [(\Delta t)^2 - (\Delta x)^2]^{1/2}$$

This calculation gives the result for the time discrepancy between laboratory clocks and the traveling clock

$$\Delta t' - \Delta t = [(\Delta t)^2 - (\Delta x)^2]^{1/2} - \Delta t$$

in complete agreement with Eq. 51.

Now return to consider the validity of the traveling-clock method of defining synchronization of clocks. Mr. Engelsberg is free to define synchronization in any way he wishes. However, if he uses the traveling-clock method to synchronize Big Ben and Little Ben he will find the following difficulties: (1) The settings one gives to laboratory clocks by this method of synchronization will depend on the *speed* of the traveling clock. Let the traveling clock move ten times faster than the speed given in the example above. Then the discrepancy between Little Ben and nearby lattice clocks will be not 0.4 milliseconds but about 40 milliseconds. Two Little Bens side by side that are synchronized using traveling clocks moving at different speeds will not agree with each other! (2) Even if traveling clocks are limited to a given speed, the results of this method of synchronization will depend on the *path* of the traveling clock. The longer the path taken by the traveling clock at its fixed speed, the earlier will Little Ben read as compared to nearby lattice clocks. (3) If the traveling clock makes a *round trip* from Big Ben, it will not be synchro-

nized with Big Ben on its return! (The clock paradox, Ex. 27.) There are other inconveniences that result from Mr. Engelsberg's method of synchronization, but these are enough to show its inappropriateness for any simple description of what goes on in spacetime.

30. Time dilation and construction of clocks

In describing the phenomenon of time dilation in Ex. 10 we made no distinction between spring clocks, quartz crystal clocks, biological clocks (aging), atomic clocks, radioactive clocks, and a clock in which the ticking element is a pulse of light flashing back and forth between two mirrors. Let all these clocks be adjusted to run at the same rate when at rest in the rocket frame. When these clocks fly past standard clocks in the laboratory frame, show that the phenomenon of time dilation (Ex. 10) occurs quite independently of the inner workings of the clocks. (Discussion: How does it happen that the construction of the clocks never came into discussion before? With flashes of light flying back and forth from one clock to another for purposes of synchronization, is any clock machinery really needed? Did one ever need anything more than a first light pulse, say from an electric spark, and half-silvered mirrors at measured locations here and there (Fig. 45) to create definite time delays?)

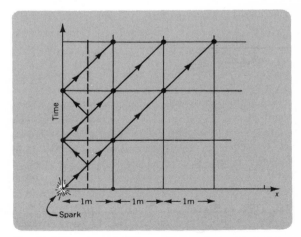

Fig. 45. Measurement of time using no clocks. Dashed line is world line of half-silvered mirror.

31. Earthbound inertial reference frames

A reference frame is inertial within some region of space and time if test particles at rest remain at rest within some specified accuracy throughout that region of spacetime. A spaceship in free fall near the earth has been shown to be effectively an inertial frame for time periods of a few seconds. Many experiments involving fast-moving particles and light itself are observed in earthbound laboratories, which are not in free fall! The force of gravity is present in an earthbound laboratory. Nevertheless, some of these experiments require so little time that a test particle released as the experiment begins does not fall very far before the experiment is over. For the purposes of many experiments, therefore, the earthbound laboratory is an inertial frame with considerable accuracy.

(a) An elementary particle with a velocity 0.96 that of light passes through a cubical spark chamber with edges 1 meter long. How far will a separate test particle released from rest fall in the gravitational field of the earth in this time? Compare your answer

with the dimensions of an atomic nucleus (a few times 10^{-15} meters). Summarize by stating the dimensions of the spacetime region in which the laboratory or earthbound frame is idealized to be inertial and the specified accuracy. How big would the spark chamber have to be in order that the separate test particle would drop a *measurable* amount from rest in the time that an elementary particle of speed 0.96 c traverses the chamber?

(b) In the Michelson-Morley experiment (Ex. 33) a beam of light is reflected back and forth between pairs of mirrors about 2 meters apart so that it travels a total distance of 22 meters. How far will a test particle fall from rest in the gravitational field of the earth during the time that a particular photon traverses the Michelson-Morley equipment? To what accuracy is the earthbound frame inertial in the spacetime region in which the Michelson-Morley experiment is carried out?

32.* Size of an inertial frame

How large can a given region of space be ($\Delta x = \Delta y = \Delta z = L$, meters), how *long* can it be studied (Δt, meters!), and how *close* can it be to a center of gravitational attraction, before a detectable discrepancy, ϵ, from an ideal inertial reference system shows up?

(a) *One kind of discrepancy: relative acceleration perpendicular to the line of attraction.*
  (1) Special case. Two ball bearings are released from rest from a common height of 250 meters

above the earth and 25 meters apart (Fig. 46). Show that they will move closer together by a distance of about 10^{-3} meter before striking the earth. (Analyze by the method of similar triangles or by some other method. This is the example treated on page 9 of the text.) The time to fall 250 meters at an acceleration of 9.8 meters per second per second is about 7 seconds or 21×10^8 meters of light-travel time. In summary, a falling railway coach can be treated as an inertial reference system under these conditions:

ϵ (smallest discrepancy given instruments can detect)	Conditions that are adequate to guarantee that discrepancy from ideal inertial frame cannot be detected			
	r (distance from center of earth)	Δx (horizontal spread)	Δy and Δz (spread of region in other two directions)	Δt (time of observation)
$\epsilon \geq 1 \times 10^{-3}$ meter	$r \geq r_e =$ 6.4×10^6 meters	$\Delta x =$ $L \leq 25$ meters	Assumed zero in analysis; therefore have to be assumed zero here in default of further analysis (part c)	$\Delta t \leq$ 21×10^8 meters (7 seconds)

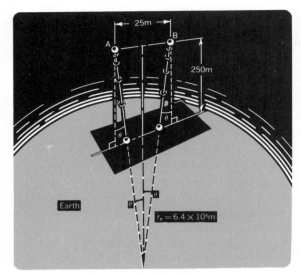

Fig. 46. Ball bearings released side by side near the earth move *closer together* as they descend. (Figure is not drawn to scale.)

(2) More general case. Test particle B is displaced Δx relative to test particle A. They have the same distance r from the center of attraction, and are studied for a time Δt. Denote by a the common acceleration of the two particles towards the center of attraction in meters per second per second, or by $a^* = a/c^2$ the value of the same acceleration measured in meters of distance per meter of time per meter of time. Show that the acceleration of particle B *relative to* A $(\Delta a^x)^*$ (meters of distance per meter of time per meter of time) is given by the formula

(52) $$(\Delta a^x)^* = -(\Delta x/r)a^*$$

(Assume that the relevant angles are so small that the sine and the tangent and the angle itself can all be identified with one another.)

(b) *Another kind of discrepancy: relative acceleration parallel to the line of attraction.*

(1) General case. Test particle B is displaced by the amount Δz relative to A and parallel to r. Therefore B is further away from the center of attraction than A and experiences a smaller attraction. Consequently B is left behind A— or, as seen by an observer on A, B has a relative acceleration in the positive z direction. Show that this relative acceleration (in meters of distance per meter of time per meter of time) is

(53) $$(\Delta a^z)^* = +(2\,\Delta z/r)\,a^*$$

(Hint: Use the fact that a^* falls off according to Newton's inverse square law of gravitation; thus, $a^* = \text{constant}/r^2$. Evaluate at r and at $r + \Delta z$ and take the difference. Take advantage of the fact that Δz is very small (a few meters) compared to r (thousands of kilometers) to simplify the result!)

(2) Special case. (Page 9 of text.) One test particle is 250 meters above the surface of the earth, the other 275 meters. How much will the 25 meter separation between the particles be increased in the approximately 7 seconds it takes for the first particle to hit the ground? (Hint: By what factor do the expressions for Δa^z in part b,1, and Δa^x in part a,2, differ from each other?) Use your result to complete—or, if you wish, to revise—the table in part a,1.

(c) *Case in which the region of experimentation is far from the center of the earth.*

The space corporation increases the scope of the experiments with test particles and light rays. The research group finds that the region used for previous experiments is not large enough for the new program and 7 seconds is not long enough. Management agrees to its recommendation for a space $\Delta x = 200$ meters, $\Delta y = 200$ meters, $\Delta z = 100$ meters and a time of 100 seconds, with the same tolerance as before, $\epsilon = 1 \times 10^{-3}$ meters = 1 millimeter. To how many earth radii from the center of the earth must the equipment be boosted by rockets to make the departures from ideality less than the tolerable upper limit? (Some possible questions to ask along the way: How does a^* vary with the distance r from the center of the earth? How do $(\Delta a^x)^*$ and $(\Delta a^z)^*$ vary with r? How do Δx and Δz depend upon $(\Delta a^x)^*$ and $(\Delta a^z)^*$ and the time Δt?)

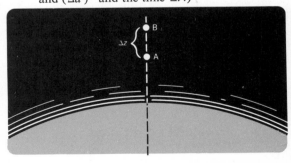

Fig. 47. Ball bearings released one above the other near the earth move *farther apart* as they descend. (Figure is not drawn to scale.)

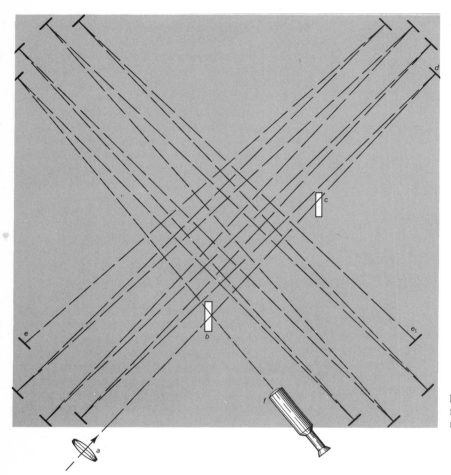

Fig. 48. Michelson-Morley interferometer mounted on a rotating marble slab.

33.* The Michelson-Morley experiment†

(a) An airplane moves with air speed c (not the speed of light) from point A to point B on the earth. A stiff wind of speed v is blowing from B toward A. Show that the time for a round trip from A to B and back to A under these circumstances is greater by a factor $1/(1 - v^2/c^2)$ than the corresponding round-trip time in still air. Paradox: The wind helps on one leg of the flight as well as hinders on the other: Why, therefore, is the round-trip time not the same in the presence of wind as in still air? Give a simple physical reason for this difference. What happens when the wind speed is nearly equal to the speed of the airplane?

(b) The same airplane now makes a round trip between A and C. The distance between A and C is the same as the distance from A to B, but the line from A to C is perpendicular to the line from A to B, so that in moving between A and C the plane flies *across* the wind. Show that the round-trip time between A and C under these circumstances is greater by a factor $1/(1 - v^2/c^2)^{1/2}$ than the corresponding round-trip time in still air.

(c) Two airplanes with the same air speed c start from A at the same time. One travels from A to B and back to A, flying first against and then with the wind (wind speed v). The other travels from A to C and back to A, flying across the wind. Which one will arrive

---

†A. A. Michelson and E. W. Morley, American Journal of Science, **34**, 333 (1887). The logical position of the experiment in the theory of relativity is outlined by H. P. Robertson, in Reviews of Modern Physics, **21**, 378 (1949).

home first, and what will be the difference in their arrival times? Using the binomial theorem show that if $v \ll c$, then an approximate expression for this time

difference is $\Delta t = \dfrac{L}{2c} \left(\dfrac{v^2}{c^2} \right)$, where L is the round-trip

distance between A and B (and between A and C).

(d) The South Pole Air Station is the supply depot for research huts on a circle of 300-kilometer radius centered on the air station. Every Monday many supply planes start simultaneously from the station and fly radially in all directions at the same altitude. Each plane drops supplies and mail to one of the research huts and flies directly home. A Fussbudget with a stopwatch stands on the hill overlooking the air station. He notices that the planes do not all return at the same time. This discrepancy perplexes him because he knows from careful measurement that (1) the distance from the air station to every research hut is the same, (2) every plane flies with the same air speed as every other plane—300 kilometers per hour, and (3) every plane travels in a straight line over the ground from station to hut and back. The Fussbudget finally decides that the discrepancy is due to the wind at the high altitude at which the planes fly. With his stopwatch he measures the time from the return of the first plane to the return of the last plane to be 4 seconds. What is the wind speed at the altitude where the planes fly? What can the Fussbudget say about the *direction* of this wind?

(e) In their famous experiment Michelson and Morley attempted to detect the so-called *ether drift*—the motion of the earth through the "ether," with respect to which light was supposed to have the velocity c. They compared the round-trip times for light to travel equal distances parallel and perpendicular to the direction of motion of the earth around the sun. They reflected the light back and forth between nearly parallel mirrors. (This would correspond to part c if each airplane made repeated round trips.) By this means they were able to use a total round-trip length of 22 meters for each path. If the "ether" is at rest with respect to the sun, and if the earth moves at 30×10^3 meters per second in its path around the sun, what is the approximate difference in time of return between light flashes that are emitted simultaneously and travel along the two perpendicular paths? Even with the instruments of today, the difference predicted by the ether-drift hypothesis would be too small to measure directly, and the following method was used instead.

(f) The original Michelson-Morley *interferometer* is diagramed in Fig. 48. Nearly monochromatic light (light of a single frequency) enters through the lens at a. Some of the light is reflected by the half-silvered mirror at b and the rest of the light continues toward d. Both beams are reflected back and forth until they reach mirrors e and e_1 respectively, where each beam is reflected back upon itself and retraces its path to mirror b. At mirror b parts of each beam combine to enter telescope f together. The transparent piece of glass at c, of the same dimensions as the half-silvered mirror b, is inserted so that both beams pass the same number of times (three times) through this thickness of glass on their way to telescope f.

Suppose that the perpendicular path lengths are exactly equal and the instrument is at rest with respect to the ether. Then monochromatic light from the two paths that leaves mirror b in some relative phase will return to mirror b in the same phase. Under these circumstances the waves entering telescope f will *add* and the image in this telescope will be *bright*. On the other hand, if one of the beams has been delayed a time corresponding to one-half period of the light, then it will arrive at mirror b one-half period later, and the waves entering the telescope will *cancel*, so the image in the telescope will be *dark*. If one beam is retarded a time corresponding to one whole period, the telescope image will be bright, and so forth. What time interval corresponds to one period of the light? Michelson and Morley used sodium light of wavelength 5890 angstroms (one angstrom is equal to 10^{-10} meter). From the equations $\nu\lambda = c$ and $\nu = 1/T$ show that one period of sodium light corresponds to about 2×10^{-15} seconds.

Now there is no way to "turn off" the alleged ether drift, adjust the apparatus, and then turn on the alleged ether drift again. Instead of this, Michelson and Morley floated their interferometer in a pool of mercury and rotated it slowly about its center like a phonograph record while observing the image in the telescope (Fig. 48). In this way if light is delayed on either path when the instrument is oriented in a certain direction, light on the *other* path will be delayed by the same amount of time when the instrument has rotated 90 degrees. Hence the *total change* in delay time between the two paths observed as the interferometer rotates should be *twice* the difference calculated using the expression derived in part c.

By simple refinements of this method Michelson and Morley were able to show that the time change between the two paths as the instrument rotated corresponded to less than *one one-hundredth* of the shift from one dark image in the telescope to the next dark image. Show that this result implies that the motion of the ether at the surface of the earth—if it exists at all—is less than one sixth of the speed of the earth in its orbit. In order to eliminate the possibility that the ether was flowing past the sun at the same rate as the earth was moving its orbit, they repeated the experiment at intervals of three months, always with negative results.

(g) Does the Michelson-Morley experiment, by itself, disprove the theory that light is propagated through an ether? Can the ether theory be modified to agree with the results of this experiment? How? What further experiment can be used to test the modified theory?

34.* The Kennedy-Thorndike experiment†

The Michelson-Morley experiment was designed to detect any motion of the earth relative to a hypothetical fluid—the ether—a medium in which light was supposed to move with characteristic speed c. No such relative motion of earth and ether was detected. Partly as a result of this experiment the concept of ether has since been discarded. In the modern view, light requires no medium for its transmission.

What significance does the negative result of the Michelson-Morley experiment have for us who do not believe in the ether theory of light propagation? Simply this: (1) The round-trip speed of light measured on earth is the same in every direction—the speed of light is *isotropic*. (2) The speed of light is isotropic not only when the earth moves in one direction around the sun in, say, January (call the earth with this motion the "laboratory frame"); but also when the earth moves in the *opposite* direction around the sun six months later, in July (call the earth with this motion the "rocket frame"). (3) The generalization of this result to any pair of inertial frames in relative motion is contained in the statement, *the round-trip speed of light is isotropic both in the laboratory frame and in the rocket frame.*

This result leaves an important question unanswered: Does the round-trip speed of light—which is isotropic in both laboratory and rocket frames—also have *the same numerical value* in laboratory and rocket frames? The assumption that this speed has the same numerical value in both frames played a central role in

†The report of the original experiment is found in the Physical Review, **42**, 400, (1932). The logical position of the experiment in the theory of relativity is outlined by H. P. Robertson in the Reviews of Modern Physics, **21**, 378 (1949).

demonstrating the invariance of the interval (Section 5). But is this assumption valid?

(a) An experiment to test the assumption of the equality of the round-trip speed of light in two inertial frames in relative motion was conducted in 1932 by Roy J. Kennedy and Edward M. Thorndike. The experiment uses an interferometer with arms of *unequal* length (Fig. 49). Assume that one arm of the interferometer is Δl longer than the other arm. Show that a flash of light entering the apparatus will take a time $2\Delta l/c$ longer to complete the round trip along the longer arm than along the shorter arm. The difference in length Δl used by Kennedy and Thorndike was approximately 16 centimeters. What is the approximate difference in time for the round trip of a light flash along the alternative paths?

(b) Instead of a pulse of light, Kennedy and Thorndike used continuous monochromatic light of period $T = 1.820 \times 10^{-15}$ seconds ($\lambda = 5461$ angstroms) from a mercury source. Light that traverses the longer arm of the interferometer will return approximately how many periods n later than light that traverses the shorter arm? If in the actual experiment the number of periods is an integer, the reunited light from the two arms will *add* and the field of view seen through the telescope will be *bright*. In contrast, if in the actual experiment the number of periods is a half-integer, the reunited light from the two arms will *cancel* and the field of view of the telescope will be *dark*.

(c) The earth continues on its path around the sun. Six months later the earth has reversed the direction of its velocity relative to the fixed stars. In this new frame of reference will the round-trip speed of light have the same numerical value c as in the original frame of reference? One can rewrite the answer to part b for the original frame of reference in the form

$$(54) \qquad c = (2/n)(\Delta l/T)$$

where Δl is the difference in length between the two interferometer arms, T is the time for one period of the atomic light source, and n is the number of periods that elapse between the return of the light on the shorter path and the return of the light on the longer path. Suppose that as the earth orbits the sun no shift is observed in the telescope field of view from, say, light toward dark. This means that n is observed to be constant. What would this hypothetical result tell about the numerical value c of the speed of light? Point out the *standards* of distance and time used in determining this result, as they appear in Eq. 54. Quartz has the greatest stability of dimension of any known material. Atomic time standards have proved to be

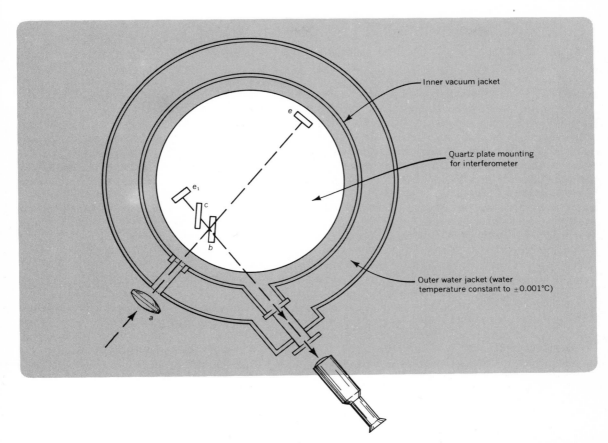

Inner vacuum jacket

Quartz plate mounting
for interferometer

Outer water jacket (water
temperature constant to $\pm 0.001°C$)

Fig. 49. Schematic diagram of apparatus used for the Kennedy-Thorndike experiment. Parts of the interferometer have been labeled with letters corresponding to those used in describing the Michelson-Morley interferometer (Ex. 33). The experimenters went to great lengths to insure the optical and mechanical stability of their apparatus. The interferometer is mounted on a plate of quartz, which changes dimension very little when temperature changes. The interferometer is enclosed in a vacuum jacket so that changes in atmospheric pressure will not alter the effective optical path length of the interferometer arms (slightly different speed of light at different atmospheric pressure!). The inner vacuum jacket is surrounded by an outer water jacket in which the water is kept at a temperature that varies less than ± 0.001 degree centigrade. The entire apparatus shown in the figure is enclosed in a small darkroom (not shown) maintained at a temperature constant within a few hundredths of a degree. The small darkroom is in turn enclosed in a larger darkroom whose temperature is constant within a few tenths of a degree. The overall size of the apparatus can be judged from the fact that the difference in length of the two arms of the interferometer (length be compared with length be_1) is 16 centimeters.

the most dependable earth-bound timekeeping mechanisms.

(d) In order to carry out the experiment outlined in the preceding paragraphs, Kennedy and Thorndike would have had to keep their interferometer operating perfectly for half a year while continuously observing the field of view through the telescope. Uninterrupted operation for so long a time was not feasible. The actual durations of their observations varied from eight days to a month. There were several such periods of observation at three-month intervals. From the data obtained in these periods, Kennedy and Thorndike were able to estimate that over a single six-month observation the number of periods n of relative delay would vary by less than the fraction 3/1000 of one period. Take the differential of Eq. 54 to find the largest fractional change dc/c of the round-trip speed of light between the two frames consistent with this estimated change in n (frame No. 1—the "laboratory" frame—and frame No. 2—the "rocket" frame—being in the present analysis the earth itself at two different times of year, with a relative velocity twice the speed of the earth in its orbit: 2×30 kilometers per second).

Historical note: At the time of the Michelson-Morley experiment in 1887 no one was ready for the idea that physics—including the speed of light—is the same in every inertial frame of reference. According to today's standard Einstein interpretation it seems obvious that both the Michelson-Morley and the Kennedy-Thorndike experiments should give null results. However, when Kennedy and Thorndike made their measurements in 1932, two alternatives to the Einstein theory were open to consideration (designated here as theory A and theory B). Both A and B assumed the old idea of an absolute space, or "ether," in which light has the speed c. Both A and B explained the zero fringe shift in the Michelson-Morley experiment by saying that all matter that moves at a velocity v relative to "absolute space" undergoes a shrinkage of its space dimensions in the direction of motion to a new length equal to $(1 - v^2/c^2)^{1/2}$ times the old length ("Lorentz-FitzGerald contraction hypothesis"). The two theories differed as to the effect of "motion through absolute space" on the running rate of a clock. Theory A said, no effect. Theory B said that a standard seconds clock moving through absolute space at velocity v has a time between ticks of $(1 - v^2/c^2)^{1/2}$ seconds. On theory B the ratio $\Delta l/T$ in Eq. 54 will not be affected by the velocity of the clock, and the Kennedy-Thorndike experiment will give a null result, as observed ("complicated explanation for simple effect"). On theory A the ratio $\Delta l/T$ in

Eq. 54 will be multiplied by the factor $(1 - v_1^2/c^2)^{1/2}$ at a time of year when the "velocity of the earth relative to absolute space" is v_1; and multiplied by $(1 - v_2^2/c^2)^{1/2}$ at a time of year when this velocity is v_2. Thus the fringes should shift from one time of year ($v_1 = v_{\text{orbital}} + v_{\text{sun}}$) to another time of year ($v_2 = v_{\text{orbital}} - v_{\text{sun}}$) unless by accident the sun happened to have "zero velocity relative to absolute space"—an accident judged so unlikely as not to provide an acceptable explanation of the observed null effect. Thus the Kennedy-Thorndike experiment ruled out theory A (length contraction alone) but allowed theory B (length contraction plus time contraction)—and also allowed the much simpler Einstein theory of equivalence of all inertial reference frames.

The "sensitivity" of the Kennedy-Thorndike experiment depends upon the theory under consideration. In the context of theory A the observations set an upper limit of about 15 kilometers per second to the "speed of the sun through absolute space" (sensitivity reported in the Kennedy-Thorndike paper). In the context of Einstein's theory the observations say that the round-trip speed of light has the same numerical magnitude—within an error of about 2 meters per second—in inertial frames of reference having a relative velocity of 60 kilometers per second.

35.* The Dicke experiment†

(a) The Leaning Tower of Pisa is about 55 meters high. Galileo says, "the variation of speed in air between balls of gold, lead, copper, porphyry, and other heavy materials is so slight that in a fall of 100 cubits [about 46 meters] a ball of gold would surely not outstrip one of copper by as much as four fingers. Having observed this I came to the conclusion that in a medium totally devoid of resistance all bodies would fall with the same speed."‡ Taking four fingers to be equal to seven centimeters, find the *maximum fractional difference* in the acceleration of gravity $\Delta g/g$ between balls of gold and copper that would be con-

---

†R. H. Dicke, "The Eötvös Experiment," Scientific American, **205**, 84 (December, 1961). See also P. G. Roll, R. Krotkov, and R. H. Dicke, Annals of Physics, **26**, 442 (1964). The first of these articles is a popular exposition written early in the course of the present experiment. The second article reports the final results of the experiment and takes on added interest because of its account of the elaborate precautions required to insure that no influence that might affect the experiment was disregarded.

‡Galileo Galilei, *Dialogues Concerning Two New Sciences,* translated by Henry Crew and Alfonso de Salvio (Northwestern University Press, Evanston, Illinois, 1950).

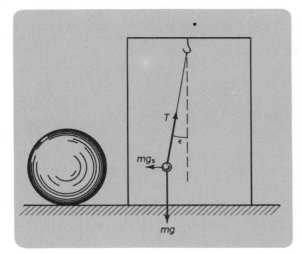

Fig. 50. Nearby massive sphere results in static deflection of plumb line from vertical.

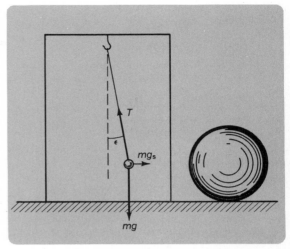

Fig. 51. Rolling the sphere to the other side results in static deflection of plumb line in opposite direction.

sistent with Galileo's experimental result. The result of the more modern Dicke experiment is that this fraction is not greater than 3×10^{-11}. Assume that the fraction has the more recently determined maximum value. Determine how far behind the first ball the second one will be when the first reaches the ground if they are dropped simultaneously from the top of a 46-meter vacuum chamber. Under these same circumstances, how far would balls of different material have to fall in a vacuum in a uniform gravitational field of 10 meters per second per second for one ball to lag behind the other one by a distance of 1 millimeter? Compare this distance with that of the moon from the earth (3.8×10^8 meters). Clearly the Dicke experiment was not carried out using falling balls!

(b) A plumb bob of mass m hangs on the end of a long line from the ceiling of a closed room (Fig. 50). A very massive sphere at one side of the closed room exerts a horizontal gravitational force mg_s on the plumb bob, where $g_s = GM/R^2$, M being the mass of the large sphere, and R the distance between plumb bob and the center of the sphere. This horizontal force causes a static deflection of the plumb line from the vertical by the small angle ϵ. (Similar practical example: In northern India the mass of the Himalaya Mountains results in a slight sideways deflection of plumb lines, causing difficulties in precise surveying!) The sphere is now rolled around to a corresponding position on the other side of the room (Fig. 51) causing a static deflection of the plumb by an angle ϵ of the same magnitude but in the opposite direction. Now the angle ϵ is very small. (Deflection due to the

Himalayas is about 5 seconds of arc, which equals 0.0014 degrees!) However, as the sphere is rolled around and around outside the closed room, an observer inside the room can measure the gravitational field g_s due to the sphere by measuring with greater and greater precision the total deflection angle $2\epsilon \approx 2 \sin \epsilon$ of the plumb line. Derive the equation that he will need in this calculation of g_s.

(c) We on earth have a large sphere effectively rolling around us once every day. It is the most massive sphere in the solar system: it is the sun itself! What is the value of the gravitational acceleration $g_s = GM/R^2$ due to the sun at the position of the earth? (Some constants useful in this calculation appear inside the front cover of this book.)

(d) One additional acceleration must be considered that, however, will not enter our final comparison of gravitational acceleration g_s for different materials. This additional acceleration is the centrifugal acceleration due to the motion of the earth around the sun. When you round a corner in a car you are pressed against the side of the car on the outward side of the turn. This outward force—called the *centrifugal pseudo-force* or the *centrifugal inertial force*—is due to the acceleration of your reference frame (the car) toward the center of the circular turn. This centrifugal inertial force has the value mv^2/r where v is the speed of the car and r is the radius of the turn. Now the earth moves around the sun in a path that is nearly circular. The sun's gravitational force mg_s acts on a plumb bob in a direction *toward* the sun; the centrifugal inertial force mv^2/R acts in a direction *away* from the sun. Compare the "centrifugal acceleration" v^2/R at the position of

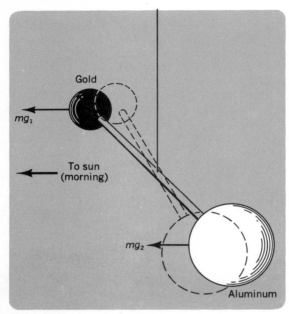 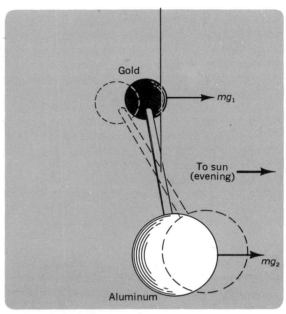

A. Hypothetical effect: morning

B. Hypothetical effect: evening

Fig. 52. Schematic diagram of the Dicke experiment. Any difference in the gravitational acceleration of the sun for gold and aluminum should result in opposite sense of net torque on torsion pendulum in the evening compared with the morning. Large aluminum ball has the same mass as small high-density gold ball.

the earth with the oppositely directed gravitational acceleration g_s calculated in part c. What is the net acceleration toward or away from the sun of a particle riding on the earth as observed in the (accelerated) frame of the earth?

(e) Of what use is the discussion thus far? A plumb bob hung near the surface of the earth experiences a gravitational acceleration g_s toward the sun—and an equal-but-opposite centrifugal acceleration v^2/R away from the sun. Therefore—in the accelerating reference frame of the earth—the bob experiences no net force at all due to the presence of the sun. Indeed this is the method by which we constructed an inertial frame in the first place (Section 2): Let the frame be in free fall about the center of gravitational attraction. A particle at rest on the earth's surface is in free fall about the sun and therefore experiences no net force due to the sun. What then does all this have to do with measuring the equality of gravitational acceleration for particles made of different substances—the subject of the Dicke experiment? Answer: Our purpose is to detect the difference—if any—in the gravitational acceleration g_s toward the sun for different materials. The centrifugal acceleration v^2/R away from the sun is presumably the same for all materials and therefore need not enter any *comparison* of different materials. Consider

a torsion pendulum suspended from its center by a thin quartz fiber (Fig. 52,A). A light rod of length l supports at its ends two bobs of equal mass made of different materials—say aluminum and gold. *Suppose* that the gravitational acceleration g_1 of the gold due to the sun is slightly greater than the acceleration g_2 of the aluminum due to the sun. Then there will be a slight net torque on the torsion pendulum due to the sun. For the position of the sun shown in Fig. 52,A, show that the net torque is *counterclockwise* when viewed from above. Show also that the magnitude of this net torque is given by the expression

$$(55) \qquad \text{torque} = mg_1 \frac{l}{2} - mg_2 \frac{l}{2} = m(g_1 - g_2)\frac{l}{2}$$

$$= mg_s \left(\frac{\Delta g}{g_s}\right)\frac{l}{2}$$

Suppose that the fraction $(\Delta g/g_s)$ has the maximum value, 3×10^{-11}, consistent with the results of the final experiment, that l has the value 0.06 meters, and that each bob has a mass of 0.03 kilograms. What is the magnitude of the net torque? Compare this to the torque provided by the added weight of a bacterium of mass 10^{-15} kilogram placed on the end of a meter stick balanced at its center in the gravitational field of the earth.

(f) The sun moves around the heavens as seen from the earth. Twelve hours later the sun is located as shown in Fig. 52,B. Show that under these changed circumstances the net torque will have the same magnitude as that calculated above but now will be *clockwise* as viewed from above—in a sense opposite to that of part e! This change in the sense of the torque every twelve hours allows a small difference $\Delta g = g_1 - g_2$ in the acceleration of gold and aluminum to be detected using the torsion pendulum. As the torsion pendulum jiggles on its fiber because of random motion, passing trucks, earth tremors and so forth, one needs to consider only those deflections that keep step with the changing position of the sun.

(g) A torque on the rod causes an angular rotation of the quartz fiber of θ radians given by the formula

$$\text{torque} = k\theta$$

where k is called the *torsion constant* of the fiber. Show that the maximum angular rotation of the torsion pendulum from one side to the other during one rotation of the earth is given by the expression

$$\theta_{\text{tot}} = \frac{mg_s l}{k}\left(\frac{\Delta g}{g}\right)$$

(h) In practice Dicke's torsion balance can be thought of as consisting of 0.030 kilogram gold and aluminum bobs mounted on the ends of a beam 6×10^{-2} meter in length suspended in a vacuum on a quartz fiber of torsion constant 2×10^{-8} newton meter per radian. A statistical analysis of the angular displacements of this torsion pendulum over long periods of time leads to the conclusion that the fraction $\Delta g/g$ for gold and aluminum is less than 3×10^{-11}. To what mean maximum angle of rotation from side to side during one rotation of the earth does this correspond? Random motions of the torsion pendulum—noise!—are of much greater amplitude than this; hence the need for the statistical analysis of the results using a programmed computer.

36.* Down with relativity!

Mr. Van Dam is an intelligent and reasonable man with a knowledge of high school physics. He has the following objections to the theory of relativity. Answer each of Mr. Van Dam's objections decisively— *without criticizing him!* If you wish, you may present a single connected account of how and why one is driven to relativity, in which these objections are all answered.

(a) "A says B's clock goes slow, and B says that A's clock goes slow. This is a logical contradiction. Therefore relativity should be abandoned."

(b) "A says B's meter sticks are contracted, and B says A's meter sticks are contracted. This is a logical contradiction. Therefore relativity should be abandoned."

(c) "Relativity does not even have a *unique* way to *define* space and time coordinates. Therefore anything it says about velocities (and hence about motions) is without meaning."

(d) "Relativity postulates that light travels with a standard speed regardless of the inertial frame from which its progress is measured. This postulate is certainly wrong. Anybody with common sense knows that travel at high speed in the direction of a receding light pulse will decrease the speed with which the pulse recedes. Hence light *cannot* have the same speed for observers in relative motion. With this disproof of the basic postulate all of relativity collapses."

(e) "There isn't a single experimental test of the *results* of special relativity."

(f) "Relativity offers no way to describe an event without coordinates—and no way to speak about *coordinates* without referring to one or another particular *reference frame*. However, physical events have an existence *independent* of all choice of coordinates and all choice of reference frame. Hence relativity— with its coordinates and reference frames—cannot provide a valid description of these events."

(g) "Relativity is concerned only with how we *observe* things, not what is *really* happening. Hence it is not a scientific theory, since science deals with *reality*."

E. APPROXIMATIONS AT LOW VELOCITY

37. Euclidean analogy—a worked example.

There is a very small angle, θ_r, between the respective axes of two rotated Euclidean frames. Use the series expansions of Table 8 to find an approximate set of transformation equations between the coordinates of a given point with respect to two reference frames. Neglect powers of θ_r higher than the first.

Solution: From Table 8, for small θ_r
$$\sin \theta_r \approx \theta_r$$
$$\cos \theta_r \approx 1$$

Therefore the Euclidean transformation equations (inverse of Eqs. 29) become

$$x' = x \cos \theta_r - y \sin \theta_r \approx x - \theta_r y$$
(56)
$$y' = x \sin \theta_r + y \cos \theta_r \approx \theta_r x + y$$

This approximate transformation can be made as accurate as desired by making θ_r sufficiently small.

38. The Galilean transformation

Suppose that β_r is very small. Then $\beta_r = \tanh \theta_r \approx \theta_r$. Use the series expansions of Table 8 to show that if terms that contain powers of θ_r higher than the first are neglected, the transformation equations become

(57)
$$x' = x - \beta_r t$$
$$(\beta_r \ll 1)$$
(58)
$$t' = -\beta_r x + t$$

Now use everyday, nonrelativistic Newtonian arguments to derive the transformation equations between two reference frames. These are called the *Galilean transformation equations*

(59)
$$x' = x - v_r t_{\text{sec}}$$
(Galilean transformation)
(60)
$$t'_{\text{sec}} = t_{\text{sec}}$$

where v_r is the relative speed between the two frames in meters per second.

Transformation equations 57 and 58 appear to be completely inconsistent with Eqs. 59 and 60. Is this first impression *correct*, and if not, why not? (Discussion: Why does v_r in the Galilean transformation (Eq. 59) replace β_r in Eq. 57? How does Eq. 58 look when rewritten in terms of v_r and t_{sec}? How do everyday velocities compare with the speed of light?)

39.* Limits of accuracy of a Galilean transformation

Make a more accurate approximation of the transformation equations at low relative velocities by allowing terms in θ_r^2 to remain but, again, neglecting terms with higher powers of θ_r. (This is called a *second order approximation* in θ_r. Notice from the series expansion of $\tanh \theta$ in Table 8 that even to second order in θ_r, $\beta_r \approx \theta_r$.) Show that the coefficients for x and t in Eqs. 57 and 58 agree with the improved second-order approximation to better than 1 percent for velocities β_r less than 1/7.

If a sports car can accelerate uniformly from rest to 60 miles per hour (about 27 meters per second) in 7 seconds, roughly how many days would it take to reach $\beta = 1/7$ at the same constant acceleration? How many days would be required to reach this speed at the greatest acceleration that the human body can stand for reasonable periods (about 7 g, or 7 times the acceleration of gravity)?

40.* Collisions Newtonian and relativistic —and the domain within which the two predictions agree to one percent

Proton A collides elastically with proton B, which is initially at rest. The outcome of the collision cannot be predicted. It depends upon the closeness of the encounter. In most events proton A will be deviated by only a slight angle α_A from its original direction of motion. Then proton B will be given only a slight kick off to the side, at an angle α_B (relative to the forward direction) that is close to 90 degrees. Occasionally there is a very close encounter in which B acquires nearly all the energy and goes off at a very small angle α_B to the forward direction. Between these two ex-

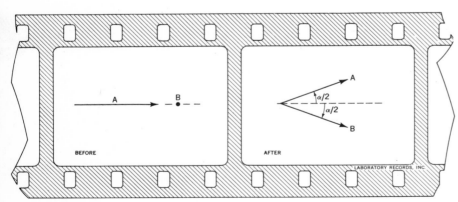

Fig. 53. Laboratory frame record of a symmetric elastic collision.

Fig. 54, A. Photograph of a nonrelativistic symmetric elastic collision between a moving proton and a second proton initially at rest. Initial speed of the incident proton is about $\beta = 0.1$. The angle between outgoing protons is 90 degrees, as predicted by Newtonian mechanics. From C. F. Powell and G. P. S. Occhialini, *Nuclear Physics in Photographs* (Oxford University Press, Oxford, 1947).

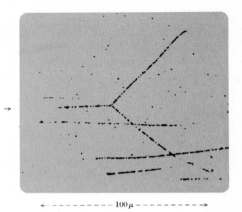

<----------- 100μ ----------->

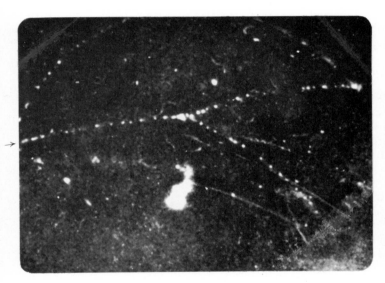

Fig. 54, B. Expansion chamber photograph of a relativistic and approximately symmetric elastic collision between a moving electron and a second electron initially at rest. Initial speed of the incident electron is about $\beta = 0.97$. The angle between outgoing electrons is much less than the 90 degree angle predicted by Newtonian mechanics. The curved path of the charged electrons is due to the presence of a magnetic field used to determine the momentum of each electron. Document Hermann Publishers, Paris.

tremes there occurs from time to time a "symmetric collision" in which the two identical particles come off with identical speeds along paths that make identical angles $\alpha_A = \alpha_B = \alpha/2$ with the forward direction (Fig. 53). *Question: How great is the angle of deflection in a symmetric collision? Discussion:* According to *Newtonian mechanics the total angle of separation, is 90 degrees in every elastic collision (symmetric or not!). That this angle will be less than 90 degrees for a fast impact is one of the most interesting and decisive predictions of relativity.* Figure 54,A, shows a low-velocity collision whose 90 degree angle of separation satisfies the Newtonian prediction. In contrast, Fig. 54,B, shows a high-velocity collision whose angle of separation is decisively less than 90 degrees. This circum-

stance means that *the difference between the separation angle from 90 degrees provides a useful measure of the departure from Newtonian mechanics.* For example, ask this question: How high must the velocity in such collision experiments be before the separation angle deviates from 90 degrees by as much as 1/100 of a radian? It greatly simplifies the analysis of this question to look at the symmetric collision pictured above from a frame of reference so chosen that one can capitalize on *symmetry arguments.* For this purpose climb onto a rocket and travel to the right with a velocity just great enough to keep up with the forward velocities of A and B after the collision. Viewed from this rocket, particles A and B therefore have *no forward velocity component:*

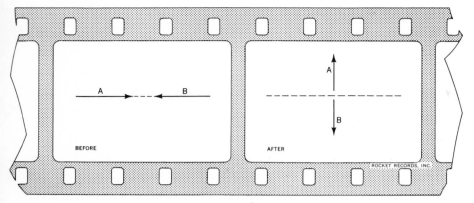

Fig. 55. Rocket frame records of the symmetric elastic collision of Fig. 53. Rocket frame is so chosen that particles A and B have no forward velocity component after the collision.

As to the lateral (up-down) velocity components of A and B, note that these were equal in magnitude and opposite in direction in the laboratory frame. Moreover, this symmetry feature of the velocity diagram cannot be altered by viewing the collision from a rocket frame moving to the right. Therefore the velocities of A and B after the collision, as viewed in the rocket frame, are equal and opposite. This conclusion is payoff No. 1 from arguments based on *symmetry*. Now for payoff No. 2—again achieved by viewing the collision in the rocket frame of reference: In this frame, and *before* the collision, A and B have velocities that are equal in magnitude and opposite in direction. Why? What inconsistency would result if these speeds were *not* equal? *Symmetry* would be violated, as one can see in the following way.

The diagram of the velocity in the rocket frame *after* the collision has *left-right symmetry*. In other words, by looking at the particles separating after the collision it is impossible to tell from what directions the particles arrived at the point of collision.

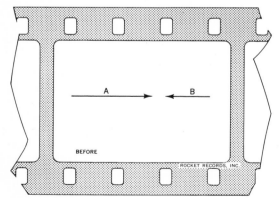

Fig. 56. Rocket record as it would be if, before the collision, particles A and B have different speeds: an incorrect assumption.

Instead of A coming from the left and B coming from the right, A could as well be coming from the right and B from the left (for example, if the viewer went around in back and looked at the collision from the other side).

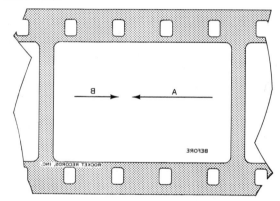

Fig. 57. Rocket record of Fig. 56 looked at from the other side.

But the colliding particles are identical—what is called B in the diagram above could as well have been called A, and conversely:

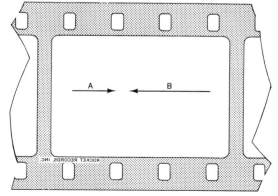

Fig. 58. Rocket record of Fig. 57 with labels A and B for identical balls interchanged.

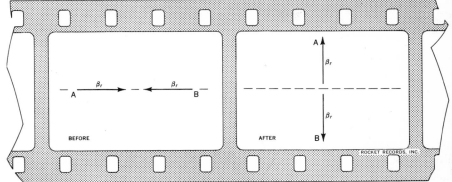

Fig. 59. Conclusion of symmetry arguments: In the rocket frame in which balls A and B have no forward velocity component after the collision, all speeds before the collision and all speeds after the collision have the same value.

Now note that we have in Figs. 56 and 58 two different initial conditions that result in one and the same outcome (Fig. 53). Moreover, these initial conditions differ only in that a suitable increase in the speed of the observing rocket transforms Fig. 56 into the appearance of Fig. 58. But the *outcome* of Fig. 56 cannot continue to look the same as the outcome of Fig. 58 after this increase in the speed of the observer. There is therefore an *inconsistency* in assuming that Fig. 56 and Fig. 58 were different in the first place. To avoid this inconsistency one must conclude that in the rocket frame *A and B have the same speed before the collision*, as drawn in Fig. 55.

Not only do A and B have equal speeds in the rocket frame before the collision—and equal speeds after the collision—but also these speeds before and after the collision are the *same*. If they were not, the following difficulty would arise. (Third use of a symmetry argument—here not symmetry in space but symmetry in time!) Make a moving picture of the collision, develop and print it, and run it *backwards* through the projector. If originally the particles *lost* speed in the collision, they will now be seen to *gain* speed. Such a difference between the two directions of time is a characteristic feature of so-called *irreversible processes*, such as (1) the flow of heat from a hotter object to a cooler one, (2) the aging of an animal, (3) the breaking of an egg, and (4) an inelastic encounter. However, we have limited attention here to *elastic* collisions. Therefore we now accept for study only those events that are *reversible* according to the following definition:

A *reversible* process is one in which it is impossible to distinguish one direction of time from the other by a difference between a film of the process run through the projector in one direction and the same film run through the projector in the other direction.

Because the collision of the two protons is *elastic*, all four speeds in Fig. 59 are *identical*.

This result is very compact and simple. The reasoning

leading up to this result can be summarized in a form equally compact and simple. Merely cite these two words: "By symmetry!" Symmetry reasoning of this kind simplifies the analysis of a great variety of physical problems.

The reasoning so far, being based as it is on symmetry considerations, is the same in Newtonian and in relativistic mechanics. The difference between the accounts appears when the now completed rocket-velocity diagram is transformed back to the laboratory frame. In Newtonian mechanics velocities add as *vectors*. Therefore we have only to add the horizontal velocity β_r of the rocket frame after the collision to find the velocities of A and B in the laboratory frame after the collision:

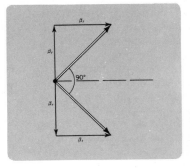

Fig. 60. Newtonian (nonrelativistic) analysis of resultant velocities in the laboratory frame after the collision.

Evidently the angle of separation α is indeed always 90 degrees in Newtonian mechanics, independent of the velocity of the original impact. Not so in relativity!

Show that the incident proton can have a velocity as great as $\beta = 2/7$ without making the angle between v_A and v_B in a symmetric collision depart from the Newtonian value of 90 degrees by as much as 0.01 radian— that is, show that Newtonian mechanics gives good accuracy for a particle with $(2/7)c$ colliding with a particle at rest (or particles with velocity $(1/7)c$ colliding with each other). The results of Ex. 20 may be useful.

41.* Examples of the limits of Newtonian mechanics

Use the particle speed $\beta = 1/7$ (Ex. 39) as an approximate maximum limit for the validity of Newtonian mechanics. Fill in the table below, following the example of the completed first entry.

Example of motion	β	Is Newtonian analysis of this motion adequate?
Satellite circling the earth at a speed of 18,000 miles per hour.	1/37,200	Yes, because $\beta < 1/7$
Earth circling the sun at an orbital speed of 30 kilometers per second.		
Electron circling a proton in the orbit of smallest radius in a hydrogen atom. (Hint: The speed of the electron in the inner orbit of an atom of atomic number Z, where Z is the number of protons in the nucleus, is derived in Ex. 101 in Chap. 2 (accurate for low velocities) $$v = (Z/137)c$$ which is accurate for low velocities; for hydrogen $Z = 1$.)		
Electron in the inner orbit of the gold atom, for which $Z = 79$.		
Electron moving with kinetic energy of 5000 electron-volts. (Hint: One electron-volt is equal to 1.6×10^{-19} joules. Try using the Newtonian expression for kinetic energy.)		
A proton or neutron moving with kinetic energy of 10 MeV (million electron-volts) in a nucleus.		

F. SPACETIME PHYSICS: MORE OBSERVATIONS

42. Time dilation with μ-mesons— a worked example

In a given sample of μ-mesons (mu-mesons: elementary particles produced in some nuclear reactions), half will decay to other elementary particles in 1.5 microseconds (measured with respect to a reference frame in which the μ-mesons are at rest). Half of the remainder will decay in the next 1.5 microseconds, and so on.

(a) Consider μ-mesons produced by the collision of cosmic rays with gas nuclei in the atmosphere at a height 60 kilometers above the surface of the earth. The μ-mesons move vertically downward with a speed approaching that of light. Approximately how long will it take them to reach the earth as measured by an observer at rest on the surface of the earth? If there were no time dilation, approximately what fraction of the mesons produced at a height of 60 kilometers would remain undecayed by the time they reached the earth?

(b) Idealize the rather complicated actual experimental situation to following roughly equivalent situation: All the mesons are produced at the same height (60 kilometers); all have the same speed; all travel straight down; of these 1/8 reach sea level without undergoing decay. Question: How can there possibly be so great a discrepancy between the prediction of part a and this observation? And how great is the *difference* between the velocity of these μ-mesons and the velocity of light?†

Solution: The μ-mesons travel with nearly the speed of light. They therefore travel 60 kilometers in approximately

$$\frac{60 \times 10^3 \text{ meters}}{3 \times 10^8 \text{ meters/second}} = 2 \times 10^{-4} \text{ seconds}$$

The "half-life" of μ-mesons is 1.5×10^{-6} seconds as observed in a reference frame in which they are at rest. If there were no time dilation the travel time to earth would be $2 \times 10^{-4}/1.5 \times 10^{-6}$ = 133 half-lives. The passage of each half-life reduces the number of remaining μ-mesons by one-half. Therefore after 133 half-lives there

---

†A film about this experiment is available. See David H. Frisch and James H. Smith, "Measurement of the Relativistic Time Dilation Using μ-Mesons," American Journal of Physics, **31**, 342 (May 1963). The original experiment is reported by B. Rossi and D. B. Hall, in Physical Review, **59**, 223 (1941).

should be only the fraction

$$1/2 \times 1/2 \times 1/2 \times 1/2 \cdots = 1/2^{133} \approx 10^{-40}$$

remaining. In fact, there are $1/8 = 1/2^3$ remaining, as determined by experiment (part b). Therefore in the rocket frame in which the μ-mesons are at rest, only 3 half-lives have passed

$$\Delta t' = 3 \times (1.5 \times 10^{-6} \text{ seconds})$$
$$\times (3 \times 10^8 \text{ meters/second})$$
$$= 1.35 \times 10^3 \text{ meters}$$

The motion of the meson, seen in the frame of reference attached to it, is naturally zero

$$\Delta x' = 0$$

Therefore the interval of proper time from formation to arrival at the ground is

$$\Delta \tau = [(\Delta t')^2 - (\Delta x')^2]^{1/2} = 1.35 \times 10^3 \text{ meters}$$

But this interval has the same numerical value in the laboratory frame as in the meson frame; thus,

$$\Delta \tau = [(\Delta t)^2 - (\Delta x)^2]^{1/2} = 1.35 \times 10^3 \text{ meters}$$

or

(61) $$[(\Delta x/\beta)^2 - (\Delta x)^2]^{1/2} = 1.35 \times 10^3 \text{ meters}$$

We know the distance of travel in the laboratory frame, $\Delta x = 6 \times 10^4$ meters. Consequently we can find the velocity β from Eq. 61. Square both sides of the equation and divide by $(\Delta x)^2$, finding

$$(1/\beta^2) - 1 = [1.35 \times 10^3/(6 \times 10^4)]^2$$

or

$$\frac{1 - \beta^2}{\beta^2} = 5.06 \times 10^{-4}$$

Clearly β is nearly equal to one. Therefore set

$$1 - \beta^2 = (1 + \beta)(1 - \beta) \approx 2(1 - \beta)$$

from which

$$\frac{1 - \beta^2}{\beta^2} \approx \frac{2(1 - \beta)}{\beta^2} \approx 2(1 - \beta) \approx 5 \times 10^{-4}$$

or

$$1 - \beta \approx 2.5 \times 10^{-4}$$

The difference in speed between the mesons and light is given by this small fraction.

43. Time dilation with π^+-mesons

Laboratory experiments on particle decay are

much more conveniently done with π-mesons than with μ-mesons, as is seen from the following table.

Particle	Time for half to decay (measured in rest frame)	"Characteristic distance" (speed of light multiplied by foregoing time)
μ-meson (207 times electron mass)	1.5×10^{-6} second	450 meters
π-meson (273 times electron mass)	18×10^{-9} second	5.4 meters

In a given sample of π^+-mesons half will decay to other elementary particles in 18 nanoseconds (measured in a reference frame in which the π^+-mesons are at rest). Half of the remainder will decay in the next 18 nanoseconds, and so on. In the Penn–Princeton proton synchrotron π^+-mesons are produced when a proton beam strikes an aluminum target *inside* the accelerator. Mesons leave this target with nearly the speed of light. If there were no time dilation and if no mesons were removed from the resulting beam by collisions, what would be the greatest distance from the target at which half of the mesons would remain undecayed? The π-mesons of interest in a particular experiment have $\cosh\theta = 1/(1 - \beta^2)^{1/2} = 15$ where θ is the velocity parameter. By what factor is the predicted distance from the target for half decay *increased* by time dilation over the previous prediction—that is, by what factor does this dilation effect allow one to increase the separation between his detecting equipment and the target?

44.* Aberration of starlight

The angle between one *remote* star (B) and other *remote* stars (A, C) appears to change from one time of year to another because the earth changes its velocity over a six-month period by 2×30 kilometers per second = 60 kilometers per second. Show that the angle of aberration, ψ (relative to angles as measured by an observer on the sun), is given by the equation $\sin\psi = \beta$. Here β is the speed of the earth in its orbit about the sun. Although the aberration of starlight can be observed experimentally, the aberration angle ψ is so small that it is not at present possible to confirm by experiment that the relativistic prediction above is the correct one—or that the almost equal Newtonian prediction $\tan\psi = \beta$ is not the correct one.

45. Fizeau experiment

Light moves more slowly through a transparent material medium than through a vacuum. Let β' represent this reduced speed of light in the medium. Idealize to a case in which this reduced velocity is independent of the wavelength of the light. Place the medium in a rocket moving at velocity β_r to the right relative to the laboratory frame, and let light travel through the medium, also to the right. Use the law of addition of velocities to find an expression for the velocity β of the light in the laboratory frame. Show that for small relative velocity β_r between the rocket and laboratory frames, the velocity of the light with respect to the laboratory frame is given approximately by the expression

$$(62) \qquad \beta \approx \beta' + \beta_r[1 - (\beta')^2]$$

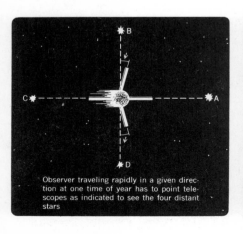

Observer traveling rapidly in a given direction at one time of year has to point telescopes as indicated to see the four distant stars

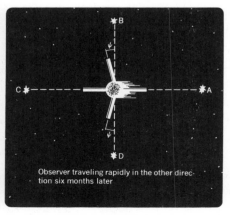

Observer traveling rapidly in the other direction six months later

Fig. 61. Aberration of starlight. Both diagrams show positions as observed in a reference frame in which the sun is at rest.

This expression has been tested by Fizeau using water flowing in opposite directions in the two arms of an interferometer similar (but not identical) to the interferometer used by Michelson and Morley (Ex. 33).†

46. Cerenkov radiation

No particle has been observed to travel faster than the *speed of light in a vacuum.* However particles have been observed that travel in a material medium faster than the speed of light *in that medium.* When a charged particle moves through a medium faster than light moves in that medium it radiates *coherent* light in a cone whose axis lies along the path of the particle. (Note the similarity to waves created by a motorboat speeding across calm water!) This is called Cerenkov radiation (C—Russian—is pronounced as "ch"). Let β be the speed of the particle in the medium and β' be the speed of light in the medium. From this information use Fig. 62 to show that the half-angle ϕ of the light cone is given by the expression

(63) $$\cos \phi = \beta'/\beta$$

---

†H. Fizeau, Comptes Rendus, **33,** 349 (1851). A fascinating discussion (in French) of some central themes in relativity theory—delivered more than fifty years before Einstein's first paper.

Fig. 63. Cerenkov radiation from a beam of 700-MeV electrons traveling through air. The beam is very much narrower than the circle of Cerenkov light seen on the screen. The beam emerges at the lower left—through a thin aluminum foil—from the vacuum inside the Stanford University linear electron accelerator. The beam itself is visible in the picture through the excitation and ionization it causes as it passes through the air. In addition to this excitation of air molecules the electrons emit Cerenkov radiation in a narrow forward cone. The cone of light from the left hand portion of the beam intercepts the screen in a circular ring which constitutes the outer portion of the disk of light on the screen. Electrons nearer the screen emit radiation at the same angle, which strikes the screen in smaller concentric rings because the emitting electrons are nearer to the screen. The result of radiation from electrons near and far is a solid disk of light. The Cerenkov angle ϕ for the most distant electrons should correspond to the half-angle subtended by the circle at the exit window from the vacuum system. The speed β of the 700-MeV electrons differs from 1—the speed of light—by less than one part in a million (determined using expressions from Chapter 2). Therefore there is little error in giving β the value 1. The speed β' of light in air can be calculated from the observed index of refraction of light in air: $n = 1/\beta' = 1.00029$. The Cerenkov formula becomes

$$\cos \phi = \beta'/\beta \approx \beta' = 1/n = 1/1.00029$$

For small ϕ we can replace these expressions by approximate ones
$$\cos \phi \approx 1 - \phi^2/2 = (1 + 2.9 \times 10^{-4})^{-1} \approx 1 - 2.9 \times 10^{-4}$$

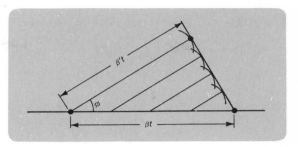

Fig. 62. Calculation of Cerenkov angle ϕ.

Consider the plastic Lucite for which $\beta' = 2/3$. What is the minimum velocity that a charged particle can have if it is to produce Cerenkov radiation in Lucite? What is the *maximum* angle ϕ at which Cerenkov radiation can be produced in Lucite? Measurement of the angle provides a good way to measure the velocity of the particle.†

---

†For details on the experimental uses of Cerenkov radiation see Chapter VII of *Techniques of High Energy Physics,* edited by David M. Ritson, (Interscience Publishers, New York, 1961).

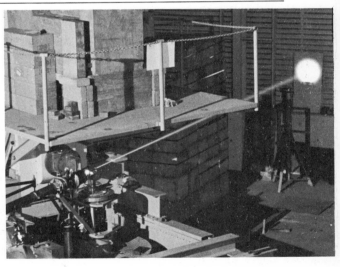

from which the calculated value of the angle is $\phi_{\text{calc}} \approx 2.4 \times 10^{-2}$ radian. The distance from exit window to screen is approximately 40 feet and the radius of the spot is about 10.5 inches, or 0.88 foot. The observed angle is thus

$$\phi_{\text{obs}} \approx 0.88/40 = 2.2 \times 10^{-2} \text{ radian}$$

which compares well with the calculated value. (The time exposure photograph was taken by A. M. Hudson of Occidental College and is reproduced here with his permission.)

47.* Deflection of starlight by the sun

Estimate the deflection of starlight by the sun using an elementary analysis. Discussion: Consider first a simpler example of a similar phenomenon. An elevator car of width L is released from rest near the surface of the earth. At the instant of release a narrow beam of light is fired horizontally from one wall of the car toward the other wall. After release the elevator car is an inertial frame. Therefore the light beam will cross the car in what is a straight line *with respect to the car*. With respect to the *earth*, however, the beam of light is falling—because the elevator is falling. Therefore, in a gravitational field, a beam of light must fall. As another example a ray of starlight in its passage tangentially across the earth's surface will receive a gravitational deflection (over and above any refraction by the earth's atmosphere). However, the time to cross the earth is so short, and in consequence the deflection so slight, that this effect has not yet been detected on the earth. At the surface of the sun, however, the acceleration of gravity has the much greater value of 275 meters per second per second. More-over, the time of passage across the surface is much increased because the sun has a greater diameter, 1.4×10^9 meters. Determine an "effective time of fall" from this diameter and the speed of light. From this time of fall deduce the net *velocity* of fall toward the sun produced by the end of the whole period of gravitational interaction. (The maximum acceleration acting for this "effective time" produces the same net effect [calculus proof!] produced by the actual acceleration—changing in magnitude and direction along the path—in the entire passage of the ray through the sun's field of force.) Comparing this lateral velocity with the forward velocity of the light deduce the *angle of deflection*. The accurate analysis of special relativity gives the *same result*. However, Einstein's 1915 general relativity predicted a previously neglected effect, associated with the change of *lengths* in a gravitational field that produces something like a supplementary *refraction* of the ray of light and *doubles* the predicted deflection. (Deflection observed in 1947 eclipse of the sun: $(9.8 \pm 1.3) \times 10^{-6}$ radian; in the 1952 eclipse: $(8.2 \pm 0.5) \times 10^{-6}$ radian.)

G. GEOMETRIC INTERPRETATION

48. Geometric interpretation

Develop a geometric interpretation of the Lorentz transformation using the following outline.

(a) Show that in the laboratory spacetime diagram the world line of the origin of the rocket frame will be the line marked t' in Fig. 64. This is the locus of all events that occur at the origin of the rocket frame, that is, *it is the rocket t' axis*. Show that the locus of events that occur at $x' = 1$ meter in the rocket frame is a line that parallels the t' axis in Fig. 64, and similarly for $x' = 2, 3, 4$ meters.

(b) Show that the slope of the t' axis relative to the t axis in Fig. 64 is given by the expression (meters of distance traveled for each)/(meter of light-travel time) $= \beta_r = \tanh \theta_r$. What happens to the slope β_r in the two cases: (1) the rocket travels very slowly and (2) the rocket travels at a speed very close to the speed of light.

(c) Now for the crucial step! Where shall we locate the rocket x' axis in the laboratory spacetime diagram? The principle of relativity says that the measured speed of light must be the same in the two frames. The dotted line in Fig. 65 is the world line of a flash of light. Show that the principle of relativity requires that the rocket x' axis be tilted upward at the same slope as

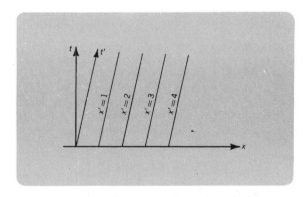

Fig. 64. Location of the rocket time axis in the laboratory spacetime diagram.

Fig. 65. Location of the rocket space axis in the laboratory spacetime diagram.

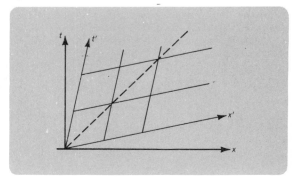

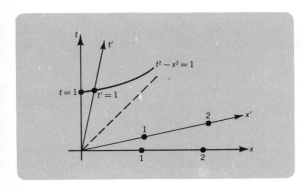

Fig. 66. Calibration of rocket space and time axes.

the rocket t' axis is tilted to the right. Show that the loci of events that occur at rocket times $t' = 1, 2, 3$ meters respectively lie parallel to the rocket x' axis as shown.

(d) Calibrate the rocket axes! Draw the hyperbola $t^2 - x^2 = 1$ (Fig. 66). At the place where the hyperbola crosses the laboratory t axis (where $x = 0$), we have $t = 1$ meter of time. But the interval $t^2 - x^2$ is an invariant so that $(t')^2 - (x')^2 = 1$ also. Therefore at the place where the hyperbola crosses the rocket t' axis (where $x' = 0$), we have $t' = 1$ meter of time. Because of the symmetry and the linearity of the transformation equations, we can use the distance along the rocket t' axis from the origin to $t' = 1$ as a unit distance to lay off along *both* the t' and the x' axes. This completes the derivation of the construction. Next: apply it!

(e) Show that if two events are simultaneous in the laboratory frame they will lie on a line parallel to the laboratory x axis of the spacetime diagram (Fig. 67). Show that if two events are simultaneous in the rocket frame they will lie on a line parallel to the rocket x' axis of the spacetime diagram. Hence the two observ-

ers will not necessarily agree on which events are simultaneous. This is the *relative synchronization of clocks.*

(f) Using lines of simultaneity in Fig. 67, show that at rocket time $t' = 1$ meter, the observer in the rocket frame determines that the clock at the laboratory origin has not yet reached one meter of time (i.e., the laboratory clock runs slow), whereas the observer in the laboratory frame observes that the clock at the laboratory origin already reads *more* than one meter of time (i.e., the rocket clock runs slow). This is *time dilation.*

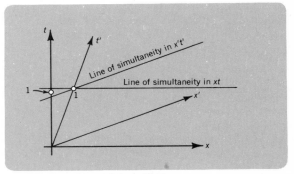

Fig. 67. Illustration of time dilation.

(g) A meter stick lies at rest in the laboratory frame with one end at the origin of that frame (Fig. 68). Measurement of its length in the laboratory frame will give a result like *ab* in Fig. 68. Measurement of its length in the *rocket frame* (i.e., determining the position of the endpoints at the "same time") will give a result like *de* in the figure. Show that this measurement results in an observed *Lorentz contraction* in the rocket frame. Using Fig. 69 show that a meter stick at rest in the rocket frame with one end at the origin of that frame will be Lorentz contracted when observed in the laboratory frame.

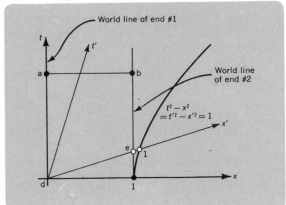

Fig. 68. A meter stick at rest in laboratory frame appears Lorentz-contracted when observed in rocket frame.

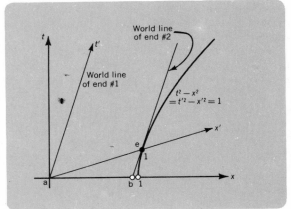

Fig. 69. A meter stick at rest in rocket frame appears Lorentz-contracted when observed in laboratory frame.

(h) Sketch spacetime diagrams for the relativity of simultaneity, time dilation, and Lorentz contraction in the limiting cases that the relative velocity between laboratory and rocket frames is very small and very large.

(i) Return to the spacetime diagram of Fig. 22 in the chapter, which describes the motion of particles and light flashes in two dimensions. Show that the rocket "plane of simultaneity" is tilted relative to the laboratory plane of simultaneity. Explain the implications of this tilt for the relative simultaneity of events that occur at different positions on the x axis of the laboratory spacetime diagram, and for the relative simultaneity of events that occur at different positions on the y axis of the laboratory spacetime diagram.

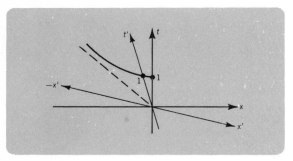

Fig. 70. Location of space and time axes for rocket frame moving in negative laboratory x direction.

(j) Consider a rocket frame moving in the *negative* x direction in the laboratory frame. Verify the features of Fig. 70, in particular the *opposite* sense of the relative synchronization of clocks and the *same* sense of time dilation when compared with the rocket moving in the positive x direction.

49. The clock paradox II— a worked example†

When Peter returned from his fourteen years of traveling (Ex. 27) he was still young enough to learn some relativity. But the more he studied the more puzzled he became. He and his brother Paul, being in relative motion, "each should see the other's clocks running slow." This simple slogan, put in Paul's mouth, made it easy enough to understand why "Peter's clocks—and Peter's aging processes—ran slow," so that Peter was the younger of the two on his

†See E. Lowry, American Journal of Physics, **31**, 59 (1963).

return. "But if the slogan is valid," Peter asked, "then would not I—if I had investigated—have found *Paul's* clocks running slow? So how did he age more than I?" *Question:* What is the way out of Peter's difficulties?

Solution: As Peter studied more, with this paradox worrying him, he learned that words like "observer" and "observed time" do not have the simple meaning he had at first attributed to them. He should not think of how he might directly have kept day-to-day track of Paul's aging back on earth, either by radio messages or by other methods. That procedure, while conceivable, does not lend itself to the simplest analysis, Peter discovered. The observer in relativity theory, he found, is to be understood as a whole framework of rods and recording clocks moving along with uniform velocity—with the same velocity as Peter himself as he recedes from the earth, $\beta_r = 24/25 = 0.96$. That parade of clocks ("Peter's clocks and Peter's reference frame") zooms by the earth. As each clock passes Paul it punches out (1) the reading of Paul's clock and (2) its own reading and location. The shorthand phrase "Peter observes Paul" means that Peter collects these cards—or the information on them—at some later time.

"So what?" Peter asked himself at this point. "In any case I know that the reading of Paul's clock increases from one punchout to the next only $(1 - \beta_r^2)^{1/2} = 7/25$ as much as the increase in readings of my own clock. So Paul is the man who should have been younger at the end of my journey, not me. But look at his gray hair! Where am I going wrong?"

Running over in his mind once again the events of his journey, Peter could not help but remember the moment when he had stopped his outward trip and started his return to the earth. "*I* stopped and *I* turned back; but," he suddenly asked himself, "what about my inertial reference frame? How can an inertial frame turn back?" He looked into this issue more and more carefully. He found himself forced to conclude that the reference frame employed for the first part of his flight—and especially the lattice clock alongside him that had recorded information for the seven outbound years—must have kept on their swift way like a stream of superhighway traffic as one car makes a U-turn into the returning lanes. Another stream of clocks accompanied him home

—a second inertial reference frame. For all the seven years of return one of these clocks remained faithfully alongside. When it took over escort duty, it adopted the seven-year reading of the outbound clock. It read fourteen years at the time when Peter rejoined Paul.

The inbound parade of clocks was passing the earth all these seven years. One by one as they went by they punched out their readings and the readings of Paul's clock. The punch cards made a growing pile on the ground at Paul's feet. As those seven years went by for Peter's inbound escort, the cards showed that Paul's clocks ran off only 7/25 of this time; that is (7/25) of 7 years or 1.96 years.

"What on earth is the matter with my reasoning?" Peter asked aloud at this point. "Now I find myself concluding that Paul should have aged 1.96 years on my outbound trip, and 1.96 years on my inbound trip, or altogether 3.92 years. Yet I *know* I aged fourteen years, and I *know* he aged more than I did. What have I overlooked?" So saying, he drew a spacetime diagram (Fig. 71), and at least had the answer to his difficulty—the time AB that he had so far left out of account. This time, Peter saw, corrects for the difference between the standards of simultaneity of his outgoing and returning reference frames. A separate calculation, using the results of Ex. 11, gives for this time the value 46.08 years. This supplement has to be added to Paul's aging as measured by Peter's two sets of recording clocks. Peter's final calculation for Paul's age (including his age of 21 years when the trip began) gave

$$21 + 1.96 + 46.08 + 1.96 = 71 \text{ years}$$

He could thankfully rejoice in his own comparative youth of $21 + 14 = 35$ years (uncorrected for the time required to learn spacetime physics!). The present analysis does not purport to be the simplest way to calculate the aging of the twins. For that one goes back to Paul's analysis, outlined in Ex. 27. There one has to consider only a single inertial reference frame, the frame with its origin at Paul. The present analysis illustrates how *any* correct method of analysis leads to the same result as any other correct method of analysis.

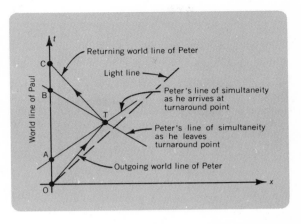

Fig. 71. Peter's bookkeeping on Paul's aging process. During Peter's outbound journey (OT in diagram) his clock flashes a new year seven times. An array of synchronized clocks escort him. Each makes its own seventh year flash somewhere along the "line of simultaneity" AT and punches out a record. The Peter clock which punches out a record at A sees Paul's clock reading only 1.96 years ("slowing of a clock as viewed from a moving reference frame"). On the return journey a different array of synchronized clocks escorts Peter ("second inertial reference frame"). Each of them flashes a seven year sign as it crosses the line of simultaneity BT. The one which travels alongside Peter makes seven more flashes along the world line TC, the last of them signaling fourteen years of travel just as Peter rejoins Paul at C. During the period BC, while the clocks of Peter's inbound reference frame indicate the passage of seven years, Paul has aged only another 1.96 years (again the "slowing of a clock as viewed from a moving reference frame"). But the bookkeeping done so far by Peter's two inertial reference frames is incomplete. Neither one of them does the job of counting the time lapse AB. It is 46.08 years ("correction for change in standard of simultaneity" between Peter's outgoing and incoming inertial reference frames). Thus the slowing of Paul's clocks as observed by Peter's two sets of recording clocks in no way keeps Peter from ending up younger than Paul.

H. FREE-FOR-ALL!

50. Contraction or rotation?†

Consider a cube, at rest in the rocket frame, whose edge measures 1 meter in that frame. In the *laboratory* frame the cube is Lorentz contracted in the direction of motion, as shown in Fig. 72. This Lorentz contraction can be determined, for example, from the locations of four clocks at rest and synchronized in the laboratory frame with which the four corners of the cube, E, F, G, H, coincide *when all four clocks read the same time.* In this way time lags in the travel of light from different corners of the cube are eliminated from the observation procedure. Now for a different observing procedure!

Stand in the laboratory frame and *look* at the cube with one eye as the cube passes overhead (Fig. 72). What one sees at any time is light *that enters his eye at that time, even if it left the different corners of the cube at different times.* Hence, what one *sees* visually may not be the same as what he *observes* using a lattice-

†For a more complete treatment of this topic, and references, see Edwin F. Taylor, *Introductory Mechanics*, (John Wiley and Sons, New York, 1963), p. 346.

work of clocks. If the cube is viewed from the bottom then the distance GO is equal to the distance HO, so light that leaves G and H simultaneously will arrive at O simultaneously. Hence, when one sees the cube to be overhead he will see the Lorentz contraction of the bottom edge.

(a) Light from E that arrives at O simultaneously with light from G will have to leave E earlier than light from G left G. How much earlier? How far has the cube moved in this time? What is the value of the distance x in Fig. 73?

(b) Suppose that one chooses to interpret the projection in Fig. 73 as a rotation of a cube that is *not* Lorentz contracted. Find an expression for the angle of apparent rotation ϕ of this uncontracted cube in Fig. 74. Interpret this expression for the two limiting cases $\beta \longrightarrow 0$ and $\beta \longrightarrow 1$.

(c) Is the word "really" an *appropriate* word in the following quotations?

(1) An observer in the rocket frame says, "The cube is *really* neither rotated nor contracted."

(2) An observer using the laboratory latticework of clocks says, "The cube is *really* Lorentz con-

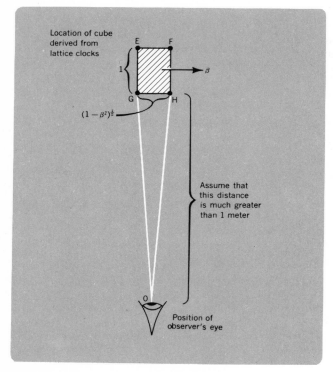

Fig. 72. Position of eye of visual observer watching "cube" pass overhead.

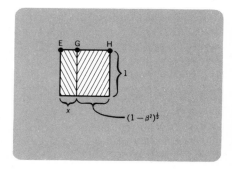

Fig. 73. What visual observer sees as he looks up from below.

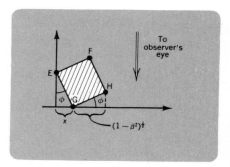

Fig. 74. How visual observer can interpret the projection of Fig. 73.

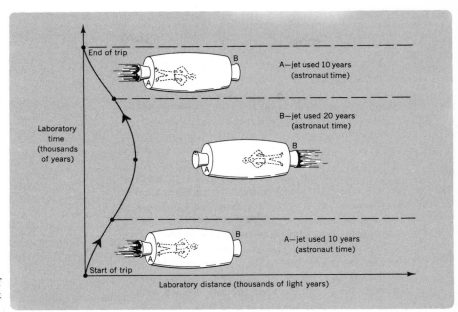

Fig. 75. Round-trip world line of rocket which experiences constant acceleration or deceleration.

Labels in figure:
- End of trip
- A—jet used 10 years (astronaut time)
- B—jet used 20 years (astronaut time)
- A—jet used 10 years (astronaut time)
- Laboratory time (thousands of years)
- Start of trip
- Laboratory distance (thousands of light years)

tracted but not rotated."

(3) The visual observer in the laboratory frame says, "The cube is *really* rotated but not Lorentz contracted."

What can one rightfully say—in a sentence or two—to make each observer think it reasonable that the other observers should come to conclusions different from his own?

51.** Clock paradox III

Can one go to a point 7000 light years away—*and return*—without aging more than 40 years? "Yes" is the conclusion reached by an engineer on the staff of a large aviation firm in a recent report. In his analysis the traveler experiences a constant "1-g" acceleration (or deceleration, depending upon the stage reached in his journey—see spacetime diagram of Fig. 75). Assuming this limitation, is he right in his conclusion? (For simplicity, limit attention to the first or "A"-jet phase of the motion—the first 10 years of astronaut time—and double the distance covered in that time to find how far it is to the most remote point reached in the course of the journey.)

(a) The acceleration is *not* $g = 9.8$ meters per second per second relative to the laboratory frame. If it were, how many times faster than light would the spaceship be moving at the end of ten years (1 year $= 31.6 \times 10^6$ seconds)? *If the acceleration is not specified with respect to the laboratory, then with respect to what is it*

specified? Discussion: Look at the bathroom scales on which one is standing! The rocket jet is always turned up to the point where these scales read one's *correct* weight. Under these conditions one is being accelerated at $g = 9.8$ meters per second per second with respect to a spaceship that (1) instantaneously happens to be riding alongside with identical velocity, but (2) is *not* being accelerated, and, therefore (3) *provides the* (momentary) *inertial frame of reference relative to which the acceleration is g.* (Hereafter this acceleration is translated from g—expressed in meters per second per second—to $g^* = g/c^2$—measured in meters of distance per meter of time per meter of time.)

(b) *How much velocity does the spaceship have after a given time?* This is the moment to object to the question and to rephrase it. *Velocity β is not the simple quantity to analyze. The simple quantity is the velocity parameter θ.* It is simple because it is *additive* in this sense: Let the velocity parameter of the spaceship in Figure 76 with respect to the imaginary instantaneously comoving inertial frame change from 0 to $d\theta$ in an astronaut time $d\tau$. Then the velocity parameter of the spaceship with respect to the *laboratory* frame changes in the same astronaut time from the initial value θ to the subsequent value $\theta + d\theta$. Now relate $d\theta$ to the acceleration g^* in the instantaneously comoving inertial frame. In this frame $g^* d\tau = d\beta = \tanh (d\theta) \approx d\theta$ so that

(64) $$d\theta = g^* \, d\tau$$

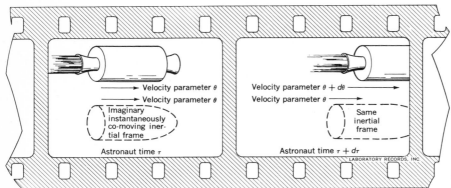

Velocity parameter θ
Velocity parameter θ
Imaginary instantaneously co-moving inertial frame
Astronaut time τ

Velocity parameter $\theta + d\theta$
Velocity parameter θ
Same inertial frame
Astronaut time $\tau + d\tau$
LABORATORY RECORDS, INC.

Fig. 76. Laboratory record of accelerating rocket.

Each lapse of time $d\tau$ on the astronaut's watch is accompanied by an additional increase $d\theta = g^* \, d\tau$ in the velocity parameter of the spaceship. In the laboratory frame the total velocity parameter of the spaceship is simply the sum of these additional increases in the velocity parameter. Assume that the spaceship starts from rest. Then its velocity parameter will increase linearly with *astronaut* time according to the equation

$$(65) \qquad \theta = g^* \, \tau$$

This expression gives the velocity parameter θ of the spaceship in the *laboratory* frame at any time τ in the *astronaut's* frame.

(c) *What laboratory distance x does the spaceship cover in a given astronaut time τ?* At any instant the velocity of the spaceship in the laboratory frame is related to its velocity parameter by the equation $dx/dt = \tanh \theta$ so that the distance dx covered in *laboratory* time dt is

$$dx = \tanh \theta \, dt$$

Remember that the time between ticks of the astronaut's watch $d\tau$ appear to have the larger value dt in the laboratory frame (time dilation) given by the expression

$$dt = \cosh \theta \, d\tau$$

Hence the laboratory distance dx covered in *astronaut* time $d\tau$ is

$$dx = \tanh \theta \cosh \theta \, d\tau = \sinh \theta \, d\tau$$

Use the expression $\theta = g^* \tau$ from part b

$$dx = \sinh (g^* \tau) \, d\tau$$

Sum (integrate) all these small displacements dx from zero astronaut time to a final astronaut time to find

$$(66) \qquad x = \frac{1}{g^*} [\cosh (g^* \tau) - 1]$$

This expression gives the *laboratory distance x* covered by the spaceship at any time τ in the astronaut's frame.

(d) Convert g^* (in meters per meter per meter) to $g = g^* c^2$ (meters per second per second) and τ (meters) to $\tau_{\text{sec}} = \tau/c$ (seconds) in the expression of part c. Determine whether the engineer is correct in his conclusion reported at the beginning of this exercise. (One year is 31.6×10^6 seconds).

52.* The tilted meter stick

A meter stick that lies parallel to the x axis moves in the y direction of the laboratory frame with speed β^y. In the rocket frame the stick is tilted upward in the positive x' direction. Explain why this is, first without using any equations. Let the center of the meter stick pass the point $x = y = x' = y' = 0$ at a time $t = t' = 0$, as shown in the figures. Next calculate the angle θ' at which the meter stick is inclined to the x' axis in the rocket frame. Discussion: Where and when does the right end of the meter stick cross the x axis as observed in the *laboratory* frame? Where and when does the right end of the meter stick make this crossing as observed in the *rocket* frame? The experimentally observed Thomas precession of the electron in an atom—described in Ex. 103—can be explained in the same way as the phenomenon of the tilted meter stick.

53.* The meter-stick paradox†
   Note: Ex. 52 should be completed before Ex. 53.

A meter stick lies along the x axis of the laboratory frame and approaches the origin with velocity β_r. A very thin plate parallel to the xz laboratory plane moves upward in the y direction with speed β^y. The

---

†See R. Shaw, American Journal of Physics, **30**, 72 (1962).

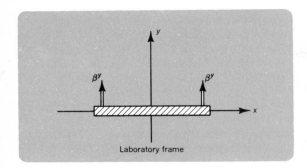

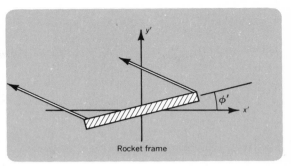

Fig. 77, A. Meter stick moving transverse to its length as observed in laboratory frame.

Fig. 77, B. Meter stick as observed in rocket frame.

plate has a circular hole with a diameter of one meter centered on the y axis. The center of the meter stick arrives at the laboratory origin at the same time in the laboratory frame as the rising plate arrives at the plane $y = 0$. Since the meter stick is Lorentz contracted in the laboratory frame it will easily pass through the hole in the rising plate. Therefore there will be no collision between meter stick and plate as each continues its motion. However, someone who objects to this conclusion can make the following argument: In the *rocket* frame in which the meter stick is at rest the meter stick is not contracted, while in this frame the hole in the plate *is* Lorentz contracted. Hence the full-length meter stick cannot possibly pass through the contracted hole in the plate. Therefore *there must be a collision* between the meter stick and the plate. Resolve this paradox using your answer to the preceding problem. Answer unequivocally the question: Will there be a collision between the meter stick and the plate?

54.** The thin man and the grid†

A certain man walks very fast—so fast that the relativistic length contraction makes him very thin. In the street he has to pass over a grid. A man standing at the grid fully expects the fast thin man to fall through the holes in the grid. Yet to the fast man he himself has his usual size and it is the *grid* that has the relativistic contraction. To him the holes in the grid are much narrower than to the stationary man, and he certainly does not expect to fall through them. Which man is correct? The answer hinges on the relativity of rigidity.

Idealize the problem as a one-meter rod sliding lengthwise over a flat table. In its path is a hole one meter wide. If the Lorentz contraction factor is ten, then in the table (laboratory) frame the rod is 10 centimeters long and will easily drop into the one-

†W. Rindler, American Journal of Physics, **29**, 365 (1961).

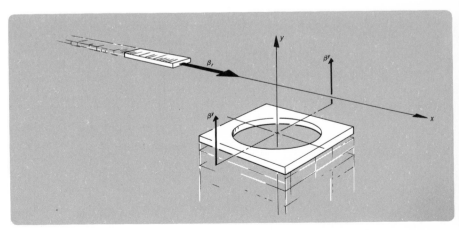

Fig. 78. Will the "meter stick" pass through the "one-meter-diameter hole" without collision?

meter hole. Assume that in the laboratory frame the meter stick moves fast enough so that it remains essentially horizontal as it descends into the hole (no "tipping" in the laboratory frame). Write an equation in the laboratory frame for the motion of the bottom edge of the meter stick assuming that $t = t' = 0$ at the instant that the *back* end of the meter stick leaves the edge of the hole. For small vertical velocities the rod will fall with the usual acceleration g. In the meter stick (rocket) frame the rod is one meter long whereas the hole is Lorentz contracted to a 10-centimeter width so that the rod cannot possibly fit into the hole. Transform the laboratory equations into the rocket frame and show that the rod will "droop" over the edge of the hole in that frame—that is, it will not be rigid. Will the rod ultimately descend into the hole in both frames? Is the rod *really* rigid or nonrigid during the experiment? Is it possible to derive any physical characteristics of the rod (e.g. its flexibility or compressibility) from the description of its motion provided by relativity?

Momentum and Energy

2

10. Introduction; Momentum and Energy in Units of Mass

Physics is concerned with matter and motion and the forces that cause motion. What then is the relation between force and motion? It is not necessary in this brief account to catalogue electric and magnetic and all the other kinds of force. Instead, we ask a more urgent question. How can one tell whether any force at all is acting on a particle? And, if a force is acting on a particle, what feature of the world line of that particle reveals the presence of this force? And finally, how do changes in the energy and momentum of the particle measure the strength of this force?

To understand the nature of the concept, "force," try to imagine how one could get along without it! Force is most obviously needed to explain why a particle speeds up or slows down. A test particle, subject to no forces, is defined precisely by the fact that it does not speed up or slow down. Relative to an inertial frame it continues to be in a state of rest or in motion at constant velocity. It traces out a straight world line. This world line appears in Fig. 79 for the special case of a particle moving in the x direction. In contrast, Fig. 80 plots the world line of a particle that evidently *does* change its velocity and therefore *is* subject to a force. No one has ever found such a change in velocity to take place without something to cause it—typically either a collision with a nearby particle or a force caused by a distant particle. Therefore, force can be said to be a form of *interaction* (Fig. 81). This way of speaking is further justified by two additional circumstances: (1) When the presence of A brings about a change in the velocity of B, the presence of B also causes an alteration in the velocity of A. (2) After the interaction has ended and the particles have sepa-

Momentum change of one object as symptom of interaction with another object

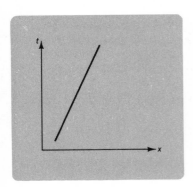

Fig. 79. World line of a particle subject to no forces.

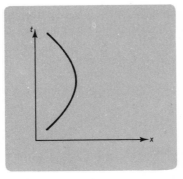

Fig. 80. World line of a particle subject to a force.

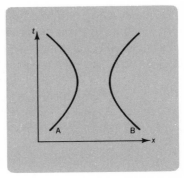

Fig. 81. World lines of two interacting particles.

rated, the change of *momentum* of one particle is equal in magnitude and opposite in direction to the change of momentum of the other particle. Thus, instead of talking about forces between particles, we can talk about their changes of momentum. Indeed to discuss both momentum *and* forces in the context of relativity is to complicate the story. In this account we analyze momentum alone.

Momentum defined so it will be conserved

How is momentum to be defined? Early workers in Newtonian mechanics defined momentum as the mass of a particle times its velocity. What makes this definition useful is the fact that momentum so defined is conserved in low-velocity collisions. However, observations show that momentum defined, according to Newtonian principles, as mass times velocity is *not* conserved in high-velocity collisions. We must therefore choose: We must abandon *either* the Newtonian expression for momentum *or* the law of conservation of momentum. The law of conservation of momentum has become so important to us that we shift to it as a new foundation. We *start* with the law of conservation of momentum and from it *derive* the expression for *momentum defined as that vector quantity which is conserved in all frames of reference.*

This requirement that momentum be conserved in all frames of reference will be used *three* times in this chapter, and each time its use will produce a revolution in our way of looking at nature. In the next section the requirement will be applied to a glancing elastic collision in two dimensions to derive the *relativistic expression for momentum* of a particle. In Section 12 the conservation requirement will be applied to a one-dimensional collision to derive the *relativistic expression for energy* of a particle. In Section 13 the conservation requirement will be applied to an inelastic collision to derive the *equivalance of energy and rest mass.* One asks, how can the law of conservation of momentum be worthwhile if momentum and energy are so *defined* as to make the law hold true. This question takes us to the heart of the nature of the laws and theories of physics.[†] For an answer, look at an object that, like a billiard ball, bats about, colliding with one body after another. In analyzing the first collisions, we use the conservation law to find out or define the unknown momenta of the several objects. The situation is quite different in the subsequent collisions. The momenta in these collisions are already known. There the law of conservation of momentum is upheld, not by definition, but by the inner workings of the world's machinery. All the laws and theories of physics have this deep and subtle character, in that they both define for us the needful concepts and make statements about these concepts. Contrariwise, the absence of some body of theory, law, and principle deprives us of a means properly to use or even to define concepts. How far out of date is that view of science which used to say, "Define your terms before you proceed."! The truly creative nature of any forward step in human knowledge is such that theory, concept, law, and method of measurement—forever inseparable—are born into the world in union.

Multiple checks test that conservation law is not mere circular reasoning

Thus physics provides a way to *harmonize* the experimental facts. No single experiment suffices to establish a conservation law. At least two are needed—

[†]See Henri Poincare, *The Foundations of Science*, translated by G. B. Halsted (Science Press, Lancaster, Pennsylvania, 1946), pp. 310 and 333.

one to establish the definition of the conserved quantity, the other to verify that this quantity really is conserved. In this chapter we will be concerned with the first of these experiments, the one necessary to establish definitions. The *checking* of these definitions proceeds daily and hourly in the ongoing enterprise of experimental physics.

In Newtonian mechanics the momentum of a particle is defined as mass times velocity. In Chapter 1 we measured velocity β in units of meters of distance traveled per meter of light-travel time. In terms of this velocity the Newtonian expression for momentum is $m\beta$. This expression says nothing new about momentum (and is *not* the relativistic expression for momentum!), but makes it clear that time is measured in meters. *If time is measured in meters, momentum has the units of mass.* Conversion to conventional units (for instance, kilogram-meters per second) requires multiplication by the conversion factor c (the speed of light) to convert β to v, thus: (Newtonian momentum in conventional units) $= m\beta c = mv$.

Similarly, in Newtonian mechanics the kinetic energy of a particle is defined as mass times velocity squared divided by two. In terms of velocity β measured in meters per meter, the Newtonian expression for kinetic energy is $1/2\ m\beta^2$. This expression says nothing new about energy (and is *not* the relativistic expression for energy), but makes it clear that time is measured in meters. *If time is measured in meters, energy has the units of mass;* and energy and momentum have the same units. Conversion to conventional units (for instance, joules) requires multiplication by the conversion factor c^2 (the square of the speed of light) to convert β^2 to v^2, thus: (Newtonian kinetic energy in conventional units) $= 1/2\ m\beta^2 c^2 = 1/2\ mv^2$.

Momentum and energy most conveniently expressed in units of mass

The symbols for momentum (p) and kinetic energy (T) in units of mass will be given without subscripts. Thus, in the Newtonian limit of low velocity,

(67)
$$\left.\begin{array}{l} p = m\beta \\ T = 1/2\ m\beta^2 \end{array}\right\} \quad \text{(for low velocity—units of mass)}$$

On the other hand, the symbols for momentum and energy in conventional units will be given the subscript *con*—intentionally unwieldy to make the use of conventional units distasteful. Thus, in the Newtonian limit of low velocity,

(68)
$$\left.\begin{array}{l} p_{con} = mv \\ T_{con} = 1/2\ mv^2 \end{array}\right\} \quad \text{(for low velocity—conventional units)}$$

In this chapter the relativistic expressions for momentum and energy will be derived in units of mass. Expressions for momentum and energy in units of mass are easily converted to conventional units by multiplication by c and c^2 respectively. A summary of results in both sets of units is tabulated inside the back cover of this book.

11. Momentum

How much can one deduce about momentum simply from what he knows about the structure of spacetime, in advance of any experiments? Specifically, if there exists for each particle such a vector quantity as the momentum, the

Symmetry shows momentum is parallel to velocity

sum of which for all particles is conserved when these particles interact, then how must the momentum of each particle depend upon its velocity? Momentum is a vector quantity, so we must first determine the *direction* of the momentum vector of a particle and second the way in which its *magnitude* depends upon the speed of the particle. We begin by reasoning that the momentum vector of a particle points in the direction in which the particle is moving. This conclusion can be supported by an *argument from symmetry*—a powerful tool in physics—in the following way. In an inertial frame, space is the same in all directions; we say that space is *isotropic*. Since this is so, the only unique direction associated with the motion of a particle that moves in a straight line is the direction in which the particle is moving. If the momentum vector of a particle did not point in the direction of motion but, say, at an angle of thirty degrees from this direction, then there would be a large number of vectors—all thirty degrees from the direction of motion, all of them equivalent—any one of which could represent the momentum. But space is isotropic. Therefore we could not choose any one of these vectors in preference to any other of these vectors. But we have assumed that the momentum is determined uniquely, both in magnitude and in direction, by the velocity. Thus we have come against a contradiction. There is only one escape. The line of the momentum vector must lie along the line of motion of the particle. Of the two possible directions along the line of motion of a particle we arbitrarily *choose*, as the direction of the momentum vector, the *same* direction as the velocity of the particle.† The conclusion, finally, is that *the momentum vector of a particle points in the direction of its velocity*.

Momentum conservation law used to find how momentum depends on velocity

Now we know the *direction* in which the momentum vector of a particle points. The second problem is to find the *magnitude* of this momentum vector. We do this by requiring that total momentum be conserved in an elastic collision. This requirement—coupled with the invariance of the interval in Lorentz geometry—will be sufficient to show that the Newtonian expression for momentum

$$p = m\beta \quad (= m \tanh \theta) = m \times \text{(displacement per unit of time)}$$

must be replaced by the relativistic formula

(69) $p = m \sinh \theta = m\beta/(1 - \beta^2)^{1/2} = m \times$ (displacement per unit of proper time)

For small velocity β (small velocity parameter θ) the exact relativistic expression becomes approximately equal to the Newtonian expression.

Total momentum is zero before collision in suitably chosen frame

Let the colliding objects be two identical balls A and B and let the collision be not head-on (rare!) but glancing (typical). One can always find a reference frame moving at such a velocity that *before* the collision the two balls have equal and opposite velocities (Fig. 82). In this frame the *total* momentum of the two identical balls is zero.

---

†We *could*, of course, choose, as the direction of the momentum vector of a particle, the direction *opposite* to its direction of motion. Such a choice would be consistent with the symmetry of the problem and would lead to no physical contradiction if used for all particles. Under such circumstances the momentum of each particle and the total momentum of a system of particles would point in the direction opposite to the corresponding momenta defined above. It is customary to have the momentum vector of a particle lie in the *same* direction as its velocity.

Fig. 82. Glancing elastic collision as observed in a frame moving in such a way that *before* collision the two balls have equal speeds but move in opposite directions. Argument in the text shows that *after* elastic collision the two balls again move with their original speed and again move in opposite directions as observed in that same frame.

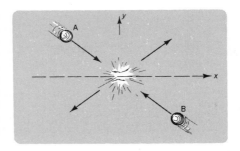

The conclusion that the total momentum is zero can be confirmed by the following symmetry argument: Suppose the total momentum is not zero in this "velocity-symmetric" frame. Then a contradiction will arise, as spelled out in the following argument. A second pair of balls started off exactly as in Fig. 82—except with B located where A is in the figure, and A located where B is—will present no new features. Therefore the total momentum will have the same magnitude, and point in the same direction, as does the total momentum in Fig. 82 (not shown because in reality this total momentum is zero!) But the picture of this new collision can be derived from Fig. 82 by turning the book upside down (rotation of 180° in its own plane!). This operation reverses the direction of the total momentum. Consequently the total momentum vector must be identical to the total momentum vector as rotated through 180°! This contradiction can be resolved only if the total momentum vector has zero magnitude. Thus *before* the collision the two identical particles have equal and opposite momenta.

What happens *after* the collision? The balls must then move in opposite directions and with equal speeds. If they did not, their momenta would not add up to zero and total momentum would not be conserved in the collision—contrary to our requirement. Consider (for the present only) collisions that are *elastic* according to the following prescription: Take a motion picture of the collision. Run it backwards. Nothing will be changed about the collision except this: Particle A now passes from right to left, particle B from left to right instead of the other way around. In this sense an elastic collision is one that is *reversible*. If the collision pictured in Fig. 82 is elastic in this sense, then each ball changes its direction of motion but not (except temporarily) its speed; the overall effect of the collision is simply to rotate the velocity vectors of both particles. The x direction of the reference frame can be chosen to lie in such a direction that the x component of velocity of each particle does not change in the collision, and the y component of velocity of each particle reverses direction, as shown in the figure.

We wish to study the total y component of momentum and its conservation in this collision. To do this most simply, observe the collision in a frame in which ball A moves only in the y direction. This is a rocket frame that moves to the right relative to the frame of Fig. 82 with the same velocity as the x component of velocity of ball A. The collision as observed in this rocket frame is shown in Fig. 83.

There is also a frame in which *ball B* moves only in the y direction. This is a laboratory frame that moves to the left relative to the frame of Fig. 82 with the same velocity as the x component of velocity of ball B. The collision as observed in this laboratory frame is shown in Fig. 84.

Appearance of collision in three different frames

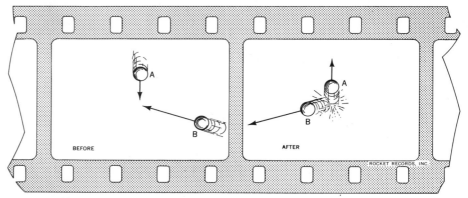

Fig. 83. Collision of Fig. 82 observed in rocket frame.

Our objective is to find out about the momentum of a particle—which may have a velocity very close to the speed of light—from what we know from Newtonian physics about the momentum of a particle of very low velocity. For this purpose a glancing collision is ideal. We can so arrange the encounter that the struck particle has arbitrarily low velocity not only before the collision but also afterwards (particle B in Fig. 84). Therefore the momentum of the struck particle can be obtained from the Newtonian formula $p = m\beta$ as well after the collision as before it. This circumstance will make it easy to determine the momentum change of the slow particle (B) in the collision and will thus —by the use of the law of conservation of momentum—allow us to get at the momentum change, and even the momentum, of the fast particle (A). Granted the symmetry of the diagram, one knows that the momentum transferred to B is twice its momentum before it is struck; or

$$1/2 \text{ (momentum change of B)} = m\, dy/dt$$

Momentum proportional to displacement per unit of proper time

Particle A transfers momentum to B, not by any alteration in the magnitude of its own momentum, but by a change in the *direction* of its momentum vector. In other words, the momentum transfer is the short and known side of a momentum triangle. The other two (equal) sides of the triangle are long and unknown. But the long and short sides of a similar triangle are known—the triangle of displacements. The proportional relation between the sides of similar

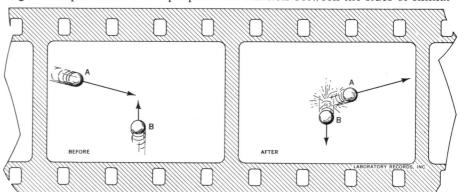

Fig. 84. Collision of Fig. 82 observed in laboratory frame.

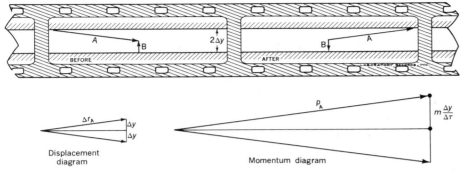

Fig. 85. Derivation of relativistic expression for momentum from the law of conservation of momentum as applied to a glancing collision. Particle B is moving so slowly that the Newtonian expression for momentum gives an arbitrarily good approximation to its momentum: (momentum) $= m(\Delta y_B/\Delta t_B)$. Here Δt_B is the time required for the flight of particle B through the distance Δy_B from the lower boundary to the point of collision. This laboratory time is arbitrarily close in value to the *proper* time, $\Delta \tau_B$, for the flight—again because the velocity of B can be chosen to be arbitrarily slow. (Example: $\Delta \tau$ and Δt differ by 5 parts in 100,000 for $\beta = 0.01$) Therefore the momentum of B can also be written in the form $m(\Delta y_B/\Delta \tau_B)$. Knowing the momentum of B one can find the momentum p_A of A by comparing the momentum diagram above with the diagram for the displacement of A ("similar triangles"). The y displacement of A has been adjusted to be the same as the y displacement of B (symmetric positioning of the "floor" and "ceiling" on which B and A, respectively, impact): $\Delta y_A = \Delta y_B = \Delta y$. Also *the proper time from collision to impact is the same for A as for B:* $\Delta \tau_A = \Delta \tau_B$.

[PROOF: (1) The motion of A in the rocket frame is identical to the motion of B in the laboratory frame (compare Figs. 83 and 84). Consequently these *proper times* of flight are equal:

$$(\Delta \tau_A)_{\text{rocket frame}} = (\Delta \tau_B)_{\text{laboratory frame}}$$

(2) But the *proper* time between two events (collision and impact) has the same value in all frames of reference; or

$$(\Delta \tau_A)_{\text{laboratory frame}} = (\Delta \tau_A)_{\text{rocket frame}}$$

Consequently (3)

$$(\Delta \tau_A)_{\text{laboratory frame}} = (\Delta \tau_B)_{\text{laboratory frame}}$$

as was to be shown. Of course the *laboratory* clock indicates very different durations for the flights of A and B when A moves very close to the speed of light:

$$(\Delta t_A)^2_{\text{laboratory frame}} = (\Delta \tau_A)^2_{\text{laboratory frame}} + (\Delta x_A)^2_{\text{laboratory frame}} \gg (\Delta \tau_A)^2_{\text{laboratory frame}}$$
$$= (\Delta \tau_B)^2_{\text{laboratory frame}} = (\Delta t_B)^2_{\text{laboratory frame}}]$$

Therefore the momentum of A is at last known directly in terms of quantities which refer exclusively to the motion of A:

$$p_A = m(\Delta r_A/\Delta \tau_A)$$

Translating from finite differences to a derivative, and recalling that momentum has the same direction as displacement, one obtains the vector equation

$$\boldsymbol{p} = m \, d\boldsymbol{r}/d\tau$$

This is the relativistic formula for momentum, valid for a particle of arbitrarily great energy.

triangles yields at once (Fig. 85) an expression for the momentum of the high energy particle A

(70)
$$\boldsymbol{p} = m \, d\boldsymbol{r}/d\tau$$
$$= m \text{ times displacement per unit of proper time}$$

The individual components† of this vector are

(71)
$$p^x = m \, dx/d\tau$$
$$p^y = m \, dy/d\tau$$
$$p^z = m \, dz/d\tau$$

in the laboratory frame of reference.

In the rocket frame of reference the components of the momentum are given by expressions similar to Eqs. 71, except that they contain dx', dy', and dz', the components of displacement as measured in the rocket frame. The lapse of proper time, $d\tau'$, between two nearby events on the track of the particle has the same value when calculated from rocket measurements as when calculated from laboratory measurements ("invariance of the interval"). Therefore there is no need to distinguish $d\tau'$ from $d\tau$. Moreover, the value of dy' (rocket frame) is the same as the values of dy (laboratory frame); similarly, $dz = dz'$. Consequently *the components*, $p^y = m \, dy/d\tau$ *and* $p^z = m \, dz/d\tau$, *of the momentum transverse to the relative motion of the rocket and laboratory frames are independent of that relative motion.*

Momentum is analogous to displacement in this respect, that transverse components of both vectors are unaffected by the motion of the observer. There is a simple reason for this similarity in properties of the two vectors! The momentum is obtained from the displacement (Δx, Δy, Δz) by multiplication with a factor ($m/\Delta \tau$) that has the same value in all inertial frames.

Mass most usefully defined as the velocity-independent factor in the momentum

From the analysis of momentum in Fig. 85 it was clear that the quantity m is the mass as mass is understood in Newtonian physics. Thus *m is a constant*, the same at all speeds, all places, and all times. Any difference between the spacetime formula for momentum (for example, $m \, dx/d\tau$) and the corresponding Newtonian formula ($m \, dx/dt$) is therefore to be attributed to the difference between proper time and laboratory time, not to any difference in the value of m in the two descriptions of nature. In some older treatments the Newtonian expression for momentum ($m \, dx/dt$) was corrected, not by changing dt to $d\tau$—as today is considered the simple method—but by introducing a "modified mass" depending upon velocity in such a way that one is justified in still using the Newtonian type of formula; thus,

$$p^x \text{ (relativistic)} = m_{\text{modified}} \, (dx/dt)$$

This modified mass has to have the value

(72)
$$m_{\text{modified}} = m \, (dt/d\tau) = m/(1 - \beta^2)^{1/2}$$

This notation is still used from time to time. However, the most useful quan-

---

†Why p^x and not p_x? In the four-dimensional geometry of spacetime—unlike the Euclidean geometry of space—the position of the label is important (details on standard notation are included in the footnote on page 118).

tities in the analysis of physics are often those, such as m and $d\tau$, that have the same value in all frames of reference. Today this fact is more and more widely recognized. Therefore *we will normally understand by the term "mass" the velocity-independent quantity m.*

How much difference is there between the relativistic and the Newtonian expressions for momentum? The relativistic expression for momentum must reduce to the Newtonian expression for low-velocity particles. A low-velocity particle moves much less than one meter of distance dr in one meter of time dt. Therefore the proper time $d\tau = [(dt)^2 - (dr)^2]^{1/2} = (1 - \beta^2)^{1/2} \, dt$ for any displacement dr of such a particle is very nearly equal to the time dt itself

Relativistic momentum reduces to Newtonian value in low-velocity limit

$$d\tau \approx dt \qquad \text{(low-velocity particle)}$$

(agreement to 5 parts in 100,000 for $\beta = 0.01$; perfect agreement for $\beta \longrightarrow 0$). Under these circumstances the relativistic expression for momentum, $p = m \, dr/d\tau$, becomes identical with the Newtonian expression, $p = m \, dr/dt$, it being understood that the quantity m is the same in the two cases (invariant m!).

It is sometimes convenient to express the magnitude of the momentum in terms of the velocity parameter θ of the particle or in terms of the particle speed $\beta = \tanh \theta$; thus

$$p = m \frac{dr}{d\tau} = m \frac{dr}{[(dt)^2 - (dr)^2]^{1/2}} = \frac{m(dr/dt)}{[1 - (dr/dt)^2]^{1/2}} = \frac{m\beta}{[1 - \beta^2]^{1/2}}$$

$$= \frac{m \tanh \theta}{[1 - \tanh^2 \theta]^{1/2}} = \frac{m \tanh \theta}{\left[\dfrac{\cosh^2 \theta}{\cosh^2 \theta} - \dfrac{\sinh^2 \theta}{\cosh^2 \theta}\right]^{1/2}} = \frac{m \tanh \theta \cosh \theta}{[\cosh^2 \theta - \sinh^2 \theta]^{1/2}} = m \sinh \theta$$

so that

(73) $p = m \sinh \theta = \dfrac{m\beta}{(1 - \beta^2)^{1/2}}$ (relativistic momentum in units of mass)

In contrast the Newtonian expression for momentum has the form

(74) $p = m\beta = m \tanh \theta$ (Newtonian momentum in units of mass)

These two expressions for momentum differ by the factor $dt/d\tau = \cosh \theta = 1/(1 - \beta^2)^{1/2}$. This factor measures the ratio between laboratory time and proper time as recorded by a clock moving with the particle. This is the time-dilation factor of Ex. 10. The presence of this factor in the relativistic formula for the momentum tells one that a particle can transport an arbitrarily great amount of momentum into a collision process if it travels arbitrarily close to the speed of light. One would not suspect this result if he were guided only by the incorrect, Newtonian, formula for momentum, $p = m\beta$, for m is a constant and β cannot exceed unity.

The expression for the momentum of a high-velocity particle thus differs importantly from the Newtonian prediction. However, the procedure for determining the mass of a new particle—involved in a collision process—differs in no point of principle between relativistic and Newtonian theory. The basic idea can be stated in various terms: (1) the principle of action and reaction, (2) the principle that connects the kick of a gun with the momentum of the bullet, (3) the law of conservation of momentum.

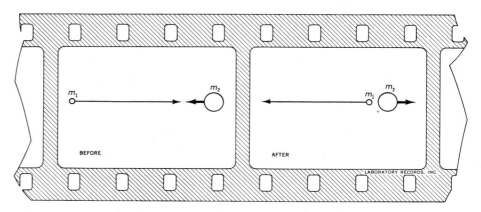

Fig. 86. Velocities before and after a head-on elastic collision as seen from the reference frame in which the total momentum is zero.

Mass of unknown particle determinable from elastic collision with a standard particle

Specifically, consider a head-on and elastic collision between (1) a standard particle, of mass m_1 (this mass arbitrarily assigned by an International Committee on Weights and Measures), and (2) the particle under investigation, with a mass m_2, which at present is unknown, but is to be determined. To say that the collision is head-on and elastic means that there exists a frame of reference in which the velocity record shows the before-after symmetry illustrated in Fig. 86. This symmetry implies that the total momentum reverses sign in the collision. But the total momentum stays constant in the collision. Therefore the total momentum must be zero. Consequently the momenta of the two particles individually, as observed after the collision, must satisfy the condition

$$m_1 \, (dx/d\tau)_1 + m_2 \, (dx/d\tau)_2 = 0$$

From this formula one deduces the value of the unknown mass in units of the known mass:

$$(75) \qquad m_2/m_1 = \frac{(-dx/d\tau)_1}{(dx/d\tau)_2} = \frac{-\Delta x_1}{[(\Delta t_1)^2 - (\Delta x_1)^2]^{1/2}} \frac{[(\Delta t_2)^2 - (\Delta x_2)^2]^{1/2}}{\Delta x_2}$$

Here Δx_1 and Δx_2 are the distances traveled by the two particles from the point of collision to the points of detection; and Δt_1 and Δt_2 are the respective times of flight. For elastic collisions at nonrelativistic velocities, the right-hand side of Eq. 75 reduces to the Newtonian value

$$(76) \qquad m_2/m_1 = -\beta_1/\beta_2 = \frac{-(\Delta x_1/\Delta t_1)}{(\Delta x_2/\Delta t_2)} \qquad \text{(Newtonian limit)}$$

The full simplicity of the relativistic concept of momentum does not become apparent until momentum is seen as the space part of a momentum-energy 4-vector. And only then does one see that checks of the balance of energy in collision processes serve as indirect tests of momentum conservation; tests that are added to all the myriad direct experimental tests of momentum conservation.

12. The Momentum-energy 4-vector

To see momentum and energy as parts of a larger unity it is helpful to recall how one sees space and time as parts of a larger unity. One considers the passage of a particle from an event A in spacetime to a nearby event B. The *4-vector* that leads from A to B is the unifying idea.† The components of this 4-vector, the displacements dx, dy, dz, and dt, have differing values according as the 4-vector is examined from one or another frame of reference. Despite this arbitrariness in the means that we use to describe the 4-vector AB, the 4-vector itself is well defined. Not only does the interval AB have the same magnitude in all frames of reference. More significantly, the *locations* of events A and B themselves—and therefore the positioning of the 4-vector AB in spacetime—are as well defined as the location of two town gates, regardless of what coordinates one uses, or even regardless of whether one uses any coordinates at all.

In a similar way we expect to see the momentum and the energy of a particle at any given phase of its history as components—and merely components—of a 4-vector, which has a reality above all questions of coordinates. Moreover, the connection of this "energy-momentum 4-vector" with the displacement 4-vector AB is no remote and indirect one. Nothing could be more direct than the following chain of ideas:

Energy as fourth component of momentum-energy 4-vector

  (1) displacement 4-vector AB with components

$$dt, dx, dy, dz$$

   illustrated in Fig. 87.

  (2) unit tangent vector obtained by dividing the 4-vector AB by the proper interval $d\tau = [(dt)^2 - (dx)^2 - (dy)^2 - (dz)^2]^{1/2}$ between one end of this displacement and the other; components

$$(dt/d\tau), (dx/d\tau), (dy/d\tau), (dz/d\tau)$$

   are illustrated in Fig. 88.

---

†In 1872, in his inaugural lecture as professor at the University of Erlangen, Felix Klein initiated the decisive new point of view towards geometry which illuminates modern mathematics. His key idea distinguishes one kind of geometry from another by the *law of transformation of components*. One sees very clearly, for example, the difference between Euclidean geometry and the Lorentz geometry of the real physical world in the definition today employed for a vector:

A *4-vector* is *defined* by giving in every inertial reference frame four numbers (numbers which differ from frame to frame!) such that these numbers transform from one frame to another by the Lorentz transformation formula (Eq. 32).

A *3-vector* is *defined* by giving in every Euclidean coordinate system three numbers (components: numbers which differ from coordinate system to coordinate system!) such that these numbers transform from one coordinate system to another by the appropriate formula for Euclidean rotation (Eq. 29).

Given that a quantity is a vector, and knowing its components in only a single frame of reference, one can at once *deduce* its components in every other frame of reference from the appropriate three- or four-dimensional law of transformation of components.

(3) energy-momentum 4-vector, obtained by multiplying this unit vector by the constant m; components

(77)

$$E = p^t = m(dt/d\tau)$$
$$p^x = m(dx/d\tau)$$
$$p^y = m(dy/d\tau)$$
$$p^z = m(dz/d\tau)$$

are illustrated in Fig. 89.

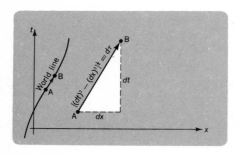

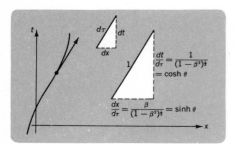

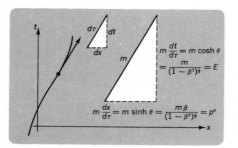

Fig. 87. Displacement 4-vector AB between two events A and B on the world line of a particle. Pictured here for the special case in which the y and z components of displacement dy and dz are both equal to zero.

Fig. 88. Unit tangent vector to the world line of a particle. Obtained by dividing the displacement 4-vector AB of Fig. 87 by the invariant proper time interval $d\tau$. The time and space components of the unit tangent vector have the values

$$\frac{dt}{d\tau} = \frac{dt}{[(dt)^2 - (dx)^2]^{1/2}} = \frac{1}{[1 - (dx/dt)^2]^{1/2}} = \frac{1}{[1 - \beta^2]^{1/2}} = \frac{1}{[1 - \tanh^2\theta]^{1/2}}$$

$$= \frac{1}{\left[\dfrac{\cosh^2\theta}{\cosh^2\theta} - \dfrac{\sinh^2\theta}{\cosh^2\theta}\right]^{1/2}} = \frac{\cosh\theta}{[\cosh^2\theta - \sinh^2\theta]^{1/2}} = \cosh\theta$$

and

$$\frac{dx}{d\tau} = \frac{dx}{[(dt)^2 - (dx)^2]^{1/2}} = \frac{dx/dt}{[1 - (dx/dt)^2]^{1/2}} = \frac{\beta}{[1 - \beta^2]^{1/2}} = \frac{\tanh\theta}{[1 - \tanh^2\theta]^{1/2}}$$

$$= \frac{\tanh\theta}{\left[\dfrac{\cosh^2\theta}{\cosh^2\theta} - \dfrac{\sinh^2\theta}{\sinh^2\theta}\right]^{1/2}} = \frac{\tanh\theta \ \cosh\theta}{[\cosh^2\theta - \sinh^2\theta]^{1/2}} = \sinh\theta$$

(In the special case chosen here the total space component of displacement dr is equal to the x displacement dx. More generally the space part of displacement dr has the value $[(dx)^2 + (dy)^2 + (dz)^2]^{1/2}$. Then it is the total space part of the unit tangent vector which has the value

$$\frac{dr}{d\tau} = \frac{\beta}{(1 - \beta^2)^{1/2}} = \sinh\theta).$$

Fig. 89. The energy-momentum 4-vector. Obtained by multiplying the unit tangent vector of Fig. 88 by the constant mass m of the particle. The time component is called the "relativistic energy" and is given the label E.

The details of this chain of ideas and alternative expressions for the space and time components of all three 4-vectors appear in the figures. No one can question that the 4-vector (dt, dx, dy, dz) remains a 4-vector after division by a factor $d\tau$ and multiplication by a factor m, both of which are the same in all frames of reference.

So much for a quick introduction to the relation between momentum and energy. Now for an important question. Why can one call the time component of the preceding 4-vector by the name *energy*? For two reasons: First, because this time component has the correct units—the units of mass. Second, and more important, because the total time component is conserved in all collisions. Proof that the sum of the E values for all particles is conserved in a collision rests on a simple principle: *When three components of a 4-vector are conserved in all frames, the fourth component is also conserved* (Table 9). We know that the three (space) components of the total momentum of a system are conserved

E-conservation in one frame follows from momentum conservation in all frames

Table 9. Zero momentum change in two frames guarantees zero energy change in all frames.

RELEVANCE TO THE DISCUSSION OF MOMENTUM AND ENERGY

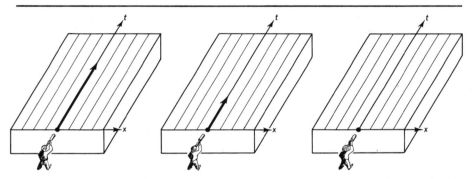

The vanishing of the x component of a vector in *one* frame of reference is of no help at all in drawing any conclusion about the t component of that vector. Here are three vectors of different magnitudes—one of them even of zero magnitude—all of which look alike to someone who is aware only of the x component.

The law of conservation of momentum states that the total of the momenta after the collision is equal to the total of the momenta before that collision. Equivalently, there is a certain quantity — the change in the total momentum in the collision—which is known to be zero. This is only part of the story. We want to have full information on a complete 4-vector (which is equal to the change in the total energy-momentum 4-vector in the collision). Looking at the space component alone (or in the diagram, verifying only that the x component of this 4-vector vanishes) does not help to show that the time component vanishes (that is, that the energy change is zero).

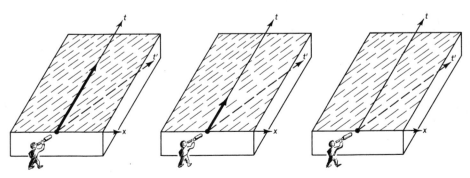

A look at the same vector from another frame of reference discloses at once the difference between vectors, which all looked alike in the previous frame of reference. Let it be known that the space component of a 4-vector vanishes in two different reference frames. Then one is assured that the 4-vector itelf is truly zero (right-hand case).

The vanishing of the space component ("momentum component") of a certain 4-vector (this 4-vector being the change in the total energy-momentum 4-vector in the collision) in two different reference frames is enough to guarantee that this 4-vector itself altogether vanishes. Thus, from the fact that momentum is conserved in laboratory and rocket frames one concludes that energy is conserved in all frames.

in all frames. Therefore the total time-component is also conserved. Details of this demonstration follow.

The Lorentz equations for transforming the elements of a displacement from laboratory to rocket frame can be written (Eqs. 37)

$$dt' = -dx \sinh \theta_r + dt \cosh \theta_r$$
$$dx' = \quad dx \cosh \theta_r - dt \sinh \theta_r$$
$$dy' = dy$$
$$dz' = dz$$

These equations remain valid when both sides are multiplied by the invariant mass m and divided by the invariant interval $d\tau = d\tau'$:

$$m\frac{dt'}{d\tau} = -m\frac{dx}{d\tau} \sinh \theta_r + m\frac{dt}{d\tau} \cosh \theta_r$$
$$m\frac{dx'}{d\tau} = \quad m\frac{dx}{d\tau} \cosh \theta_r - m\frac{dt}{d\tau} \sinh \theta_r$$
$$m\frac{dy'}{d\tau} = m\frac{dy}{d\tau}$$
$$m\frac{dz'}{d\tau} = m\frac{dz}{d\tau}$$

But $m\dfrac{dx}{d\tau}$, $m\dfrac{dy}{d\tau}$, and $m\dfrac{dz}{d\tau}$ are the components of the relativistic momentum and $m\dfrac{dt}{d\tau}$ —the time component of the new 4-vector—is what we have chosen to call the "relativistic energy E". Thus we arrive at the following important equations connecting momentum and the new quantity "E" in one frame with momentum and E' in another inertial frame.

Lorentz transformation of momentum and energy (78)

$$E' = -p^x \sinh \theta_r + E \cosh \theta_r$$
$$p'^x = \quad p^x \cosh \theta_r - E \sinh \theta_r$$
$$p'^y = p^y$$
$$p'^z = p^z$$

("Lorentz transformation of momentum and energy")

Now let two particles collide: p_1^x and p_2^x are the x components of momentum of these particles respectively before the collision as measured in the *laboratory* frame, while E_1 and E_2 are the "relativistic energies" in this frame. Similarly $p_1'^x$ and $p_2'^x$ are the x components of momentum of these particles before the collision as measured in the *rocket* frame. The two sides of the second equation (of Eqs. 78) for each particle can be added to give the total x momentum in the rocket frame before the collision.

$$(p_1'^x + p_2'^x) = (p_1^x + p_2^x) \cosh \theta_r - (E_1 + E_2) \sinh \theta_r$$

The same equation can be written for the particles that rebound from the collision (two particles for an elastic collision; one particle if amalgamation occurs; many particles if fragmentation takes place). These *before* and *after* equations can be analyzed as follows:

(79) $\begin{pmatrix} \textit{before collision:} \\ \text{total } x \text{ momentum} \\ \text{as observed in} \\ \text{rocket frame} \end{pmatrix} = \begin{pmatrix} \textit{before collision} \\ \text{total } x \text{ momentum} \\ \text{as observed in} \\ \text{laboratory frame} \end{pmatrix} \cosh \theta_r - \begin{pmatrix} \textit{before collision:} \\ \text{total relativistic} \\ \text{energy as observed} \\ \text{in laboratory frame} \end{pmatrix} \sinh \theta_r$

STEP 1: these terms   STEP 2: these terms   CONCLUSION: these
are equal—   are equal—   terms are equal—
conservation of   conservation of   proves the *conservation*
momentum!   momentum!   *of relativistic energy!*

(80) $\begin{pmatrix} \textit{after collision:} \\ \text{total } x \text{ momentum} \\ \text{as observed in} \\ \text{rocket frame} \end{pmatrix} = \begin{pmatrix} \textit{after collision:} \\ \text{total } x \text{ momentum} \\ \text{as observed in} \\ \text{laboratory frame} \end{pmatrix} \cosh \theta_r - \begin{pmatrix} \textit{after collision:} \\ \text{total relativistic} \\ \text{energy as observed} \\ \text{in laboratory frame} \end{pmatrix} \sinh \theta_r$

Now—for the second time in this chapter—we *demand* that momentum be conserved in the collision as observed in both laboratory and rocket frames. With this requirement, each of the momentum brackets in Eq. 79 is equal to the corresponding momentum bracket in Eq. 80. If both equations are to hold true, with corresponding momentum brackets being equal, then the energy brackets must be equal also. Therefore the total relativistic energy in the laboratory frame is the same after the collision as before the collision: *total relativistic energy is conserved in the collision.*

We draw three conclusions from this analysis. First, we can assign to any particle of mass m a "relativistic energy,"

Features of total relativistic energy

$$E = m(dt/d\tau)$$

Second, when there are several particles in free motion, the relativistic energy of the system is the sum of the relativistic energies of the separate particles. Third, when these particles collide and separate, with changes in the individual energies of the several particles, the total relativistic energy of the system is the same after the collision as it was before (conservation of relativistic energy).

The additive relation between the energy of a collection of free particles and the energies of the individual particles traces back to the additive connection between total momentum and the momenta of these particles individually. This additivity indicates that the ability to calculate the energy of single particles is sufficient to allow evaluation of the energy of a collection of such particles.

The expression for the relativistic energy of one particle can be written in a variety of ways, the circumstances determining which form is most useful. Thus we have (Fig. 89)

Alternative expressions for energy

(81) $$E = m(dt/d\tau) = m/(1 - \beta^2)^{1/2} = m \cosh \theta$$

What can be learned from these expressions about the relation between relativistic energy, E, and velocity? Between E and energy defined by the Newtonian expression? Between E and momentum?

For very small β, expand the expression for relativistic energy in a "power series" in powers of β using the binomial theorem or some other method:

$$E = m/(1 - \beta^2)^{1/2} = m(1 - \beta^2)^{-1/2} = m\left(1 + \frac{\beta^2}{2} + \frac{3}{8}\beta^4 + \cdots\right)$$

For sufficiently small velocity β this series can be approximated to any desired accuracy by the first two terms

$$(82) \qquad\qquad E \approx m(1 + \beta^2/2) = m + 1/2\, m\beta^2 \qquad\qquad \text{(low velocity)}$$

But $1/2\, m\beta^2$ is simply the Newtonian expression for kinetic energy in units of mass. Thus the relativistic energy E is *related* to the kinetic energy of the particle. But E is *not equal* to the kinetic energy of the particle, because of the presence of the extra term m. This extra term remains, even for a particle at rest—a particle that has no kinetic energy at all. For this reason the term m is called the *rest energy* E_{rest} *of the particle*.

$$(83) \qquad\qquad\qquad E_{\text{rest}} = m \qquad\qquad \text{(rest energy—units of mass)}$$

The rest energy of a particle in conventional units $E_{\text{rest con}}$ is obtained by multiplying the rest energy in units of mass by the conversion factor c^2. This gives the famous expression

$$(84) \qquad\qquad\qquad E_{\text{rest con}} = mc^2 \qquad\qquad \text{(rest energy—conventional units)}$$

Table 10. Energy which must be imparted to a hydrogen atom ($m = 1.67 \times 10^{-27}$ kilogram) to give it a speed close to the speed of light.

β	Distance traveled from the starting line by a light flash, in a race with the particle, at the time the particle is 1 centimeter behind	$\dfrac{E_{\text{con}}}{mc^2}$	$\dfrac{T_{\text{con}}}{mc^2}$	T_{con} (joules)	An everyday equivalent of this energy
0.5	2 centimeters	1.15	0.15	2×10^{-11}	—
0.99	1 meter	7.1	6.1	10^{-9}	—
0.99999	1 kilometer	222	221	3×10^{-8}	Kinetic energy of 1 grain of table salt dropped from a height of 1 centimeter
0.999 . . . 99 (13 nines)	10^{11} meters†	2.2×10^6	$\sim 2.2 \times 10^6$	3×10^{-4}	Kinetic energy of 1 buck-shot pellet dropped from a height of 1 centimeter
0.9999 . . . 99 (18 nines)	10^{16} meters‡	7.1×10^8	$\sim 7.1 \times 10^8$	10^{-1}	Kinetic energy of 1 buck-shot pellet dropped from a second-story window
0.9999 . . . 999 (28 nines)	10^{26} meters§	7.1×10^{13}	7.1×10^{13}	10^4	Kinetic energy of a motorcycle traveling 25 miles per hour

†About two-thirds of the distance to the sun.
‡About one light year.
§Approximate distance to the most remote galaxy photographed to date.

It is impossible to have the laws of conservation of momentum and energy upheld in all inertial frames of reference unless the rest energy is included in the bookkeeping of the energy in every frame. This is the new lesson of space-time physics that never was apparent in Newtonian physics. Newtonian mechanics does not contain an expression for the rest energy of a particle. However, in Newtonian mechanics any constant energy can be added to the energy of a particle without changing the laws which describe its motion. One may think of the low-velocity limit of the relativistic expression for energy as providing this previously arbitrary constant.

Allowance for rest energy essential in upholding conservation law

The relativistic energy of a particle in any reference frame can be thought of as made up of two parts: the rest energy m of the particle plus the additional energy that the particle has by virtue of its motion. This additional energy is the kinetic energy of the particle. The relativistic expression for kinetic energy is

Relativistic expression for kinetic energy

$$(85) \quad T = E - E_{\text{rest}} = m \cosh \theta - m = m(\cosh \theta - 1)$$
$$= m[1/(1 - \beta^2)^{1/2} - 1] \qquad \text{(kinetic energy—units of mass)}$$

This expression for relativistic kinetic energy is valid for all particle velocities. In contrast, *only for low particle velocities is the kinetic energy correctly given by the Newtonian formula,* $1/2\ m\beta^2$.

As the velocity increases and approaches the speed of light, the energy increases without limit. Therefore, even if one can draw upon unlimited supplies of energy, he cannot accelerate a particle to the speed of light. How rapidly the energy requirement increases as the velocity approaches the speed of light is shown by the numbers in Table 10.

Energy, the time component of the momentum-energy 4-vector and energy, the time dimension of the triangle in Fig. 90, can be evaluated by the familiar means by which one evaluates the side of any other triangle. The two principal methods employ *proportion* and the *Pythagorean theorem*. In evaluating energy as a function of velocity we made use of the similarity of the triangle $m\,E\,p$ and the triangle $d\tau\ dt\ dx$ (see Fig. 87). By proportion we found the relation $E/m = dt/d\tau = 1/(1 - \beta^2)^{1/2}$. Now we want to find energy as a function of momentum. For this purpose it is enough to refer to the triangle $m\,E\,p$ all by itself. However, it is necessary to recognize that the geometry is not Euclidean, but Lorentzian. The square of the hypotenuse is given, not by the sum of the squares of the other two sides, but by their difference; thus

Mass as magnitude of momentum-energy 4-vector

$$(86) \qquad m^2 = E^2 - p^2 \qquad \text{(units of mass)}$$

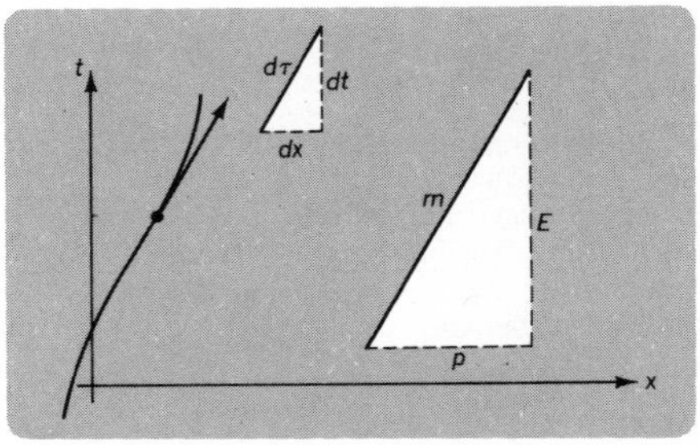

Fig. 90. The energy-momentum 4-vector.

This expression gives the squared magnitude of the momentum-energy 4-vector.† This formula is the exact analog of the formula that gives the squared magnitude of the spacetime interval between two nearby events on the world line of the particle

$$(d\tau)^2 = (dt)^2 - (dr)^2$$

In both formulas the individual quantities on the right-hand side depend upon the state of motion of the particle or the reference frame in which it is observed. In other words, the individual components of the momentum-energy 4-vector— or the energy E of the particle and its momentum p—do not have the same values in the laboratory frame as in the rocket frame. In contrast, the left-hand side of each equation—the rest mass m and the interval $d\tau$—are invariants: they have the same values in all frames of reference.

An explicit expression for energy in terms of momentum is obtained from Eq. 86 by solving for E; thus

(87) $E = (m^2 + p^2)^{1/2}$

---

†For many purposes it is convenient to have an expression for the squared magnitude of a 4-vector in terms of the four components of that vector. One has to be a little more careful about the notation for these components than one is for vectors in three-dimensional Euclidean space. The normal representation for a 4-vector in this book and in most current literature uses *upper indices*

$$p^t = E = m \, dt/d\tau, \qquad p^x = m \, dx/d\tau, \qquad p^y = m \, dy/d\tau, \qquad p^z = m \, dz/d\tau$$

There is another representation which uses *lower indices* but with the *time component reversed in sign*

$$p_t = -m \, dt/d\tau, \qquad p_x = m \, dx/d\tau, \qquad p_y = m \, dy/d\tau, \qquad p_z = m \, dz/d\tau$$

The two alternative representations, employing upper or lower labels, are also used for other 4-vectors, as, for example, the vector R from the origin of an inertial reference frame to some chosen event; thus

$$R^t = t, \qquad R^x = x, \qquad R^y = y, \qquad R^z = z$$

and

$$R_t = -t, \qquad R_x = x, \qquad R_y = y, \qquad R_z = z$$

In terms of this notation, the invariant squared interval for a spacelike separation between event and origin takes the convenient form

$$\sigma^2 = R_t R^t + R_x R^x + R_y R^y + R_z R^z = -t^2 + x^2 + y^2 + z^2$$

When the separation is timelike, the expression for the squared interval is

$$\tau^2 = -(R_t R^t + R_x R^x + R_y R^y + R_z R^z) = t^2 - x^2 - y^2 - z^2$$

The momentum-energy 4-vector is a timelike 4-vector, for a very simple reason: because two successive events on the world line of a particle are separated by a timelike interval. Therefore the squared magnitude of this 4-vector is to be calculated from a formula analogous to the equation for τ^2; thus

$$\binom{\text{squared}}{\text{magnitude}} = -(p_t p^t + p_x p^x + p_y p^y + p_z p^z)$$
$$= m^2[(dt)^2 - (dx)^2 - (dy)^2 - (dz)^2]/(d\tau)^2$$
$$= m^2$$

In *Euclidean* geometry, in which a vector has only space components, this distinction between upper and lower labels is unimportant, and frequently lower labels are used exclusively. However, in spacetime geometry, in which there *is* a difference in sign for the time component associated with the difference between upper and lower labels, it is important to maintain this distinction. Moreover, the components of a 4-vector with upper labels are ordinarily more convenient to work with, as these components often relate directly to the changes in individual coordinates.

This formula is as good at arbitrarily high momentum as at low momentum. It admits of simplification in the two extreme limits.

When the momentum p is small compared to m (that is, when β is very small compared to unity: "nonrelativistic limit") one can expand Eq. 87 by using the binomial theorem or some other method, finding

$$E = m(1 + p^2/m^2)^{1/2}$$
$$= m + (p^2/2m) + (p^4/8m^3) \cdots \qquad \text{(low } p\text{)}$$

Energy in terms of momentum; Newtonian and extreme relativistic limits

For sufficiently small momentum p this series can be approximated to any desired accuracy by the first two terms

(88) $$\qquad\qquad E \approx m + p^2/2m \qquad\qquad \text{(low } p\text{)}$$

Here the first term represents the rest energy. The second term is the Newtonian formula for the kinetic energy of a particle of momentum p.

When the momentum p is very large compared to m ("extreme relativistic limit") one can again expand the accurate formula in a power series

$$E = p(1 + m^2/p^2)^{1/2}$$
$$\approx p + (m^2/2p) + (m^4/8p^3) \cdots \qquad \text{(high } p\text{)}$$

For sufficiently high momentum p the series can be approximated to any desired accuracy by the first term

(89) $$\qquad\qquad E \approx p \qquad\qquad \text{(extreme relativistic limit)}$$

In this limit the rest mass has no influence on the relation between momentum and energy.

Should one be surprised that the legs E and p of the triangle of Fig. 90 both grow greater and greater while the hypotenuse m remains fixed at a value that is small compared to that of either leg? How can the hypotenuse of a right triangle possibly remain fixed in length while the legs increase in length without limit? Such a relationship of lengths of legs and length of hypotenuse is absolutely incompatible with Euclidean geometry. But the geometry is not Euclidean. In the Lorentz geometry of spacetime the square of the hypotenuse is equal to the *difference* of the squares of the two legs. Therefore there is no paradox in the combination of a hypotenuse of constant length with two legs, E and p, which can both increase without limit and ultimately become practically equal in magnitude.

There is another way to see that energy should become approximately equal to momentum when either quantity becomes very great compared to the rest mass. Quite generally, and without any approximation, we deduce from the formulas $p = m\beta/(1 - \beta^2)^{1/2}$ and $E = m/(1 - \beta^2)^{1/2}$ the result

Momentum as rate of transport of massenergy

(90) $$\qquad\qquad p = \beta E \qquad\qquad \text{(all velocities)}$$

From this formula it follows that p becomes arbitrarily close to E as the velocity becomes arbitrarily close to the speed of light.

One can give an illuminating interpretation to the formula (Eq. 90). There E represents the mass-energy of the particle, and β measures the speed with which this mass-energy is moving. Therefore the product, *the momentum p, represents the rate of transport of mass-energy.* It is interesting that the mass-energy factor in this formula (the quantity E in Eq. 90) differs from the mass m that a Newtonian analysis might have suggested. What accounts for the transport of mass-energy is not rest mass alone, but rest mass supplemented by the mass-equivalent of the kinetic energy; or in other words, the total mass-energy, E.

The rest mass itself does not appear in the formula $p = \beta E$. Therefore we put this formula at the center of Fig. 91, and group around it the other key formulas connecting energy, momentum, and velocity. Each relationship has its own special field of usefulness, as indicated by the captions in the diagram.

Nothing has been said in our analysis of momentum and energy about the internal structure, if there is any, of the object that carries these attributes. The object can be a rocket, or a complex organic molecule, or an elementary particle, or even a photon—the elementary quantum of light. In all these examples the motion proceeds with a speed less than that of light, except, of course, for light itself. For light traveling through a vacuum, the velocity β has a value of precisely unity. In this case the formulas $E = m/(1 - \beta^2)^{1/2}$ and $p = m\beta/(1 - \beta^2)^{1/2}$ evidently lose all usefulness. However, the relation (90) becomes extraordinarily simple; thus

Any packet of energy that moves with speed of light has zero rest mass

(91) $p = E$ (for any energy traveling with the speed of light)

Moreover, the relation $m^2 = E^2 - p^2$ tells us that in this case the rest mass is zero. We conclude that *any agency which transports energy in a straight line with the speed of light is characterized by a zero rest mass.* Today only three mechanisms for transmitting energy with the speed of light are known—elec-

Fig. 91. The quantities measured in an experiment decide which relativistic formula is convenient in the analysis of the experiment.

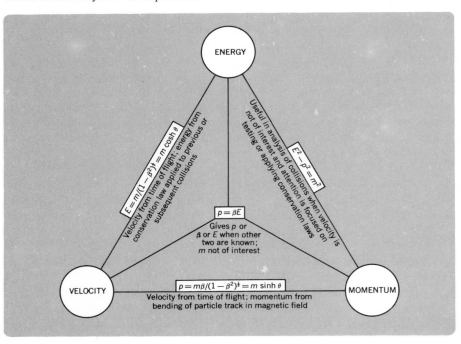

tromagnetic radiation, gravitational radiation, and neutrinos—and of these only the first and the last have so far been observed experimentally.†

The relation $p = E$ is fulfilled with 100 percent accuracy only by a radiation of zero rest mass. However, it is approximated with arbitrarily high precision by a particle that has an energy sufficiently great in comparison with its rest mass. Therefore in this extreme relativistic limit a particle of rest mass m behaves—so far as concerns the laws of conservation of momentum and energy —in practically the same way as a photon.

13. The Equivalence of Energy and Rest Mass

The total of the momenta of all particles is conserved in a collision; the total of their energies E (rest energy plus kinetic energy) is also conserved. That has been the guiding principle in our analysis of collisions. But is it correct to accept this principle when we turn from considering elastic encounters to look at an *inelastic* collision? A ball of putty is thrown with high speed against another ball of putty lying at rest on a skating rink. They stick together as they hurtle across the ice. We are quite willing to believe that the law of conservation of momentum applies to this collision; but is it reasonable to expect the law of conservation of energy to be useful in analyzing this collision? Some of the energy of impact has been converted into heat. Another portion of the original energy shows up in the energy of rotation as the two joined balls whirl like a dumbbell about their center-of-mass. How can any treatment give adequate recognition to these complications when it limits its description of the final system to the two quantities E and p, connected by the elementary formula $E^2 - p^2 = m^2$? Answer: the rest mass m of the final system is greater than the sum of the rest masses of the original colliding objects. This is a new feature of spacetime physics, never known or even imagined in Newtonian mechanics. The increase in rest mass measures precisely the energy which has gone into heat and whirling and any other forms of internal excitation of the final system. Unless one recognizes the changes in rest mass that take place in many encounters, he will be led into apparent violations of the law of conservation of energy or the law of conservation of momentum or both.

Rest mass of final system increases in an inelastic encounter

How does one evaluate the alteration of the rest mass? In the example of the two balls of putty he applies (1) the law of conservation of energy

$$E_{\text{final}} = E_{\text{initial}} = E_1 + m_2$$

(2) the law of conservation of momentum

$$p_{\text{final}} = p_{\text{initial}} = p_1 + p_2 = p_1$$

and (3) the equation

$$m_{\text{final}}^2 = E_{\text{final}}^2 - p_{\text{final}}^2$$

---

†On the detection of free neutrinos see C. L. Cowan, Jr., F. Reines, F. B. Harrison, H. W. Kruse, and A. D. McGuire, Science, **124**, 103 (1956).

For attempts presently in progress to detect gravitational radiation from outer space, see J. Weber, "Gravitational Waves," in *Gravitation and Relativity*, edited by H.-Y. Chiu and W. F. Hoffmann, (W. A. Benjamin, New York, 1964).

He obtains the result

$$
\begin{aligned}
m_{\text{final}}^2 &= (E_1 + m_2)^2 - p_1^2 \\
&= E_1^2 + 2E_1 m_2 + m_2^2 - p_1^2 \\
&= (E_1^2 - p_1^2) + 2E_1 m_2 + m_2^2 \\
&= m_1^2 + 2(m_1 + T_1) m_2 + m_2^2 \\
&= (m_1 + m_2)^2 + 2T_1 m_2
\end{aligned}
$$

(92)

Conservation laws valid whether collision is elastic, inelastic, or superelastic

Evidently the rest mass of the agglomerated system exceeds the sum of the rest masses of the original objects 1 and 2. Moreover, the amount of the excess is greater when the kinetic energy of impact, T, is large. We conclude from this example that *the laws of conservation of momentum and energy are as valid—and as useful—for inelastic encounters as for elastic processes.*

How does this unexpected bonus from the conservation laws come about? And what does it tell us about the equivalence of energy and rest mass? These questions require a closer look.

"Energy is conserved in every frame if momentum is conserved in both laboratory and rocket frames." In the proof of this theorem in Eqs. 79 and 80 it made no difference whether a single object emerged from the collision or a thousand fragments came off, or whether the two colliding particles met in an elastic encounter. There are many reactions in physics that change the number of particles. One of the most dramatic is the creation of a pair of electrons, one positive, the other negative, out of empty space during the collision of two energy-bearing agencies; for example, in the collision of two electrons

$$ e^-(\text{fast}) + e^-(\text{at rest}) = e^- + e^- + e^- + e^+ $$

Such a process is called inelastic because kinetic energy is converted into rest mass. There are also superelastic processes, in which part of the rest mass of an object (stored internal energy) is converted into kinetic energy

$$ \begin{pmatrix} \text{slow} \\ \text{electron} \end{pmatrix} + \begin{pmatrix} \text{atom containing} \\ \text{internal excitation energy} \end{pmatrix} \longrightarrow \begin{pmatrix} \text{deexcited} \\ \text{atom} \end{pmatrix} + \begin{pmatrix} \text{fast} \\ \text{electron} \end{pmatrix} $$

Finally, there are decay processes, in which one particle breaks up into two products of lesser combined rest mass

$$ K^+ \longrightarrow \pi^+ + \pi^0 $$

(positive K-meson [mass of 967 electron masses] decaying in 10^{-8} second to positive pi-meson [mass of 273 electron masses] plus neutral pi-meson [mass of 264 electron masses]).

All complications that originate, in these or other ways, from changes in the number of particles in no way affect the applicability of the laws of conservation of momentum and energy. Happily the reactants and the reaction products—and their energies and momenta—can be defined and discussed whether the reaction they have just been through or are just about to go through is elastic or inelastic. Each particle carries its momentum-energy 4-vector at all times: It does not know whether it is going to go through an inelastic or an elastic encounter. It needs to have all the bookkeeping machinery for a possible *elastic* collision. Thus, whether the collision is destined to be elastic or inelastic, one knows the momentum and energy of each particle before the collision. Therefore one also knows the *total* momentum and energy of the entire system before the collision. One likewise knows the *total* momentum and energy after the collision. Therefore one can speak of the *change*—if any— in the total energy and momentum in the collision. This change is zero in an elastic encounter. The change of energy is also zero in inelastic encounters, provided that the change of total *momentum* is zero in both laboratory and rocket frames: of this we are assured by earlier reasoning (Eqs. 79, 80). No convincing argument has ever been given for doubting that momentum—and therefore energy as well—is conserved in inelastic collisions.

What about observational evidence on conservation of momentum and energy in inelastic events? Momentum and energy have been defined in such a way that these quantities are conserved in the simplest of elastic encounters. Therefore it is too late to change the definitions to fit observations on a wider range of collision processes. Either the change in momentum and energy is zero when measured by every experiment—in which case the conservation of momentum and energy is a principle of wide-reaching significance; or the change in momentum and energy is *not* zero—in which case the experimental result would be a revolutionary upset of the principles of relativity. Experiment makes the test—and observation confirms that this change is zero. This test is repeated daily and hourly as high-energy collisions are recorded in laboratories all over the world.

For experiments that test the conservation laws and experience in interpreting them, see Exs. 90 to 100.

Innumerable observational tests of conservation laws

Table 11.   The number of yearly tests of Euclidean geometry and of Lorentz geometry.

How well tested is Euclidean geometry?	*How well tested is relativity?*
42,000 surveyors (1963 Statistical Abstracts of the United States), each making 20 surveys per year in which he identifies the n vertices of a polygonal boundary, measures the interior angle at each vertex, adds, and compares the sum with the value $(n-2)\,180°$ predicted by Euclidean geometry.	50 particle accelerators (estimated) that produce particles of energy greater than 100 MeV, each operating 100 days per year, each recording 200 collisions per day of operation in which departures from the relativistic conservation laws would be apparent.
Result: 840,000 tests per year, each with a sensitivity of one part in 10^4 or better.	*Result:* 1,000,000 tests per year, each with a sensitivity of one part in 10^4 or better.

The energy set free in the burning of coal, the combustion of gas, and the explosion of dynamite appears large on an everyday level of experience. However, when one translates these numbers into mass equivalent, he finds that less than one part in 10^9 of the rest mass has been converted into energy (see, for example, Ex. 63)—a mass change too small for detection by existing equipment. Therefore one is driven to the worlds of particle physics and nuclear physics when he looks for places to make careful tests of the conservation laws.

In particle physics many of the objects under study live for a very short time. It is not easy to determine precisely the mass of such a short-lived particle by using a conventional mass spectrometer. The mass is found instead by applying the laws of conservation of momentum and energy to a collision or transformation process in which one or more of the particles have known masses. One can still check the conservation laws in this way, for a given particle is often formed by several different reactions. However, for a direct check of energies of transmutation against the energies expected from changes in rest masses, it is better to turn to the world of nuclear physics. There mass values have been determined directly and with high precision both for stable nuclei and for some unstable nuclei. The conditions for an accurate comparison of energy release with mass changes are most favorable for the lighter nuclei. There the change of mass in the typical nuclear reaction constitutes a higher fraction of the total mass—and is therefore subject to more precise determination—than in heavier nuclei. For this reason examine the reaction of two of the lightest of atomic nuclei, a reaction which, moreover, is of great importance in this nuclear age:

Conditions for a precise test of conservation laws especially favorable in nuclear physics

$$\begin{pmatrix} \text{fast} \\ \text{deuteron} \end{pmatrix} + \begin{pmatrix} \text{deuteron} \\ \text{at rest} \end{pmatrix} \nearrow \begin{pmatrix} \text{very energetic} \\ \text{proton} \end{pmatrix} + \begin{pmatrix} \text{energetic} \\ \text{triton} \end{pmatrix}$$
$$\searrow \begin{pmatrix} \text{very energetic} \\ \text{neutron} \end{pmatrix} + \begin{pmatrix} \text{energetic} \\ \text{helium 3} \end{pmatrix}$$

or

$$(93) \qquad H^2(\text{fast}) + H^2 \begin{array}{c} \nearrow H^1 + H^3 \\ \searrow n + He^3 \end{array}$$

The alternative reactions of Eq. 93 occur with comparable frequency in a hydrogen bomb, or "fusion" weapon. They provide a large part of the energy release characteristic of a device fueled by deuterium ("heavy hydrogen," H^2). The kinetic energy of the products of such a thermonuclear reaction is hundreds of times greater than the kinetic energy of the deuterons entering the reaction.

Triton mass from conservation law checks triton mass as measured by spectrometer

The triton-producing reaction—the first of the two alternative transformations in Eq. 93—lends itself to the most precise single test of the conservation laws that we have been able to find in all of physics. Making this test possible are independent, and careful, mass spectrometer determinations of the rest masses of all particles taking part in this reaction (deuteron, proton, triton).

An equally accurate and independent determination of the rest mass of the neutron is not available. Hence we exclude from attention the second, or neutron-producing reaction in Eq. 93. It is not suitable for a highly accurate test of the equivalence of mass and energy. The neutron is an unstable particle (mean life about 17 minutes). More important, it is unresponsive (electrically neutral!) to the electric and magnetic fields in a mass spectrometer. This unresponsiveness stands in the way of any precise independent determination of the mass of the neutron.

Imagine that we were to concern ourselves here with the neutron rather than the triton. What could we hope to discover, since we lack any independently determined *precise* value of the neutron mass? We could give up trying to *check* the conservation laws. Instead, we could *apply* the conservation laws to deduce a value for the neutron mass good to about 1 part in 10^5. Why can we be assured that the conservation laws—as applied to the second reaction—provide a means so reliable for determining the mass of the neutron? Because, applied to the first reaction, the conservation laws give a value for the triton mass that checks the mass spectrometer value to better than 1 part in 10^5 (ANALYSIS OF THE REACTION $H^2 + H^2 \longrightarrow H^1 + H^3$, pages 126 and 127). This one check of maximal present day precision, together with many other checks of slightly lower accuracy elsewhere in physics, argues powerfully for the soundness of the conservation principle.

A remark has to be made about the units in the calculation on pages 126 and 127. In principle it would be natural to express all energies and momenta in kilograms, as was done in earlier calculations of this chapter. To do this here, however, it would be necessary to translate the numbers given by mass spectroscopy from "unified atomic mass units" (u; scale changed in 1961 from $0^{16} = 16.000 \cdots$ to $C^{12} = 12.000 \cdots$) to kilograms, and also to translate the kinetic energy values measured by the nuclear physicist from electron volts to kilograms. It is more convenient to express all energies in u, thus eliminating the need for one of the conversion calculations (u to kilograms). Moreover, all formulas in the text apply as well to one set of units of mass-energy as to another set, provided only that a given set of units is used consistently throughout. How then is one to translate from electron volts to u? Happily the translation can be made without knowing the mass in kilograms associated with one mass unit—or equivalently, without knowing how many atoms there are in a gram atom (Avogadro's number, N, which has a value of $(6.02252 \pm 0.00028) \times 10^{23}$). The present-day uncertainty in this number, 5 parts in 10^5, would affect all our results if we chose to translate into kilograms. The conversion factor from electron volts to unified atomic mass units is derived on page 128.

ANALYSIS† OF THE REACTION H^2 (FAST) $+ H^2 \longrightarrow H^1 + H^3$

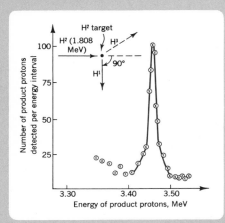

Fig. 92. Experimental evidence that protons (H^1) emerging from the reaction

$$H^2(1.808 \text{ MeV}) + H^2(\text{at rest}) \longrightarrow H^1(\text{very fast}) + H^3(\text{fast})$$

at 90 degrees from the direction of the incident deuteron (H^2) have an energy of 3.467 MeV. (The value 3.467 MeV was obtained by combining the results shown here with results of several similar determinations.) The number of protons emerging with energies in the range $E - 0.1$ MeV to $E + 0.1$ MeV is plotted as a function of E. The spread in energy arises from the finite thickness of the target, the finite width of slits used to define the beam, inhomogeneities in the magnetic fields used to define energies, etc. The experimental curve in this figure can be found in the article by D. M. Van Patter and W. W. Buechner, Physical Review, **87**, 51, (1952).

Laws of conservation of energy and momentum:

(94)	$E_2 + m_2 = \bar{E}_1 + \bar{E}_3$	energy conservation
(95)	$p_2{}^x + 0 = 0 + \bar{p}_3{}^x$	x-momentum conservation
(96)	$0 + 0 = \bar{p}_1{}^y + \bar{p}_3{}^y$	y-momentum conservation
(97)	$0 + 0 = 0 + \bar{p}_3{}^z$	z-momentum conservation

Here each subscript indicates the mass number of the isotope and a bar over a symbol means "after the reaction."

Each of the four equations (94–97) can be regarded as giving a separate piece of information about the triton—either about its energy, or about one component of its momentum. But we are not interested in all this information. We want to know one simple property of the triton, different from any of these four quantities—its rest mass. Happily, this rest mass is given by the length of the 4-vector of energy and momentum

$$(98) \qquad m_3{}^2 = \bar{E}_3{}^2 - (\bar{p}_3{}^x)^2 - (\bar{p}_3{}^y)^2 - (\bar{p}_3{}^z)^2$$

Insert into this expression the values of the components read from Eqs. 94–97 and obtain

$$m_3{}^2 = (E_2 + m_2 - \bar{E}_1)^2 - (p_2{}^x + 0 - 0)^2 - (0 + 0 - \bar{p}_1{}^y)^2 - (0 + 0 - 0)^2$$

$$= \underbrace{\bar{E}_1{}^2 - 0 - (\bar{p}_1{}^y)^2 - 0}_{m_1{}^2} + \underbrace{E_2{}^2 - (p_2{}^x)^2 - 0 - 0}_{m_2{}^2} + m_2{}^2 - 2m_2\bar{E}_1 + 2m_2E_2 - 2E_2\bar{E}_1$$

$$= \qquad\qquad m_1{}^2 \qquad\qquad + \qquad m_2{}^2 \qquad + m_2{}^2 - 2m_2\bar{E}_1 + 2m_2E_2 - 2E_2\bar{E}_1$$

$$= m_1{}^2 + 2(m_2 + E_2)(m_2 - \bar{E}_1)$$

$$(99) \qquad m_3{}^2 = m_1{}^2 + 2(m_2 + m_2 + T_2)(m_2 - m_1 - \bar{T}_1)$$

Here we have used equations of the form $E = m + T$, which relate kinetic energy to total energy.

---

†Results of the experiment presented in this calculation are published in an article by E. N. Strait, D. M. Van Patter, W. W. Buechner, and A. Sperduto, in the Physical Review, **81**, 747 (1951). The authors express their appreciation to W. W. Buechner and A. Sperduto for additional data and for discussions regarding their proper interpretation.

The values of all quantities on the right side of Eq. 99 are known. This equation thus permits a prediction of the mass m_3 of the triton. Mass values for the right side of Eq. 99 are obtained from mass spectrometer experiments (expressed in "unified atomic mass units"—symbol u—based on the isotope $C^{12} = 12.0000 \ldots u$. as the standard of mass).†

$$(100) \qquad\qquad m_2 = 2.0141019 \pm 0.0000003\ u$$

$$(101) \qquad\qquad m_1 = 1.0078252 \pm 0.0000003\ u$$

Kinetic energies were measured in the nuclear reaction experiment (Fig. 92).

$$(102) \qquad \text{(kinetic energy of incident deuteron)} = T_2$$

$$= (1.808 \pm 0.002\ \text{MeV})(1.073562 \times 10^{-3}\ u/\text{MeV}) = 0.001941 \pm 0.000002\ u$$

For derivation of the conversion factor from MeV to unified atomic mass units, see page 128.

$$(103) \qquad \text{(kinetic energy of product proton)} = \overline{T}_1$$

$$= (3.467 \pm 0.0035\ \text{MeV})(1.073562\ u/\text{MeV}) = 0.003722 \pm 0.000004\ u$$

Substitute these values into Eq. 99, keeping only the six decimal digits that correspond to the accuracy of the kinetic energy measurements. The two terms on the right of this equation become

$$
\begin{aligned}
m_1{}^2 &= 1.015712\ u^2 \\
2(2m_2 + T_2)(m_2 - m_1 - \overline{T}_1) &= \underline{8.080881 \pm 0.00003\ u^2} \\
\text{sum of these terms} = m_3{}^2 &= 9.096593 \pm 0.00003\ u^2
\end{aligned}
$$

The square root of this number is the mass of the triton predicted on the basis of this nuclear reaction.

$$(104) \qquad\qquad m_3 = 3.016056 \pm 0.000015\ u$$

Compare this mass with the mass of the triton measured by mass spectrometer.†

$$(105) \qquad\qquad m_3 = 3.0160494 \pm 0.0000007\ u$$

The two values differ by about 2 parts in 10^6, a difference less than the uncertainty in the result of the nuclear reaction experiment. So accurate a prediction of the triton mass on the basis of the relativistic conservation laws is strong evidence for the validity of these conservation laws.

---

†Mass spectrometer mass values quoted here are derived from F. Everling, L. A. König, J. H. E. Mattauch, and A. H. Wapstra, Nuclear Physics, **25**, 177 (1961). Mass values could instead have been taken from standard tables of nuclidic masses. However, mass values in standard tables constitute a "best compromise" between various kinds of data, including not only mass spectrometer results but also the results of nuclear reaction experiments such as the one under discussion here. In constructing standard tables, data from nuclear reaction experiments are interpreted using the conservation laws of relativity. Therefore mass values from standard tables cannot be used in an independent check of these conservation laws, as we would like to do here. For this reason we limit present attention to mass spectrometer mass values. After this and other similar verifications of the conservations laws, we are willing to place reliance on standard tables, which use these laws to derive the best possible mass values from available data of all kinds. Such a standard mass table can be found in L. A. König, J. H. E. Mattauch, and A. H. Wapstra, Nuclear Physics, **31**, 18 (1962).

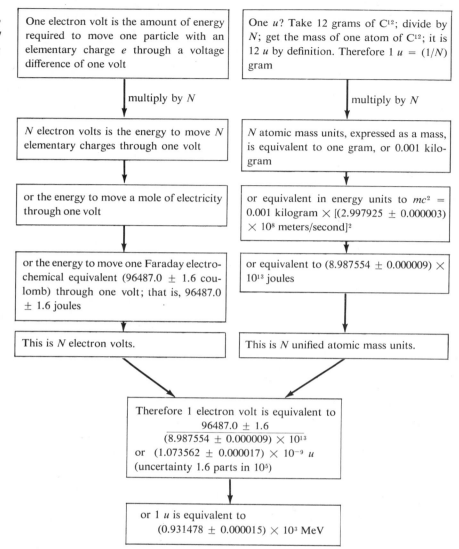

Conversion factor from electron volts to unified atomic mass units

One electron volt is the amount of energy required to move one particle with an elementary charge e through a voltage difference of one volt

One u? Take 12 grams of C^{12}; divide by N; get the mass of one atom of C^{12}; it is 12 u by definition. Therefore 1 $u = (1/N)$ gram

multiply by N

multiply by N

N electron volts is the energy to move N elementary charges through one volt

N atomic mass units, expressed as a mass, is equivalent to one gram, or 0.001 kilogram

or the energy to move a mole of electricity through one volt

or equivalent in energy units to $mc^2 =$ 0.001 kilogram $\times [(2.997925 \pm 0.000003) \times 10^8$ meters/second$]^2$

or the energy to move one Faraday electrochemical equivalent (96487.0 $\pm$ 1.6 coulomb) through one volt; that is, 96487.0 $\pm$ 1.6 joules

or equivalent to $(8.987554 \pm 0.000009) \times 10^{13}$ joules

This is N electron volts.

This is N unified atomic mass units.

Therefore 1 electron volt is equivalent to
$$\frac{96487.0 \pm 1.6}{(8.987554 \pm 0.000009) \times 10^{13}}$$
or $(1.073562 \pm 0.000017) \times 10^{-9}$ u (uncertainty 1.6 parts in 10^5)

or 1 u is equivalent to
$(0.931478 \pm 0.000015) \times 10^3$ MeV

This conversion factor is used in the calculation on pages 126 and 127 to translate the observed kinetic energies of the deuteron and triton from electron volts to u, as needed for the final check of the conservation law.

Not all kinetic energies measured: simple energy comparison not possible

In that calculation one sees the mass value of a triton as obtained from the conservation laws, compared with and checked against the mass spectrometer determination. The sample verification of spacetime physics is impressive. One cannot doubt that rest mass energy is converted into kinetic energy. But one can still be puzzled at just how this simple principle gets translated into an equation so complicated as that employed in the checking process (Eq. 99). Why did we not take the spectrometer masses of the reactants, similar mass values for the products, and compare them with the balance of kinetic energies in the transmutation process? What could be simpler!

Reactants:	H²	2.0141019 *u*	
	H²	2.0141019 *u*	
		Sum:	4.0282038 *u*
Products:	H¹	1.0078252 *u*	
	H³	3.0160494 *u*	
		Sum:	4.0238746 *u*
		Difference:	0.0043292 *u*
		equivalent to:	4.0322546 MeV

The difficulty arises only in the next step: evaluating from observation the net release of kinetic energy. The kinetic energy of the deuteron that moves before the reaction is known to be 1.808 Mev, and the kinetic energy of the proton after the reaction, 3.467 MeV. However, it was not convenient to measure at the same time the kinetic energy of the emerging triton, and this energy was not measured. If that kinetic energy was not known, then the net release of kinetic energy in the reaction was not directly measured. So how was it possible to test energy release versus change in rest mass? Or did our comparison really amount to any such direct confrontation of two energies? No!

One obtains a false impression of what is going on if he thinks of it as concerned exclusively with energy. An equally misleading way to do surveying is easily described. The plot of ground is a polygon of an odd shape laid out on a surface which is not flat. The length of a straight boundary AB is desired. The surveyor has measured only the difference in north-south coordinates of A and B. He will obviously be in difficulty if this is the limit of his information! Similarly, there is no hope of finding the mass of the triton from the deuteron-deuteron reaction data used above if one considers energy alone. He must also take into account the balance of momentum.

Finding triton mass is analogous to finding length of a sloping side of polygon

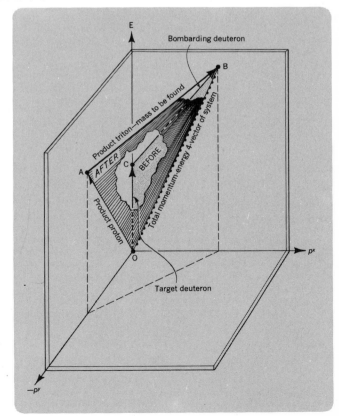

Fig. 93. Finding the triton mass—by using the conservation laws—treated as a problem in geometry. Note: Points O, B, C lie in the plane of the paper; point A lies above the plane of the paper (*y* component of momentum).

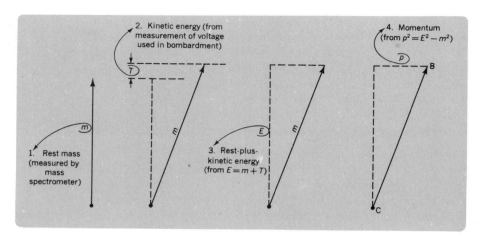

Fig. 94. Finding from experiment the energy and momentum components of the momentum-energy 4-vector of the bombarding deuteron in the $H^2 + H^2 \longrightarrow H^1 + H^3$ experiment. (The labels B, C for the two ends of the vector refer back to the labeling in Fig. 93.)

One determines the triton mass value by using the conservation laws much as a surveyor finds the length of one side of a polygon from the other measurements of the polygon by using Euclidean geometry (Fig. 93). There is one important change. In physics the geometry is to be understood as Lorentzian. Thus we have

$$(m_3)^2 = (E \text{ component of AB})^2 - (p \text{ component of AB})^2$$

In this formula the energy and momentum components of AB are found from the energy and momentum components of the other three sides of the polygon; that is, of the other three particles. How does one get the E and p values for one of these particles; for example, for the bombarding deuteron? Answer: By a procedure (Fig. 94) rather different from that normally used in surveying a plot of land! Suppose that a surveyor were required to use a method analogous to the way of measurement used in the $H^2 + H^2 \longrightarrow H^1 + H^3$ experiment. He could do so only if he employed the following unusual procedure to determine the north-south and east-west components of a boundary line CB (Fig. 94, after translation from the language of particle physics to the language of surveying!): (1) Measure the length of the line CB. (2, 3) Measure its component along the north-south direction. (4) Apply the Pythagorean theorem to evaluate the east-west component of the line CB.

We have now outlined how the components of the momentum-energy vectors of the target deuteron (OC, Fig. 93), the bombarding deuteron (CB), and the emerging proton (OA), are found. The components of the fourth, unknown, leg of the polygon (AB: the triton) are then found by a simple combination of the other three, known, 4-vectors, a calculation glorified by the phrase "application of the law of conservation of momentum and energy;" thus

$$\bar{p}_3{}^k = p_2{}^k + p_0{}^k - \bar{p}_1{}^k \qquad (k = x, y, z, t)$$

where the subscript zero refers to the initial deuteron at rest. The magnitude of this last leg gives at once the desired mass,

$$(m_3)^2 = (\bar{p}_3{}^t)^2 - (\bar{p}_3{}^x)^2 - (\bar{p}_3{}^y)^2 - (\bar{p}_3{}^z)^2$$

The determination of mass from the reaction $H^2 + H^2 \longrightarrow H^1 + H^3$ has been seen from this review to be highly geometric in character. The example illustrates a general principle. *Every application of the law of conservation of momentum and energy is a statement about a polygon built of 4-vectors in space-time.* Apart from the difference between Lorentz geometry and Euclidean geometry, the arithmetic is no different from what one uses in surveying, in trigonometry, and in every other analysis of triangles and polygons. This comparison of particle physics and surveying suggests better than can be indicated in any other way the variety of situations that one encounters in the analysis of experiments. There is no problem connected with collisions, reactions, and transformation processes that does not have an analog in elementary geometry. A few examples of such problems and their analogs have been selected and are listed in Table 12.

To give prescriptions for analyzing all the types of collisions and transmutations which can and do arise in physics is out of place here even as it would be inappropriate in a brief text on the key ideas of Euclidean geometry to list and solve all the multitude of problems that can arise there! The character of the typical problem may be described by generalizing from the analogies in Table 12: *Given* such and such sides of a polygon, plus such and such north-south and east-west and up-down projections, plus such and such angles; *predict* this or that length ("rest mass"), projection ("energy or momentum"), or angle ("velocity relative to another particle or relative to laboratory"). To go into the varied arithmetic of great numbers of such problems would not illuminate the basic principles. For particle physics, those "principles" come back in the end to two very simple features of spacetime geometry: (1) The vector sum of the momentum-energy 4-vectors of all particles involved in a reaction is zero (provided that the 4-vectors of the *products* of the reaction are treated as having reversed sign). (2) The invariant magnitude of each 4-vector is equal to the rest mass of the particle under consideration.

In the application of these ideas one is guided by the standard principles of algebra. (1) To find n distinct unknowns one must have n independent equations in which all other quantities are known. (2) If only $n - r$ independent equations are available, then r of the unknown quantities will be indeterminate. (An example is the collision of a deuteron of specified energy with a deuteron at rest, to produce a triton and a proton. Even when the rest masses of all four particles are given, it is impossible to predict the outcome of the reaction. The reason is simple. The proton may come off in any one of an infinitude of directions, at its own pleasure. The *angle of emission is indeterminate* in this problem. If one gives the angle as a separate piece of information ($\theta = 90°$ in the example) he can predict the energy. Conversely, if he gives the energy, he can predict the angle.) (3) If $n + s$ independent equations are available to predict n unknowns, then the first n equations suffice to determine the unknowns. The remaining s equations serve as *checks* on the accuracy of the measurements or the correctness of the physics or both. In applying these principles one often takes the primary quantities to be the component values E and p^x and p^y and p^z of the several particles, both as a matter of bookkeeping convenience, and as a systematic way to count the number of knowns and unknowns.

An example of how one counts off knowns and unknowns is furnished by the (deuteron) + (deuteron) $\longrightarrow$ (proton) + (triton) reaction, regarded as a means to determine the mass of the triton. Table 13 examines this example.

Every application of conservation laws refers to polygon built of 4-vectors

Conservation laws applied to analysis of collisions and transmutations: knowns vs unknowns

Table 12. Finding a mass or an energy or another physical quantity by use of the conservation laws is analogous to finding the length of one side of a polygon or an angle or another geometric quantity by use of Euclidean geometry.

Particle physics		Analog in Euclidean geometry
Process	*Problem*	
A(fast) + B(target) $\longrightarrow$ C(observed) + D(undetected)	*Known:* m_A, m_B, m_C. *Measure:* E_A and E_C and direction of p_C relative to p_A. *Calculate:* unknown mass m_D.	*Given* (for an irregular polygon of four sides which does not lie in a plane): lengths of three sides, north-south components of these three sides, and angle between two of these sides as seen by a person sighting along third side. *Find:* length of fourth side.
photon (momentum p) + electron (at rest) $\longrightarrow$ electron (set in motion) + photon (momentum $\bar{p}$)	*Given:* rest mass m of electron, initial momentum (or energy, $E = p$) of photon, and direction of emergence of the final photon. *Predict:* momentum $\bar{p}$ (or energy, $\bar{E} = \bar{p}$) of that photon ("Compton effect," see Ex. 70).	*Given* (for an irregular polygon of four sides which does not lie in a plane): lengths of all four sides, north-south components of two sides (analogous to "energy of photon and electron before collision!"), and the angle between two of these sides ("photon before and after") as seen by a person sighting along third side ("target electron"). *Find:* east-west component of one unknown side.
$_{94}Pu^{239}$ (at rest) $\longrightarrow$ $_{56}Ba^{144}$ + $_{38}Sr^{95}$ (spontaneous fission into exactly two fragments)	*Measure:* velocities of heavy and light fragments by time-of-flight experiment; also, mass of Pu^{239} by mass spectrometer. *Find:* rest masses of both fragments.	*Given:* long side of a triangle ("plutonium rest mass") and the two adjacent angles ("velocity parameters θ from velocities β = tanh θ"). *Find:* other two sides.
Same process as in previous example.	*Given:* data from measurements in previous example. *Find:* kinetic energy set free in fission.	*Given:* data given in previous example. *Find:* difference between long side and sum of other two sides.
μ (mu-meson at rest) $\longrightarrow$ e (fast electron) + ν (neutrino; speed of light) (spontaneous decay of mu-meson in $\sim 10^{-6}$ second)	*Known:* rest mass of electron. *Measure:* kinetic energy of electron ejected in this transmutation process. *Find:* rest mass of mu-meson.	*Known:* shorter two sides of a triangle ("rest mass m of electron and rest mass 0 of neutrino") and one angle ("velocity parameter θ of electron from its energy $E = m \cosh \theta$"). *Find:* long side of triangle.

Table 13. Count of knowns and unknowns in the reaction $H^2 + H^2 \longrightarrow H^1 + H^3$.

Commentary: It is assumed, as in the text, that one does not have available a mass-spectrometer value of the mass of H^3 at the time when he determines this mass from the balance of momentum and energy in the reaction. Quantities which have been measured are marked YES in the table; those which have not, are marked NO.

For each of the four particles there are five symbols (four components and the mass), a total of twenty quantities. Of these ten are known (marked YES in the table), and ten are unknown. There are exactly ten equations to use in finding these ten unknowns. Therefore, it is not surprising that one can combine the information in these ten equations to obtain a unique equation (Eq. 99) for the desired triton mass m_3 in terms of measured quantities.

		$E = p^t$	p^x	p^y	p^z	Invariant magnitude of 4-vector
Reactants (list all components of 4-vector of momentum and energy with positive sign in table)	H^2 (target)	NO (measured m_2, not E_2 directly)	YES (zero!)	YES (zero)	YES (zero)	m_2 YES (Eq. 100) (spectrometer)
	H^2 (fast)	NO (measured KE; see below)	NO	YES (zero)	YES (zero)	$m_2{}^* = m_2$ YES (spectrometer)
Products of reaction (list all components with negative sign)	H^1 (measured)	NO (measured KE; see below)	YES (zero)	NO	YES (zero)	m_1 YES (Eq. 101) (spectrometer)
	H^3 (not measured)	NO	NO	NO	NO	m_3 "NO" (Eq. 105) (to be *found*)
Sum, gives change in total energy-momentum 4-vector for system; must vanish in order for 4-vectors to form closed polygon ("conservation law")		0 (Eq. 94)	0 (Eq. 95)	0 (Eq. 96)	0 (Eq. 97)	

YIELDS FOUR EQUATIONS

Supplementary information. YIELDS SIX EQUATIONS:

$E_2{}^* - m_2{}^* = 1.808$ MeV (kinetic energy of bombarding deuteron) (Eq. 102)

$E_2 - m_2 = 0$ (kinetic energy of target deuteron—assumed to be at rest)

$\bar{E}_1 - m_1 = 3.467$ MeV (kinetic energy of product proton) (Eq. 103)

$\bar{E}_3{}^2 - \bar{p}_3{}^2 = m_3{}^2$ (momentum-energy 4-vector for product triton) (Eq. 98)

$\bar{E}_1{}^2 - \bar{p}_1{}^2 = m_1{}^2$ (momentum-energy 4-vector for product proton)

$(E_2{}^*)^2 - (p_2{}^*)^2 = (m_2{}^*)^2 = m_2{}^2$ (momentum-energy 4-vector for incident deuteron)

"Rest mass can be transformed into energy and energy can be transformed into rest mass"—this is a loose way to summarize some consequences of the two principles that are basic and really accurate: (1) the total momentum-energy 4-vector of the system is unchanged in a reaction; and (2) the invariant magnitude of the momentum-energy 4-vector of any given particle is equal to the rest mass of that particle. How much sound information about physics can be extracted from these basic principles? What troubles sometimes arise from accepting too loose a formulation of the "principle of equivalence of mass and energy"? Some answers to these two questions are given in Table 14.

Table 14

USES AND ABUSES OF THE CONCEPT OF MASS

Does *rest mass* have the same value in every inertial frame?	Yes. Given in terms of energy E and momentum p by $m^2 = E^2 - p^2$ in one frame, by $m^2 = (E')^2 - (p')^2$ in another frame. Rest mass is thus an *invariant*.
Does *energy* have the same value in every inertial frame?	No. Energy is given by $E = (m^2 + p^2)^{1/2}$ or $E = m \cosh \theta = m/(1 - \beta^2)^{1/2}$ or $E = $ (rest mass) + (kinetic energy) $= m + T$; value depends upon frame of reference from which particle (or system of particles) is viewed. Value is lowest in frame of reference in which particle (or system of particles) has zero momentum (zero *total* momentum in case of a system of particles). Only in that frame of reference is energy equal to rest mass.
Is energy zero for an object of zero rest mass? (photon: light quantum; x-ray; gamma ray).	No. Energy has value $E = (0^2 + p^2)^{1/2} = p$ (or in conventional units $E_{\mathrm{con}} = c\, p_{\mathrm{con}}$). Alternatively one can say—formally—that entire energy resides in the form of *kinetic* energy ($T = p$ in this special case of *zero* rest mass), none at all in the form of rest energy; thus, $E = $ (rest mass) + (kinetic energy) $= 0 + T = T = p$ (case of zero rest mass only!)
Does the invariance of rest mass mean that rest mass cannot change in a collision?	No. Rest mass often changes in an *inelastic* encounter. Example 1: Collision of two balls of putty—hotter and therefore very slightly more massive after collision than before. Example 2: Collision of two electrons (e^-) with sufficient violence to produce a new pair consisting of one ordinary electron and one positive electron (e^+): e^- (fast) + e^- (at rest) $\longrightarrow e^+ + 3e^-$.
How can a quantity be *invariant* and yet *change* as a consequence of a collision?	Invariance means "same value as determined from different inertial frames of reference," *not* "unchanged by impact or external forces."
Does rest mass change in *every* inelastic encounter?	No. Example: In the collision e^- (fast) + e^- (at rest) $\longrightarrow$ $2\begin{pmatrix}\text{electrons of}\\ \text{intermediate}\\ \text{speed}\end{pmatrix} + \begin{pmatrix}\text{electromagnetic energy}\\ \text{or } photons \text{ emitted}\\ \text{in the collision process}\end{pmatrix}$ rest masses of individual electrons are the same after collision as before.

Does rest mass ever change in an *elastic* collision?

No—by definition of elastic collision! Example:

$$e^- \text{ (fast)} + e^- \text{ (at rest)} \longrightarrow 2 \left(\begin{array}{c} \text{electrons of} \\ \text{intermediate} \\ \text{speed} \end{array} \right) + \left(\begin{array}{c} \text{no emitted} \\ \text{radiation} \end{array} \right)$$

Is the rest mass of a *system* composed of a number, *n*, of freely moving particles equal to the *sum* of the rest masses of the individual particles? Example: Box of hot gas.

No. Rest mass M of the system is greater than the sum of rest masses of particles—unless by chance all particles happen to be moving in same direction with a common speed. What is additive is not rest mass but *energy* and *momentum*:

$$E_{\text{system}} = \sum_{i=1}^{n} E_i$$

$$p^x{}_{\text{system}} = \sum_{i=1}^{n} (p^x)_i$$

From these sums the rest mass of the *system* can be evaluated:

$$M^2 = (E_{\text{system}})^2 - (p^x{}_{\text{system}})^2 - (p^y{}_{\text{system}})^2 - (p^z{}_{\text{system}})^2$$

Does this relation simplify when the total momentum of the system is zero? *Example 1:* Box of hot gas at rest in laboratory. *Example 2: Any* system of particles in free motion when viewed from an inertial frame so chosen as to *make* the total momentum zero!

Yes. In this case the rest mass of the *system* is given by the sum of energies of individual particles:

$$M = E_{\text{system}} = \sum_{i=1}^{n} E_i$$

Moreover, energy of each particle can always be expressed as sum of rest energy and kinetic energy:

$$E_i = M_i + T_i \qquad (i = 1, 2, \ldots, n)$$

So rest mass of a *system* exceeds sum of rest masses of its individual particles by an amount equal to the total kinetic energy of all particles (as seen in frame in which *total* momentum is zero!):

$$M = \sum_{i=1}^{n} m_i + \sum_{i=1}^{n} T_i$$

Has the "rest mass of the *system*" any *experimental* significance?

Yes. Rest mass of the system determines its inertia: resistance to acceleration by a force that acts on the system as a whole. (Example: A box of hot gas offers, in principle, more resistance to acceleration than the same box after the gas is cooled.) Rest mass of the system also governs the gravitational attraction that it exerts on a test particle. (Example 1: A hot star containing specified numbers and kinds of atoms exerts, in principle, more pull on a distant planet than does the same collection of atoms after cooling. Example 2: A cloud of electromagnetic radiation consists of photons, each with zero rest mass but with positive "kinetic energy." Therefore, rest mass of cloud of radiation is positive. It exerts a gravitational attraction on a distant object, such as a sun, and in turn responds to gravitational attraction of that sun.)

Does the explosion in space of a 20-megaton hydrogen bomb convert 0.93 kilogram of *mass* into *energy*? [$\Delta m = \Delta E/c^2 = (20 \times 10^6$ tons$) \times (10^6$ grams/ton$) \times (10^3$ calories/gram of "TNT equivalent"$) \times (4.18$ joules/calorie$)/c^2 = (8.36 \times 10^{16}$ joules$)/(9 \times 10^{16}$ meters^2/second$^2) = 0.93$ kilogram].

Yes *and* no; question needs to be stated more carefully. Rest mass of the system of expanding gases, fragments, and radiation has *same* value after explosion as before; rest mass M of system has *not changed*. However, hydrogen has been transmuted to helium and other nuclear transformations have taken place. In consequence the *makeup* of rest mass of the system,

$$M = \sum m_i + \sum T_i$$

has changed. The first term on the right—sum of rest masses of individual constituents—has *decreased* by 0.93 kg:

$$\left(\sum m_i\right)_{\text{after}} = \left(\sum m_i\right)_{\text{before}} - 0.93 \text{ kilogram}$$

The second term—sum of kinetic energies, including "kinetic energy" of photons and neutrinos that are produced—has *increased* by the same amount:

$$\left(\sum T_i\right)_{\text{after}} = \underbrace{\left(\sum T_i\right)_{\text{before}}}_{\substack{\text{original heat content} \\ \text{of bomb—practically} \\ \text{zero by comparison} \\ \text{with 0.93 kg}}} + 0.93 \text{ kilogram}$$

Thus part of the rest mass of *constituents* has been converted into energy; but the rest mass of the *system* has not changed.

Is the mass of the products of a nuclear explosion—contained in an underground cavity, allowed to cool, collected, and weighed—less than the mass of the original nuclear device?

Yes. Key point is the waiting period, which allows heat and radiation to flow away until transmuted materials have same heat content as that of original bomb. Then in the expression for the rest mass of the system

$$M = \sum m_i + \sum T_i$$

the second term—whose value rose suddenly at time of explosion, but dropped during cooling period—has undergone no net alteration as a consequence of the explosion followed by cooling. In contrast, the sum of rest masses, $\sum m_i$, has undergone a permanent decrease; and with it, the mass M of *what one weighs* (after the cooling period) has dropped (Fig. 95).

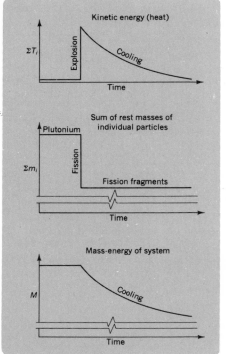

Fig. 95. Total kinetic energy, sum of rest masses of individual particles, and rest mass of system as functions of time when nuclear device explodes and products are allowed to cool.

Does Einstein's statement that mass and energy are equivalent mean that energy is the *same* as mass?

No. Value of energy depends upon inertial frame of reference from which particle (or system of particles) is regarded. Value of rest mass is independent of inertial frame. Energy is only the time *component* of a 4-vector, whereas mass measures entire *magnitude* of that 4-vector (see also Ex. 67). The *time component* gives the *magnitude* of the 4-vector only in the special case in which that 4-vector has no space component; that is, when the momentum of the particle (or the total momentum of the system of particles) is zero. Only in this special case does energy have the same value as rest mass.

Without delving into all fine points of legalistic phraseology, is the equation $E_{con} = mc^2$ what is *really* significant about the equivalence of mass and energy?

Historically, yes; today, no! In earlier days one did not recognize that joules and kilograms are two units—different only because of historical accident—for one and the same kind of quantity, mass-energy. Similarly ergs and grams are different units for the single quantity, mass-energy. The conversion factor c^2, like the factor of conversion from seconds to meters or miles to feet, can today be counted, if one wishes, as a detail of convention, rather than as a deep new principle.

If the factor c^2 is not the central feature of the relationship between mass and energy, then what *is* central?

The distinction between mass and energy is this: mass measures the magnitude of a 4-vector and energy measures the time component of the *same* 4-vector. Any feature of any discussion that emphasizes this contrast is an aid to understanding. Any slurring of terminology that obscures this distinction is a potential source of error or confusion.

The rest mass M of a system of freely moving particles is given, not by the sum of the *rest masses* m_i of the individual constituents, but by the sum of the *energies* E_i (but only in a frame in which the total momentum of the system is zero). Then why not give E_i a new name and call it the "relativistic mass" of the individual particle? With this notation

$$m_{i,\,\text{rel}} = E_i \begin{cases} = m_i + T_i \\ = (m_i^2 + p_i^2)^{1/2} \\ = m_i/(1 - \beta_i^2)^{1/2} \end{cases}$$

one can then write

$$M = \sum_{i=1}^{n} m_{i,\,\text{rel}}$$

The concept of "relativistic mass" is subject to misunderstanding and is not used here. (1) It applies the name "mass"—belonging to the *magnitude* of a 4-vector—to a very different concept, the *time component* of a 4-vector. (2) It makes increase of energy of a particle with velocity or momentum appear to be connected with some change in internal structure of the particle. In reality increase of energy with velocity originates in geometric properties of spacetime itself (Lorentz transformation!).

Can any simple diagram illustrate adequately this contrast between mass and energy?

Yes! Figure 96 shows the momentum-energy 4-vector of the same particle as seen in different reference frames. Energy differs from frame to frame. Rest mass (magnitude of 4-vector) has same value m in all frames. (Apparent difference between values of m in the three frames comes about because of trying to represent Lorentz geometry on the Euclidean page. In Lorentz geometry, square of hypotenuse is difference between squares of E' and p', or E'' and p''.)

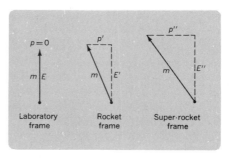

Fig. 96. Momentum-energy 4-vector of the same particle as seen in three different reference frames.

Is there any equally simple diagram to illustrate the transformation of a part of the rest mass of a plutonium nucleus into energy in the process of fission?

Yes! Figure 97. The vector sum of two timelike 4-vectors has magnitude M (rest mass of Pu^{239} before fission), which is greater than sum of magnitudes, m_1 and m_2, of the two individual 4-vectors (rest masses of fission products). Contrasts to Euclidean geometry in which the third side of a triangle always has a length that is less in value than sum of lengths of other two sides.

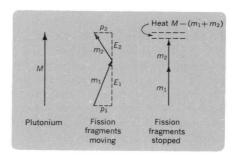

Fig. 97. The sum of the rest masses of the fission fragments of plutonium is less than the rest mass of the original plutonium nucleus.

INTRODUCTION TO THE EXERCISES OF CHAPTER 2

The velocity β and the velocity parameter θ of a particle are almost never used in solving problems involving the momentum and energy of particles moving with relativistic velocities. For one thing, it is inconvenient to deal with β since it enters the expressions for momentum and energy in the square root $(1-\beta^2)^{1/2}$. More important, a very small change in speed β can correspond to an immense change in the momentum and energy of a particle moving with nearly the speed of light. For example, if a given particle moves initially with a velocity $\beta = 0.99$, then an increase of 0.01 in this velocity corresponds to an infinite change in both the momentum and the energy of this particle. Usually problems involving fast-moving particles are stated in terms of the kinetic energy or the total energy of these particles. Then Eqs. 85 and 86

$$E^2 - p^2 = m^2$$
$$T = E - m$$

can be used to find the momentum of each particle. In this case it is most convenient not to mention velocity and not to use any formula that contains either velocity or velocity parameter.

When the speed β of a particle is required explicitly, one can find it from the expression

$$(106) \qquad \beta = \tanh \theta = \frac{\sinh \theta}{\cosh \theta} = \frac{m \sinh \theta}{m \cosh \theta} = \frac{p}{E}$$

In such cases it is often sufficient (as in Ex. 55) to find the *difference* $1 - \beta$ between the speed β of the particle and the speed of light. Substituting $p = \beta E$ into the equation $E^2 - p^2 = m^2$ we have

$$\frac{m^2}{E^2} = 1 - \beta^2 = (1 - \beta)(1 + \beta)$$

If β is very close to one, then $1 + \beta \approx 2$ and

$$(107) \qquad 1 - \beta \approx \frac{m^2}{2E^2} \qquad \text{if } \beta \approx 1$$

In collision problems (Ex. 90 and those following) it is conventional to put bars over symbols when they represent the value of these quantities "after the collision" (e.g., $\bar{p}$, $\bar{E}$).

The number of asterisks on an exercise indicates increasing order of difficulty. Numbers in parentheses after exercise titles indicate exercises that should be solved before the exercise so labeled.

A. GENERAL PROBLEMS

B. EQUIVALENCE OF ENERGY AND REST MASS

C. PHOTONS

 *70. Compton scattering (66)
 **71. Measurement of photon energy
 **72. Energy and frequency of a photon (66)
 *73. Gravitational red shift (66)
 *74. Density of the companion of Sirius (73)

D. DOPPLER SHIFT

 75. Doppler equations (66, 22)
 76. Decay of π^0 meson—a worked example
 77. The speeding light bulb (75)
 78. The physicist and the traffic light (75)
 79. Doppler shift at the limb of the sun (73, 75)
 80. The expanding universe (75)
 *81. Clock paradox using the Doppler shift (75)
 *82. Speed trap (75)
 *83. Doppler line broadening (75)
 *84. Photon energy shift due to recoil of emitter (83)
 *85. The Mössbauer effect (84)
 **86. Resonant scattering (85)
 **87. Measurement of Doppler shift by resonant scattering (86)
 **88. Mössbauer test of the gravitational red shift (73, 87)
 **89. Mössbauer test of the clock paradox (87)

E. COLLISIONS

 90. Symmetric elastic collision
 91. David and Goliath—a worked example
 92. Perfectly inelastic collision
 *93. Creation of particles by protons
 *94. Creation of particles by electrons
 *95. Photoproduction of a pair by a single photon (66, 93)
 **96. Photoproduction of a pair by two photons (95)
 **97. Positron-electron annihilation
 *98. Test of the principle of relativity (97)
 *99. Identifying particles from bubble chamber tracks
 *100. Storage rings and clashing beams (93)

F. ATOMIC PHYSICS

 *101. deBroglie and Bohr (72)
 *102. Seeing with electrons (101)
 **103. Thomas precession (52, 101)

G. INTERSTELLAR FLIGHT

 *104. Difficulties of interstellar flight (58)

A. GENERAL PROBLEMS

55. Fast electrons

The Stanford Linear Accelerator is designed to accelerate electrons to a final kinetic energy of 40 GeV (40 thousand million electron volts; one electron volt is equal to 1.6×10^{-19} joule) for use in experiments with elementary particles. Electromagnetic waves produced in large vacuum tubes ("klystron tubes") accelerate the electrons along a straight pipe-like structure 10,000 feet long (approximately 3000 meters long).

(a) Electrons increase their kinetic energy by approximately equal amounts for every meter traveled along the accelerator pipe as observed in the laboratory frame. What is this energy gain in MeV per meter? Suppose the Newtonian expression for kinetic energy were correct. In this case how far would the electron travel along the accelerator before its speed were equal to the speed of light? (The answer to this question is previewed in the text, page 16).

(b) In reality, of course, even the 40 GeV electrons which emerge from the end of the accelerator have a velocity β which is less than the velocity of light. What is the value of the difference $(1 - \beta)$ between the speed of light and the speed of these electrons? Let a 40 GeV electron from this accelerator race a flash of light along an evacuated tube 1000 kilometers long. How far ahead of the electron is the light flash at the end of this race? Express the answer in millimeters.

(d) How long is the "3000 meter" accelerator tube as observed from a rocket frame moving alongside a 40 GeV electron emerging from the accelerator?

56.* Cosmic rays

(a) At least one cosmic-ray particle has been observed (indirectly) that had an estimated energy of 16 joules (1.0×10^{20} eV).† If the carrier of this energy was a proton ($mc^2 \approx 1$ GeV), how long would it take to cross our galaxy (diameter 10^5 light years) as measured on a clock carried with the proton? Express your answer in seconds (one year $\approx 32 \times 10^6$ seconds). (In the *earth* frame the proton—traveling with nearly the speed of light—takes only a little more than 10^5 years for this crossing!)

(b) An elementary particle must have an energy of how many times its rest energy for the diameter of our galaxy to appear to it Lorentz contracted to the diame-

†John Linsley, Physical Review Letters, **10**, 146 (15 February 1963).

ter of the particle (about 1 fermi, which is equal to 10^{-15} meters)? How much mass would have to be converted to energy to give a proton the desired speed?

57. Limits of Newtonian mechanics

(a) One electron-volt (eV) is equal to the increase of kinetic energy that a singly charged particle experiences when accelerated through a potential difference of one volt. One electron-volt is equal to 1.60×10^{-19} joules. What are the rest energies of the electron and the proton (masses listed inside front cover) in units of million electron-volts (MeV)?

(b) The kinetic energy of a particle of a *given velocity* β is not correctly given by the expression $1/2\ m\beta^2$. The error

$$\frac{\left(\begin{array}{c}\text{relativistic expression}\\ \text{for kinetic energy}\end{array}\right) - \left(\begin{array}{c}\text{Newtonian expression}\\ \text{for kinetic energy}\end{array}\right)}{\left(\begin{array}{c}\text{Newtonian expression}\\ \text{for kinetic energy}\end{array}\right)}$$

is one percent when the Newtonian kinetic energy has risen to a certain fraction of the rest energy. *What fraction?* (An approximate answer will suffice, obtained by examining the next term in the "binomial" or "power series" expansion of the correct formula for energy as a function of velocity β, or by any other clearly indicated line of reasoning.) Let this point—where the error is one percent—be arbitrarily called the "limit of Newtonian mechanics." At what kinetic energy does a proton reach this limit (energy in MeV)? An electron?

58.* The relativistic rocket

What limits does the theory of relativity impose on the performance and speed of a rocket? Idealize the operation of a rocket as the ejection of a series of identical pellets—each of rest mass m—one after the other. Each ejection can then be analyzed as an "inelastic collision in reverse." Let the pellet shooter who rides on the rocket use an identical procedure in firing each pellet. Then it is reasonable to suppose that the *backward velocity* is the same for each pellet when observed in the inertial frame in which the rocket is at rest (pictured in Fig. 98 in the "laboratory frame" before the rockets are turned on). This backward velocity of the pellet is called the *exhaust velocity* β_{ex}.

(a) Using the symbols in the figure, write down the equations for conservation of momentum and conservation of energy. Do not forget the initial rest energy M_1 but, since this is an *inelastic* collision in

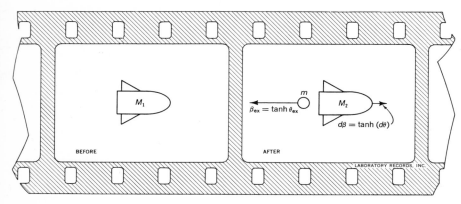

Fig. 98. Analysis of the motion of a relativistic rocket.

reverse, do *not* assume that *rest* mass is conserved. Eliminate m from these equations to derive, for incremental $d\theta$,

$$d\theta = \beta_{ex}\left(\frac{M_1 - M_2}{M_2}\right)$$

where β_{ex} is the exhaust velocity with respect to the initial rocket frame. Now $M_2 - M_1 = dM$ is the change of mass of the rocket so

$$d\theta = -\beta_{ex}\frac{dM}{M}$$

where M is the mass of the rocket at any time. If we now consider a new frame (a "rocket frame") in which the rocket is at rest, the ejection of further mass with velocity β_{ex} in that frame will cause a further change $d\theta$ in the velocity parameter. However, from Eq. 25 the new velocity parameter of the rocket in the original frame is simply the sum of all such changes in velocity parameter (velocities do not add, but velocity *parameters* do add). Also, rest masses (and changes in rest mass) are invariant, the same in all frames. Hence the final velocity parameter in the original frame can be found by summing (integrating) the velocity-parameter increments.

$$\int_0^\theta d\theta = -\beta_{ex}\int_{M_1}^M \frac{dM}{M}$$

The solution of these integrals yields the natural logarithm

(108) $\theta = \beta_{ex}\ln\dfrac{M_1}{M}$ (relativistic rocket)

or

$$\left(\begin{array}{c}\text{velocity } parameter\\ \text{attained after any}\\ \text{given amount of}\\ \text{fuel has burned}\end{array}\right)$$

$$= \left(\begin{array}{c}\text{exhaust velocity}\\ \text{of products of}\\ \text{combustion}\end{array}\right)\ln\left(\frac{\begin{array}{c}\text{initial rest}\\ \text{mass of}\\ \text{rocket}\end{array}}{\begin{array}{c}\text{present rest}\\ \text{mass of}\\ \text{rocket}\end{array}}\right)$$

This is the equation of motion for a relativistic rocket.

(b) A *nonrelativistic rocket* is one that moves with a speed very much less than the speed of light. Show that the equation above for the relativistic rocket reduces to the usual form for a nonrelativistic rocket.

(109) $v = v_{ex}\ln\dfrac{M_1}{M}$ (nonrelativistic rocket)

(c) From the original conservation laws show explicitly that rest mass is *not* conserved for the relativistic rocket. Where does it go? Show that rest mass is (approximately) conserved in the special case of the nonrelativistic rocket.

(d) Show that the speed of the relativistic rocket may approach but cannot exceed the speed of light.

(e) Consider the special case of very high exhaust velocities. Show that for β_{ex} approaching the speed of light, that is, for θ_{ex} very large, the ejected rest mass m necessary to obtain a given velocity parameter is nearly zero. Infer from this that if light is used to propel the rocket, the mass of the fuel is entirely converted into radiant energy and the equation becomes

(110) $\theta = \ln\dfrac{M_1}{M}$ (rocket propelled by light)

(f) One sometimes hears the summarizing statement: "The rocket propelled by light is the most efficient." Show how this statement is both right and wrong. Discussion: Evaluate the "efficiency" of a flashlight as a propulsion system. How efficient is it to accelerate the "ashes" (the dead batteries) along with the payload? Are there any *elementary particle interactions* that leave no "ashes" and that produce only light (e.g., gamma rays)? See page 122 and Ex. 97.

(g) For a "perfect rocket" that converts mass entirely into light, what is the smallest *mass ratio* (initial mass divided by mass at burnout) that will accelerate a rocket from rest to a speed for which the time-dilation factor is ten? What is this mass ratio for the largest exhaust velocity attainable with *chemical* rockets (about 4000 meters per second)? Note: Engineering literature often speaks of the "specific impulse" (symbol: I) of rocket fuel—for example, 260 seconds for kerosene and liquid oxygen; 350 seconds for liquid hydrogen and liquid oxygen. Multiply by 9.8 meters per second per second to convert to physics units (exhaust velocity in meters per second; or momentum in kilogram-meters per second imparted to the rocket by each kilogram of fuel ejected). This *momentum* figure—unlike the *time* figure—is as relevant on the moon where $g \approx (1/6) \times 9.8$ meters per second per second as on the earth where $g = 9.8$ meters per second per second.

59.* Center-of-mass paradox

A long tube is fixed at rest along the x axis of the *rocket* frame. Two identical cannon balls are fired into opposite ends of the tube with equal speed and simultaneously in the rocket frame. The cannon balls collide elastically at the center of the tube and bounce back toward the ends. The ends of the tube are capped before the balls return, and thereafter the balls bounce back and forth without friction.

(a) Describe the motion of the center of mass of the two balls in the *rocket* frame.

(b) Are the cannon balls fired into the tube simul-

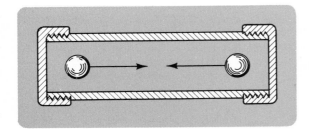

Fig. 99. Reciprocating cannon balls.

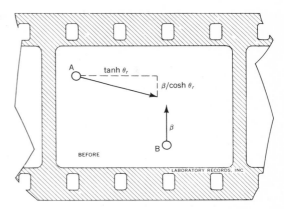

Fig. 100. Velocity components of balls A and B in the laboratory frame before the collision.

taneously in the *laboratory* frame? Describe the motion of the center of mass of the two balls in the laboratory frame. A spacetime diagram may be useful. Is the location of the center of mass an *invariant* in relativity?

(c) Now suppose that instead of being fixed in the rocket frame the tube lies on a frictionless surface. Analyze the motion of the center of mass of the *tube* in the two reference frames. How does the center of mass of the system, tube *plus* cannon balls, move in each reference frame?

60.* A second derivation of relativistic expression for momentum

(a) In Fig. 85 a time $\Delta t'$ elapses in the rocket frame between the collision of two balls and the impact of ball A with the upper wall. In the laboratory frame this elapsed time is Δt. Use the Lorentz transformation equations to find a relation between the two elapsed times $\Delta t'$ and Δt. Find a relation between the y components of velocity of ball A in the two frames (see Ex. 20). If β is the speed of ball A in the rocket frame show that the y component of velocity of ball A in the laboratory frame $\beta_A{}^y{}_{\text{lab}}$ is given by the expression

$$\beta_A{}^y{}_{\text{lab}} = \beta/\cosh \theta_r$$

(b) Now analyze the collision in the laboratory frame. From the symmetry of the collision in the laboratory and rocket frames, verify the velocity components in Fig. 100. Remember (Section 11) that the momentum of a particle must lie along the direction of motion of the particle. Therefore the triangle of *velocity* vectors of ball A before and after the collision is similar to the triangle of *momentum* vectors of ball A before and after the collision (Fig. 101). Assume that ball B is moving so slowly in the laboratory frame

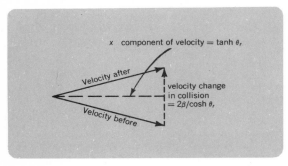
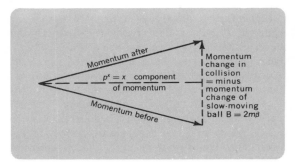

Fig. 101. Velocity and momentum diagrams of ball A as observed in the laboratory frame.

that its momentum is given by the Newtonian expression $m\beta$. Now demand that the momentum change of ball A in the collision be equal and opposite to the momentum change of ball B. From the properties of similar triangles

$$\frac{\left(\begin{array}{c}\text{horizontal dotted line}\\ \text{in momentum diagram}\end{array}\right)}{\left(\begin{array}{c}\text{vertical dotted line}\\ \text{in momentum diagram}\end{array}\right)} = \frac{\left(\begin{array}{c}\text{horizontal dotted line}\\ \text{in velocity diagram}\end{array}\right)}{\left(\begin{array}{c}\text{vertical dotted line}\\ \text{in velocity diagram}\end{array}\right)}$$

Show that this leads to the following expression for the x component of momentum of the fast-moving ball A.

$$p^x = m \sinh \theta_r$$

(c) In the limit of small y velocities p^x becomes equal to the total momentum p of ball A and the rela-

tive velocity parameter θ_r becomes equal to the velocity parameter θ of ball A. This leads to the expression for relativistic momentum of a particle

$$p = m \sinh \theta$$

61.* A second derivation of relativistic expression for energy

(a) *Newtonian momentum conservation.* Consider a head-on elastic collision between particles of *unequal* rest mass m_1 and m_2. Particle 1 rebounds from particle 2 with reduced speed, transferring momentum to particle 2. Analyze the collision first from the Newtonian point of view. Show from the figure that in the laboratory frame the Newtonian law of conservation of momentum leads to the equation

$$m_1\beta_1 + m_2\beta_2 = m_1\bar{\beta}_1 + m_2\bar{\beta}_2$$

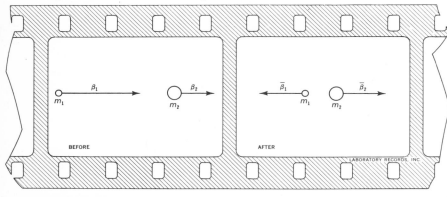

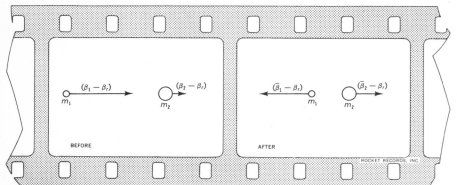

Fig. 102. Newtonian analysis of an elastic head-on collision between particles of unequal mass. Velocities before and after collision as observed in the laboratory and rocket frames using the Newtonian law of addition of velocities.

where, for the directions of motion shown in the figure, $\bar{\beta}_1$ is negative. Bars over symbols mean "after the collision." Now look at the collision from the rocket reference frame. For a small relative rocket velocity β_r, the velocity of each particle in the rocket frame is found simply by subtracting β_r from the laboratory velocity of the particle. Apply the Newtonian law of conservation of momentum to the collision as observed in the rocket frame. Show that *if Newtonian momentum is conserved in the laboratory frame it is automatically conserved in a rocket frame moving with small velocity relative to the laboratory frame.*

(b) *Conservation of relativistic momentum implies conservation of relativistic energy.* Now analyze the same collision from the relativistic point of view. Show that the law of conservation of relativistic momentum in the laboratory frame is expressed by the following equation.

(111) $m_1 \sinh \theta_1 + m_2 \sinh \theta_2$
$$= m_1 \sinh \bar{\theta}_1 + m_2 \sinh \bar{\theta}_2$$

The masses of the two particles are not changed in the collision, since the collision is elastic. For the directions of motion shown in the figure, $\bar{\theta}_1$ is negative. In relativistic mechanics the velocities of the particles in the rocket frame can be found by subtracting the *relative-velocity parameter* θ_r from their *velocity parameters* in the laboratory frame (page 51). Apply the law of conservation of momentum to the collision as observed in the rocket frame. Use Table 8 to expand all hyperbolic sine functions of the difference of two velocity parameters. Regroup the terms of the resulting equation by the common factors $\cosh \theta_r$ and $\sinh \theta_r$,

(112)   (parenthesis number one) $\cosh \theta_r$
        $-$ (parenthesis number two) $\sinh \theta_r = 0$

Here neither parenthesis contains a function of the relative-velocity parameter θ_r. Now if momentum is to be conserved in *every* rocket frame, then this equation must be true for *every* relative-velocity parameter θ_r. We can choose a rocket frame with the value of the velocity parameter anywhere between zero (for which $\cosh \theta_r = 1$ and $\sinh \theta_r = 0$) and an infinite value (for which $\cosh \theta_r$ becomes equal to $\sinh \theta_r$). The only way in which the equation above can be valid for *every* value of θ_r between these limits is for each of the parentheses *separately* to equal zero. Show that parenthesis number one is equal to zero if momentum is conserved in the *laboratory* frame. Show that parenthesis number two is equal to zero if

(113) $m_1 \cosh \theta_1 + m_2 \cosh \theta_2$
$$= m_1 \cosh \bar{\theta}_1 + m_2 \cosh \bar{\theta}_2$$

Equation 112 expresses the law of conservation of momentum in the rocket frame. Evidently momentum is conserved in all rocket frames if, and only if, both

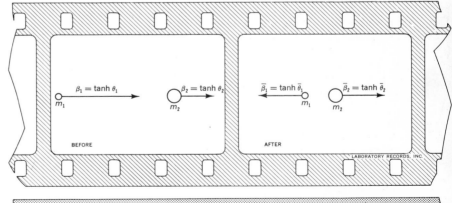

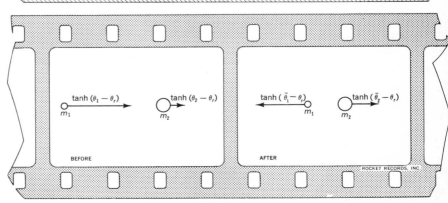

Fig. 103. Relativistic analysis of an elastic head-on collision between particles of unequal mass. Velocities before and after collision as observed in the laboratory and rocket frames using the relativistic law of addition of *velocity parameters.*

Eq. 111 and Eq. 113 are correct in the laboratory frame. Equation 111 expresses the law of conservation of momentum in the laboratory frame. Equation 113 expresses the law of conservation of—what? Identify the quantity $m \cosh \theta$ and name the new conservation law.

(c) Is the derivation above still correct if we write $\overline{m}_1$ and $\overline{m}_2$ for the rest masses of the two particles after the collision and consider the possibility that after the collision these rest masses are different than they were before the collision? Is the law of conservation of relativistic energy still valid in this case? Is the relativistic expression for *kinetic energy* conserved in such a collision?

B. EQUIVALENCE OF ENERGY AND REST MASS

62. Examples of conversion

(a) How much mass does a 100-watt bulb dissipate (in heat and light) in one year?

(b) The total electrical energy generated in the United States is something like 10^{12} kilowatt-hours per year. How much mass is this energy equivalent to? In the actual production of this electrical energy is this much mass converted to energy? Less mass? More mass? Explain your answer.

(c) A student pedaling a bicycle full throttle produces one-half horsepower of *useful* power (1 horsepower = 746 watts). The human body is about 25 percent efficient; that is, 75 percent of the food burned is converted to heat and only 25 percent is converted to useful work. How long a time will the student have to ride to lose one pound by the conversion of mass to energy? How can reducing gymnasiums stay in business?

(d) About 1.4 kilowatts of sunlight fall on one square meter of area perpendicular to this light near the earth but outside the atmosphere of the earth (1.4 kilowatts per square meter is called the *solar constant*.) How much mass does the sun radiate as light in one second? How much of the sun's mass reaches the earth per year in the form of light?

(e) Two freight trains, each of 10^6 kilogram mass, travel in opposite directions on the same track with equal speeds of 45 meters per second (about 100 miles per hour). They collide and come to rest. The rest mass of the trains plus the rest mass of the track plus the rest mass of the roadbed is increased immediately after the collision by what number of micrograms? Neglect energy lost in the forms of sound and light.

63. Relativistic chemistry

When 1 kilogram of hydrogen combines with 8 kilograms of oxygen, about 10^8 joules of energy is released. A very good chemical balance is able to detect a fractional change in mass of 1 part in 10^7. By what factor is this sensitivity more than enough—or insufficient—to detect the fractional change in rest mass in this reaction?

64.** A relativistic oscillator

An engineer decides, in order to test the laws of relativity, to construct an oscillator with a very light oscillating bob, which can move back and forth very fast. The lightest bob known with a rest mass greater than zero is the electron. The engineer uses a cubical metal box, whose edge measures one meter, that is warmed slightly so that a few electrons "boil off" from its surfaces (Fig. 104). Across the middle of the box—and electrically insulated from it—is a metal screen charged to a high positive voltage by a power supply. A voltage-control knob on the power supply can be turned to change the dc voltage V_0 between box and screen.

A vacuum pump removes air from the box so that electrons may move freely inside without colliding with air molecules. Let an electron boiled off from the inner wall of the box have very small velocity initially (assume that the initial velocity is zero). The electron is attracted to the positive screen, increases speed toward the screen, passes through a hole in the screen, slows down as it moves away from the attracting screen, stops just short of the opposite wall of the box, is pulled back toward the screen; and in this way oscillates back and forth between the walls of the box.

(a) In how short a time T can the electron be made to oscillate back and forth on one round trip between the walls? The engineer who designed the equipment claims that by turning the voltage-control knob high enough he can obtain as high a frequency of oscillation $\nu = 1/T$ as desired. Is he right?

(b) For sufficiently low voltages the electron will be nonrelativistic—and one can use Newtonian mechanics to analyze its motion. For this case the frequency of oscillation of the electron is increased by what factor when the voltage on the screen is doubled? (Discussion: At corresponding points of the electron's

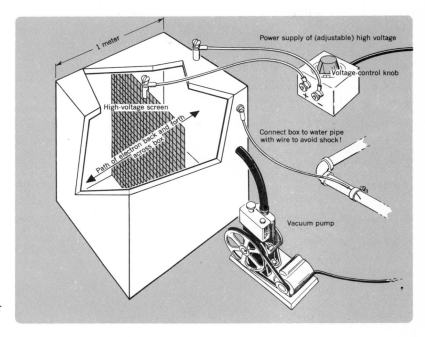

Fig. 104. Relativistic oscillator with electron as oscillating bob.

path before and after voltage doubling, how does the Newtonian *kinetic energy* of the electron compare in the two cases? How does its *velocity* compare in the two cases?)

(c) What is a definite formula for *frequency ν* as a function of *voltage* in the nonrelativistic case?

(d) What is the frequency in the *extreme* relativistic case in which over most of its course the electron is moving ... (rest of sentence suppressed!) ... ?

(e) On the same graph, plot two curves of frequency *ν* as functions of screen voltage V_0: (i) the nonrelativistic curve from part (c) to be drawn *heavily* in the region where it is *reliable* and indicated by dashes elsewhere; and similarly (ii) the extreme relativistic value from (d). From the resulting graph estimate quantitatively the voltage of *transition* from the nonrelativistic to the relativistic region. If possible give a simple argument explaining why your result does or does not make sense as regards *order of magnitude* (that is, overlooking factors of 2, π, etc.).

65.** Momentum without mass?

A small motor mounted on a board is powered by a battery mounted on top of it as shown in Fig. 105. By means of a belt, the motor drives a paddlewheel that stirs a puddle of water. The paddlewheel mecha-

nism is mounted on the same board as the motor. The motor does work at a rate dE/dt.

(a) How much mass is being transferred per second from the motor end of the board to the paddlewheel end of the board?

(b) Mass is being transferred over a distance x at a rate given by your answer to part a. What is the *momentum* associated with this transfer of mass? Since this momentum is small, Newtonian momentum concepts are adequate.

(c) Let the mounting board be initially at rest and supported by frictionless rollers on a horizontal table. The board will move! In which direction? What happens to this motion when the battery runs down? How far will the board have moved in this time?

(d) Show that an observer on the board will see the energy being transferred by the belt; an observer on the table will see the energy being transferred partly by the belt and partly by the board; an observer riding one way on the belt will see the energy being transferred partly by the belt moving in the other direction and partly by the board. Evidently it is not always possible to make a statement satisfactory to all observers about the path by which energy travels from one place to another or about the speed at which this energy moves from one place to another!

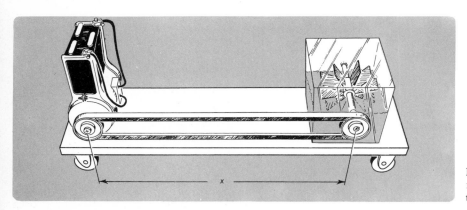

Fig. 105. Transfer of mass without net transfer of particles or radiation.

C. PHOTONS

66. Particles of zero rest mass

On what arguments does the derivation of the important relation $E^2 - p^2 = m^2$ depend? Derive from this formula a relation between momentum and energy that is valid in the case of *zero* rest mass (photons, gravitons, neutrinos). What does the resulting relation say about the slope of the world line for such a particle and hence about its speed? How does your result depend, as a limiting case, on the equality of $\sinh\theta$ and $\cosh\theta$ for large θ? Is there a "rest frame" for particles of zero rest mass?

67. Einstein's derivation of the equivalence of energy and rest mass—a worked example

Problem: From the fact that light exerts pressure and carries energy, show that this energy is equivalent to mass and hence—by extension—show the equivalence of all energy to mass. Commentary: The equivalence of energy and mass is such an important consequence that Einstein very early, after his relativistic derivation of this result, sought and found an alternative elementary physical line of reasoning† that leads to the same conclusion. He envisaged a closed box of mass M initially at rest (Fig. 106). A directed burst of electromagnetic energy is emitted from the left-hand wall. It travels down the length L of the box and is absorbed at the other end. The radiation carries an energy E. But it also carries momentum. This one sees from the following reasoning. The radiation exerts a pressure on the left-hand wall during the emission. In consequence of this pressure the box receives a push to the left, and a momentum $-p$. But

the momentum of the system as a whole was zero initially. Therefore the radiation carries a momentum p opposite to the momentum of the box. How can one use his knowledge of the transport of energy and momentum by the radiation to deduce the *mass equivalent* of the radiation? Einstein got his answer from the argument that the center of mass of the system was not moving before the transport process and therefore cannot be in motion during the transport process. But the box obviously carries mass to the left. Therefore *the radiation must carry mass to the right.* So much for Einstein's reasoning in broad outline. Now for the details.

From relativity Einstein knew that the momentum p of a directed beam of radiation is equal to the energy E of that beam (both p and E measured in units of mass; Section 10). However, to secure a derivation free of all direct reference to relativity principles, he based the conclusion $p = E$ on the following elementary argument. The pressure exerted on an ideal emitter or absorber by a directed beam of radiation is

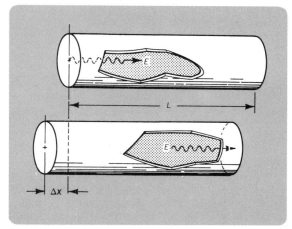

Fig. 106. Transfer of mass by radiation.

†A. Einstein, Annalen der Physik, **20**, 627 (1906).

equal to the density of energy in that beam. This one knows both from Maxwell's theory of electromagnetic radiation and from direct observation of the pressure exerted by light on a mirror suspended in a vacuum. This measurement had first successfully been carried out by E. F. Nichols and G. F. Hull between 1901 and 1903. By now the experiment has been so simplified and increased in sensitivity that it can be carried out in an elementary laboratory.† Take the resulting conclusion,

$$\begin{pmatrix} \text{density of radiant energy} \\ \text{in units of energy per} \\ \text{unit of volume} \end{pmatrix}$$

$$= \begin{pmatrix} \text{pressure exerted by directed} \\ \text{radiation on perfect emitter} \\ \text{or absorber in units of force} \\ \text{per unit of area} \end{pmatrix}$$

and multiply both sides by the area A of the emitting wall and the length l of the pulse of radiation (envisaged as much shorter than the length L of the box). Note that l is equal to the time of action of the radiation pressure multiplied by the speed of light. Thus the multiplying factor is

$$\begin{pmatrix} \text{volume occupied} \\ \text{by the pulse of} \\ \text{radiant energy} \end{pmatrix}$$

$$= \begin{pmatrix} \text{area of emitting} \\ \text{surface} \end{pmatrix} \begin{pmatrix} \text{time of action} \\ \text{of pressure on} \\ \text{surface} \end{pmatrix} \begin{pmatrix} \text{speed} \\ \text{of light} \end{pmatrix}$$

Multiply corresponding sides of the foregoing two equations and find the result

$$\begin{pmatrix} \text{energy carried} \\ \text{by radiation} \end{pmatrix}$$

$$= \begin{pmatrix} \text{force of radiation} \\ \text{on wall} \end{pmatrix} \begin{pmatrix} \text{time of action} \\ \text{of force} \end{pmatrix} \begin{pmatrix} \text{speed} \\ \text{of light} \end{pmatrix}$$

$$= \begin{pmatrix} \text{momentum transfer from radiation} \\ \text{to wall—and therefore magnitude} \\ \text{of momentum carried by} \\ \text{radiation itself} \end{pmatrix} \begin{pmatrix} \text{speed} \\ \text{of light} \end{pmatrix}$$

---

†Robert Pollock, American Journal of Physics, **31**, 901 (1963). Pollock's method of determining the pressure of light makes use of resonance to amplify a small effect to an easily measured magnitude. Dr. Pollock developed this experiment in collaboration with the same group of freshmen with whom the authors had the privilege to work out the presentation of relativity contained in this book. The authors are grateful in particular to Mark Wasserman, a member of this group, who made many helpful comments on several subsequent drafts.

or, in mass units

$$(114) \quad E = \begin{pmatrix} \text{energy of} \\ \text{directed beam} \\ \text{of radiation} \end{pmatrix} = \begin{pmatrix} \text{momentum of} \\ \text{directed beam} \\ \text{of radiation} \end{pmatrix} = p$$

Thus the radiation carries momentum and *energy* to the right while the box carries momentum and *mass* to the left. But the center of mass of the system, box plus radiation, cannot move. So the radiation must carry to the right, not merely energy, but mass. How much mass? To discover the answer is the object of these questions:

(a) What is the velocity of the box during the time of transit of the radiation?

(b) After the radiation is absorbed in the other end of the box, the system is once again at rest. How far has the box moved during the transit of the radiation?

(c) Now demand that the center of mass of the system be at the same location both before and after the flight of the radiation. From this argument, what is the mass-equivalent of the energy that has been transported from one end of the box to the other?

Solution: (a) During the transit of the radiation the momentum of the box must be equal in magnitude and opposite in direction to the momentum p of the radiation. The box moves with a very low velocity β. Therefore the Newtonian formula $M\beta$ suffices to calculate its momentum:

$$M\beta = -p = -E$$

From this relation we deduce the velocity of the box,

$$\beta = -E/M$$

(b) The transit time of the photon is very nearly $t = L$ meters of light-travel time. In this time the box moves a distance

$$\Delta x = \beta t = -EL/M$$

(c) If the radiation carried with it no mass, and the box were the sole object endowed with mass, then this displacement Δx would result in a net motion of the center of mass of the system to the left. But, Einstein reasoned, an isolated system with its center of mass originally at rest can never set itself into motion nor experience any shift in its center of mass. Therefore, he argued, there must be some countervailing displacement of a part of the mass of the system. This transport of mass to the right can be understood only as a new feature of the radiation itself. Consequently, during the time that the box is moving to the left, the radiation must transport to the right some mass m, as yet of unknown magnitude, but such as to ensure that the center of gravity of the system has not moved. The distance of transport is the full length L of the box diminished by the distance Δx through which the box has moved to the left in the meantime. But Δx is smaller than L in the ratio E/M. This ratio can be made as small as one pleases for any given transport of radiant energy E by making the mass M of the box sufficiently great. Therefore it is legitimate to take the distance moved by the radiation as equal to L itself. Thus, with arbitrarily high precision, the condition that the center of mass shall not move becomes

$$M\Delta x + mL = 0$$

Calculate the mass m and find (using Δx from part b)

$$m = -\Delta x M/L = -(-EL/M)(M/L)$$

or, finally

$$m = E$$

We conclude that the process of emission, transport, and reabsorption of radiation of energy E is equivalent to the transport of a mass $m = E$ from one end of the box to the other end. The simplicity of this derivation and the importance of the result makes this analysis one of the most interesting in all of physics.

Discussion: The mass equivalence of radiant energy implies the mass equivalence of thermal energy and—by extension—of other forms of energy, according to the following reasoning. The energy which emerges from the left wall of the box may reside there originally as heat energy. This thermal energy excites a typical atom of the surface from its lowest energy state to a higher energy state. The atom returns from this higher state to a lower state and in the course of this change sends out the surplus energy in the form of radiation. This radiant energy traverses the box, is absorbed, and ultimately converted back into thermal energy. Whatever the details of the mechanisms by which light is emitted and absorbed, the *net effect* is the transfer of heat energy from one end of the box to the other. To say that mass had to pass down the length of the box when radiation went from one wall to the other therefore implies that mass moves when *thermal* energy changes location. The thermal energy in turn is derived from chemical energy or the energy of a nuclear transformation or from electrical energy. Moreover, thermal energy deposited at the far end of the tube can be converted back into one or another of these forms of energy. Therefore these form of energy—and likewise all other forms of energy—are equivalent in their transport to the transport of mass in the amount

$$m = E$$

How can one possibly uphold the idea that a pulse of radiation transports mass? One already knows that a photon has zero rest mass, by virtue of the relation

$$\text{(rest mass)}^2 = \text{(energy)}^2 - \text{(momentum)}^2 = 0$$

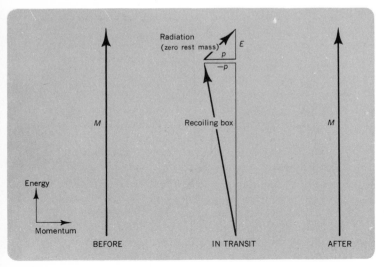

Fig. 107. Radiation transfers rest mass from place to place even though the rest mass of radiation is zero!

(earlier derivation in this problem; see also preceding exercise; also Section 12 of the text). Moreover, what is true of the individual photon is true of the pulse of radiation made up of many such photons: The energy and momentum are equal in magnitude, so that the rest mass of the radiation necessarily vanishes. Is there not a fundamental inconsistency in saying that the rest mass of the pulse is zero and saying in the same breath that radiation of energy E transports the mass $m = E$ from one place to another?

The source of our difficulty is some confusion between two quite different concepts: (1) energy, the time component of the momentum-energy 4-vector, and (2) rest mass, the magnitude of this 4-vector. When the system divides itself into two parts (radiation going to the right and box recoiling to the left) the *components* of the 4-vectors of the radiation and of the recoiling box add up to identity with the *components* of the original 4-vector of the system before emission (Fig. 107). However, the magnitudes of the 4-vectors (magnitude = rest mass) are not additive. No one dealing with Euclidean geometry would expect the length of one side of a triangle to be equal to the sum of the lengths of the other two sides. Similarly in Lorentz geometry. The rest mass of the system (M) is not to be considered as equal to the sum of the rest mass of the radiation (zero) and the rest mass of the recoiling box (less than M). But *components* of 4-vectors are additive; for example,

$$\begin{pmatrix} \text{energy} \\ \text{of system} \end{pmatrix} = \begin{pmatrix} \text{energy of} \\ \text{radiation} \end{pmatrix} + \begin{pmatrix} \text{energy of} \\ \text{recoiling box} \end{pmatrix}$$

Thus we see that the energy of the recoiling box is $M - E$. Not only is the *energy* of the box reduced by the emission of radiation from the wall; also its rest mass is reduced (see shortened length of 4-vector in diagram). Thus the radiation takes away rest mass from the wall of the box even though this radiation has zero rest mass. The result

$$\begin{pmatrix} \text{rest mass} \\ \text{of system} \end{pmatrix} \neq \begin{pmatrix} \text{rest mass of} \\ \text{radiation [zero]} \end{pmatrix} + \begin{pmatrix} \text{rest mass of} \\ \text{recoiling box} \end{pmatrix}$$

is as natural in spacetime geometry as is the inequality $5 \neq 3 + 4$ in Euclidean geometry.

What about the gravitational attraction exerted by the system on a test object? Of course the redistribution of mass as the radiation moves from left to right makes some difference in the attraction. But let the test object be at a distance r so great that any such redistribution has a negligible effect on the attraction. In other words, all that counts for the pull on a unit test object is the total mass M as it appears in Newton's formula for gravitational force

$$\begin{pmatrix} \text{force per} \\ \text{unit mass} \end{pmatrix} = GM/r^2$$

Even so, will not the distant detector momentarily experience a less-than-normal pull while the radiation is in transit down the box? Is not the rest mass of the radiation zero, and is not the rest mass of the recoiling box reduced below the original mass M of the system? So is not the total attracting mass less than normal during the process of transport? No! The rest mass of the system—one has to say again—is not equal to the sum of the rest masses of its several parts. It is instead equal to the magnitude of the total momentum-energy 4-vector of the system. And at no time does either the total momentum (in our case zero!) or the total energy of the system change—it is an isolated system. Therefore neither is there any change in the magnitude M of the total momentum-energy 4-vector (Fig. 107). So, finally, there is never any change in the gravitational attraction.

There is one minor swindle in the way this problem has been presented: the box cannot in fact move as a rigid body. If it could, then information about the emission of the radiation from *one* end could be obtained from the motion of the *other* end long before the arrival of the radiation itself—this information would be transmitted at a greater speed than that of light! Instead, the recoil from the emission of the radiation travels along the sides of the box as a *vibrational wave*, that is, with the speed of sound, so that this wave arrives at the other end long after the radiation does. In the meantime the absorption of the radiation at the second end causes a second vibrational wave which travels *back* along the sides of the box. The addition of the vibration of the box to the problem requires a more complicated analysis but does not change in any essential way the results found above.

68.* Photon integrity

Show that an isolated photon cannot split into two photons going in directions other than the original direction. (Hint: Apply the laws of conservation of momentum and energy and the fact that the third side of a triangle is shorter than the sum of the other two sides. What triangle?)

69.* The pressure of light

(a) Calculate the total force exerted by a one-watt flashlight beam.

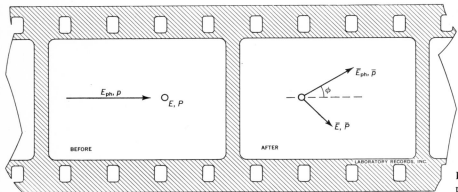

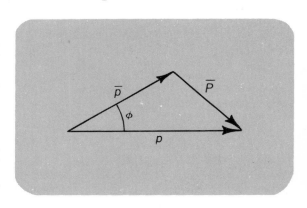

Fig. 108. Compton scattering of a photon by an electron.

(b) From the solar constant (1.4 kilowatts per square meter; see part d of Ex. 62) calculate the pressure of the sunlight on an earth satellite. Consider both reflecting and absorbing surfaces, and also "real" surfaces (partially absorbing). Why does the *color* of the light make no difference?

(c) It may be that particles *smaller* than a certain size are swept out of the solar system by the pressure of sunlight. This certain size is determined by the equality of the outward force of sunlight and the inward gravitational attraction of the sun. Estimate this size, making any assumptions necessary for your estimate. List the assumptions with your answer. Does your estimated size depend on the distance from the sun?

70.* Compton scattering

In 1923 Arthur Compton showed that X-rays (photons) scattered by free electrons have less energy after the scattering process than before.† His experiment is rated by many as the most important piece of experimental work done in physics in the 1920's. Analyze the collision between a photon of energy E_{ph} and an electron initially at rest to determine the energy of the photon that has been scattered with a change of direction measured by the angle ϕ. The angle ϕ is called the *scattering angle*. Use the following notation:

	Before the collision	*After the collision*
Electron	E, P	$\bar{E}, \bar{P}$
Photon	E_{ph}, p	$\bar{E}_{ph}, \bar{p}$

Do *not* use h or ν or λ or β or θ in your analysis—*only* the laws of conservation of momentum and energy *plus* the equations

---

†A. H. Compton, Physical Review, **22**, 411 (1923).

$$E^2 - P^2 = m^2 \qquad \text{for an electron}$$
$$E_{ph}^2 - p^2 = 0 \qquad \text{for a photon}$$

Plot the energy of the scattered photon, in units of the rest energy of the electron, as a function of the scattering angle ϕ, for the case in which the energy of the incident photon is twice the rest energy of the electron (2 × 0.511 MeV).

Fig. 109. Momentum conservation diagram for Compton scattering. Recall the law of cosines:
$$\bar{P}^2 = p^2 + \bar{p}^2 - 2p\bar{p}\cos\phi$$

Compton's original experiments showed that some photons were scattered without a measurable change of energy (Fig. 110). These photons were scattered by electrons so tightly bound to an atom that the entire atom recoiled as a unit. Show that the energy change is negligible for photons scattered by electrons tightly bound to an atom of average mass (say 10 × 2000 × mass of electron).

71.** Measurement of photon energy

A given radioactive source emits energetic photons (X-rays) or very energetic photons (gamma rays) with

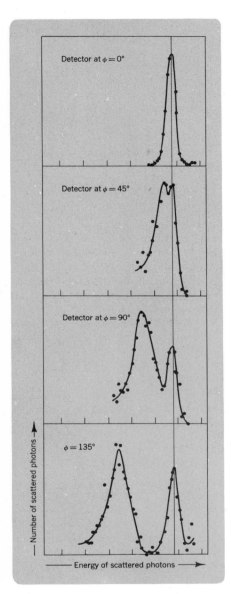

Fig. 110. Results of the Compton experiment in which photons were scattered from the electrons in a graphite target. At each angle of the detector except $\phi = 0$ there are some photons scattered with loss of energy (electron recoils by itself), and other photons scattered with little or no loss of energy (electron and atom recoil as a unit).

energies characteristic of the particular radioactive nucleus in question. Thus a precise energy measurement can often be used to determine the composition of even a tiny specimen. In the apparatus diagramed in Fig. 111 only those events are detected in which a count on detector A (knocked on electron) is accompanied by a count on detector B (scattered photon). What is the energy of the incoming photons that are detected in this way (in units of the rest energy of the electron)?

72.** Energy and frequency of a photon

Planck found himself forced in 1900 to recognize that light of frequency ν (vibrations per second) is composed of quanta (Planck's word) or photons (Einstein's later word), each endowed with an energy $E = h\nu/c^2$ (energy in units of mass) where h is a universal constant of proportionality called *Planck's constant*. How can Planck's formula possibly make sense when—as we now know—not only E but also ν depend upon the frame of reference in which the light is observed?

(a) How is photon *energy* changed by a Lorentz transformation? Consider a photon of energy E (momentum $p = E$) that moves in the positive x direction in the laboratory frame. Using the transformation equations for the energy-momentum 4-vector, find an expression for the energy E' of this photon in the rocket frame in terms of E and θ_r alone.

(b) Find how light *frequency* is changed by a Lorentz transformation. More specifically, let a train of waves (or pulses) of light travel in the positive x direction, so that in the course of one meter of light-travel time ν/c of these pulses pass the origin of the laboratory frame. It is understood that the zeroth or "fiducial" crest or pulse passes the origin at the zero of time—and that the origin of the rocket frame passes the origin of the laboratory frame at this same time. Show that the x coordinate of the nth pulse or wave crest is related to the time of observation (in meters) by the equation

$$n = \left(\frac{\nu}{c}\right)(t - x)$$

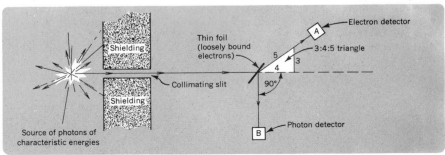

Fig. 111. Measurement of photon energy.

The same argument, applied in the rocket frame, leads to the relation

$$n = \left(\frac{\nu'}{c}\right)(t' - x')$$

Express this rocket formula in laboratory coordinates by use of the Lorentz transformation (parameter θ_r of relative velocity). Make any simplifications that are suggested by the formula (Table 8)

$$\cosh \theta \pm \sinh \theta = e^{\pm \theta}$$

where e is the base of natural logarithms: $e = 2.718281 \ldots$. Comparing the resulting formula for n in terms of x and t with the laboratory formula for n in terms of x and t, derive a simple formula for ν' in terms of ν and θ_r.

(c) Compare your answers to parts a and b. Show that for light moving in the direction of the relative motion of two frames, the transformation of the energy E of a photon between frames is identical to the transformation of the frequency ν of a light wave. This result is true for all directions of motion of light (Ex. 75). Thus if we associate photons with a light wave in one coordinate system, this association will hold in all coordinate systems. The theory of relativity does not tell us the value of Planck's constant h in the formula that relates energy (in units of mass) and frequency: $E = (h/c^2)\nu$. Experiment shows the constant h to have the value 6.63×10^{-34} joule-second. Show that if energy is measured in conventional units, the relation between energy and frequency has the form

(115) $E_{\text{con}} = h\nu$ (energy in conventional units)

(d) Show that the formula for Compton scattering (Ex. 70) becomes

(116) $$\bar{\nu} = \frac{\nu}{1 + \dfrac{h\nu}{mc^2}(1 - \cos \phi)}$$

In the 1920's there was great resistance to the idea that when the electron is "shaken" by the electric field of the photon at one frequency it should scatter (re-emit) this radiation at a lower frequency.

73.* Gravitational red shift

The two following problems assume a modest acquaintance with certain elementary facts of gravitation:

(i) A very small object—or a spherically symmetric object of any radius—with mass m_1 attracts an object of mass m_2—also small or spherically symmetric—

with a force $F = G\, m_1 m_2 / r^2$. Here r is the distance between the centers of the two objects and G is the Newtonian constant of gravitation, $G = 6.67 \times 10^{-11}$ (meter)^3/(kilogram-second^2).

(ii) The work required to move a test particle of *unit mass* from r to $r + dr$ against the gravitational pull of a fixed mass m is

$$G\, m(dr/r^2)$$

Translated from *conventional units of energy* to *units of mass* this work is

(117) $dW = (Gm/c^2)(dr/r^2) = m^*(dr/r^2)$

per unit of mass contained in the test particle.

(iii) The first factor in this formula, $m^* = Gm/c^2$, has a simple meaning. It is the mass of the center of attraction translated from units of kilograms to units of meters. For example, the mass of the earth ($m = 5.983 \times 10^{24}$ kg) expressed in length units is $m_{\text{earth}}^* = 4.44 \times 10^{-3}$ meters, and the mass of the sun ($m = 1.987 \times 10^{30}$ kg) is $m_{\text{sun}}^* = 1.47 \times 10^3$ meters.

(iv) Start the test particle at a distance r from the center of attraction and carry it to an infinite distance. The work required is

(118) $W = m^*/r$

per unit of mass contained in the test particle.

(a) What fraction of one's rest energy is converted to potential energy when he climbs the Washington Monument (555 feet or 170 meters high)? Let $g^* = (Gm_e/c^2)(1/r_e^2) = m_e^*/r_e^2$ be the acceleration of gravity in meters per meter^2 at the surface of the earth (radius r_e).

(b) What fraction of one's rest energy is converted to potential energy when he climbs a very high ladder that reaches higher than the gravitational influence of the earth? Assume that the earth does not rotate and is alone in space. Does the *fraction* of the energy that is lost in either part a or part b depend upon the original mass of the climber?

(c) Apply the result of part a to deduce the fractional energy change of a *photon* that rises vertically to a height z in a uniform gravitational field g^*. Photons have zero rest mass; one can say formally that they have only kinetic energy $E = T$. Thus photons have only one purse—the kinetic energy purse—from which to pay the potential energy tax as they rise in the gravitational field. Light of frequency ν is composed of photons of energy $E = h\nu/c^2$ (see Ex. 72). Show that the fractional energy loss for photons rising in a gravitational field corresponds to the following fractional change in frequency

$$\frac{\Delta\nu}{\nu} = -g^*z \qquad \text{(uniform gravitational field)}$$

(d) Apply the result of part b to deduce the fractional energy loss of a *photon* escaping to infinity. (To apply b for this purpose is an approximation good to one percent when this fractional energy loss itself is less than two percent.) Specifically, let the photon start from a point on the surface of an astronomical object of mass M (kg) or M^* (meters) $= GM/c^2$ and radius r. From the fractional energy loss, show that the fractional change of frequency is given by the expression

(119)
$$\frac{\Delta\nu}{\nu} = -\frac{M^*}{r}$$

This decrease in frequency is called the *gravitational red shift* because, for visible light, the shift is toward the lower frequency (red) end of the visible spectrum. Calculate the fractional gravitational red shifts for light escaping from the surface of the earth and for light escaping from the surface of the sun.

74.* Density of the companion of Sirius

Sirius (the Dog Star) is the brightest star in the heavens. Sirius and a small companion revolve about one another. By analyzing this revolution using Newtonian mechanics, astronomers have determined that the mass of the companion of Sirius is roughly equal to the mass of our sun (m is about 2×10^{30} kilograms; m^* is about 1.5×10^3 meters).

Light from the companion of Sirius is analyzed in a spectrometer. A spectral line from a certain element, identified from the pattern of lines, is shifted in frequency by a fraction 7×10^{-4} compared to the frequency of the same spectral line from the same element in the laboratory. (These figures are experimentally accurate to only one significant figure.)† Assuming that this is a gravitational red shift (formula at end of Ex. 73), estimate the average density of the companion of Sirius in grams per cubic centimeter. This type of star is called a *white dwarf*.

D. DOPPLER SHIFT

75. Doppler equations

A photon moves in the xy laboratory plane in a direction that makes an angle ϕ with the x axis, so

---

†J. H. Moore, Proceedings of the Astronomical Society of the Pacific, **40**, 229 (1928).

---

that its components of momentum are $p^x = p \cos \phi$, $p^y = p \sin \phi$, $p^z = 0$.

(a) Use the Lorentz transformation equations for the momentum-energy 4-vector and the relation $E^2 - p^2 = 0$ for a photon to show that in the rocket frame the photon has an energy E' given by the equation

(120)
$$E' = E \cosh \theta_r (1 - \beta_r \cos \phi)$$

and moves in a direction that makes an angle ϕ' with the x' axis given by the equation

(121)
$$\cos \phi' = \frac{\cos \phi - \beta_r}{1 - \beta_r \cos \phi}$$

(b) Derive the inverse equations for E and $\cos \phi$ as functions of E', $\cos \phi'$, and β_r. Compare these inverse equations to the results of Ex. 22 on the "headlight effect."

(c) If the frequency of the light in the laboratory frame is ν, what is the frequency ν' of the light in the rocket frame? This difference in frequency due to relative motion is called the *relativistic Doppler shift* (Ex. 6). Do these equations enable one to tell in what frame the *source* of the photons is at rest?

76. Decay of π^0 meson— a worked example

A π^0 meson (neutral pi-meson) moving in the x direction with a kinetic energy in the laboratory frame equal to its rest energy decays into two photons. In the rocket frame in which the meson is at rest these photons are emitted in the positive and negative y' directions. Find the energies of the two photons in the rocket frame (in units of the rest energy of the meson) and the energies and directions of propagation of the two photons in the laboratory frame.

Solution: In the rocket frame the π^0 meson is at rest before decay (no momentum). There is no way for the meson to decay into *only one* photon and conserve momentum. Decay into *two* photons will conserve momentum *provided* (a) the two photons are emitted in *opposite* directions in the frame in which the undecayed meson was at rest, and (b) these two photons have momenta of equal magnitude in that frame—and therefore have equal energy ($E' = p'$ for photons). Now the problem can be solved in the rocket frame: each photon carries away *half* of the rest energy of the meson, $E' = m/2$. In addition, the problem states that these photons move in the positive and negative y' directions ($\phi' = \pm 90°$; hence, $\cos \phi' = 0$).

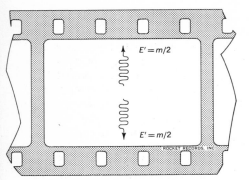

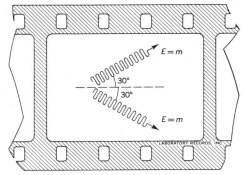

Fig. 112. Solution to the π^0-meson decay problem.

The energy and direction of motion of each photon in the *laboratory* frame can be found using the results of Ex. 75,

$$E = E' \cosh \theta_r \, (1 + \beta_r \cos \phi')$$
$$\cos \phi = \frac{\cos \phi' + \beta_r}{1 + \beta_r \cos \phi'}$$

First one must know the values of θ_r and β_r. The problem states that before decay the kinetic energy of the meson in the laboratory frame is equal to its rest mass.

$$E_\pi \equiv m \cosh \theta_r \equiv T + m = 2m$$

from which

$$\cosh \theta_r = \frac{1}{(1 - \beta_r^2)^{1/2}} = 2$$

and

$$\beta_r = \sqrt{3}/2$$

Use these results and $E' = m/2$ in the transformation equations to obtain for each photon

$$E = m$$
$$\cos \phi = \beta_r = \sqrt{3}/2$$

so that $\phi = 30°$. The energy result could have been seen immediately from the symmetry of the decay and the total energy $2m$ of the meson before its decay. Figure 112 summarizes the results. *Check* that *momentum*, as well as energy, is conserved in the laboratory frame.

77. The speeding light bulb

A neon bulb that emits red light uniformly in all directions in its rest frame approaches the observer from a very great distance moving with nearly the speed of light along a straight-line path whose perpendicular distance from the observer is b. Both the color and the number of photons which reach him per second from the light bulb vary with time. Describe

these changes qualitatively at several stages of the motion. Consider both the Doppler shift and the headlight effect (Exs. 75 and 22).

78. The physicist and the traffic light

A physicist is arrested for going through a red light. In court he pleads that he approached the intersection at such a speed that the red light looked green to him. The judge, a graduate of a physics class, changes the charge to speeding and fines the defendant one dollar for every mile per hour he exceeded the local speed limit of twenty miles per hour. What is the fine? Take the wavelength of green light to be 5300 angstroms (one angstrom equals 10^{-10} meter) and the wavelength of red light to the 6500 angstroms. Notice that the light propagates in the *negative x* direction ($\phi = \phi' = \pi$).

79. Doppler shift at the limb of the sun

The sun rotates once in about 24.7 days. The radius of the sun is about 7.0×10^8 meters. Calculate the Doppler shift that we should observe for light of wavelength 5000 angstroms ($1A = 10^{-10}$ meter) from the edge of the sun's disk (the limb) near the equator. Is this shift toward the red end or toward the blue end of the visible spectrum? Compare the magnitude of this Doppler shift with that of the gravitational red shift of light from the sun (Ex. 73).

80. The expanding universe
(Recall Ex. 6.)

(a) Light from a distant galaxy is analyzed by a spectrometer. A spectral line of wavelength 7300 angstroms is identified (from the pattern of other lines) to be one of the lines of hydrogen that, for hydrogen in the laboratory, has the wavelength 4870 angstroms. If the shift in wavelength is a Doppler shift, how fast is the observed galaxy moving relative to the earth? Notice that the light propagates in a direction opposite to the direction of motion of the galaxy ($\phi = \phi' = \pi$).

(b) There is independent evidence that the observed galaxy is five billion light years away. Estimate the time when that galaxy parted company from our own galaxy—the Milky Way—using the simplifying assumption that the speed of recession was the same throughout the past (that is, not slowed down by the gravitational attractions between one galaxy and another). The astronomer Edwin Hubble discovered in 1929† that this time—whose reciprocal is called the Hubble constant, and which may itself therefore appropriately be called the Hubble time—has about the same value for all galaxies whose distances and speeds can be measured. Hence the concept of the *expanding universe*.‡ Will allowance for the past effect of gravitation in slowing the expansion *increase* or *decrease* the estimated time back to the start of this expansion?

81.* Clock paradox using the Doppler shift§

The clock paradox (Exs. 27 and 49) can be resolved elegantly using the Doppler shift as follows. Paul remains on earth. Peter travels with a large speed β_r to a distant star and returns to earth at the same speed. Both Peter and Paul observe a distant variable star whose light gets alternately dimmer and then brighter with a frequency ν in the earth frame (ν' in the rocket frame). This variable star is very much farther away than the length of Peter's path and is in a direction perpendicular to this path in the earth frame. Both observers will count the same total number of pulsations of the variable star during Peter's round trip. Use this fact and the expression for the Doppler shift at the laboratory angle of observation $\phi = 90°$ (Ex. 75)

(122) $\nu' = \nu \cosh \theta_r (1 - \beta_r \cos \phi)$

to verify that at the end of the trip described in Ex. 27 Peter will be only 14 years older while Paul will have aged 50 years.

82.* Speed trap

A stationary radar transmitter is aimed along a

†Proceedings of the U.S. National Academy of Sciences, **15**, 168 (1929).

‡For more details see, for example, Herman Bondi, *Cosmology* (Cambridge University Press, Cambridge, England, Second Edition, 1960).

§E. Feenberg, American Journal of Physics, **27**, 190 (1959).

highway and the shift in frequency of the signal reflected back from an approaching car is used to measure the speed of the car. One such device used by New Jersey police operates at a frequency of 2455 megacycles. How much is the reflected beam shifted in frequency if a speeding car approaches at 80 miles per hour? One mile per hour equals 0.447 meters per second. (Use approximations and assume that the automobile acts like a source of the same frequency as the radiation that falls on it in its rest frame. The solution involves *two* transformations; one from road frame to car frame; the second from car frame back to road frame.) Suppose that this device can discriminate between speeds that are different from one another by not less than ten miles per hour. What is the smallest fractional change in frequency that this unit can detect?

83.* Doppler line broadening

The average kinetic energy of an atom in a gas at temperature T degrees Kelvin is $(3/2)kT$. (The constant k is called the *Boltzmann constant* and has the value 1.38×10^{-23} joules per degree Kelvin). Estimate the fractional change in frequency due to the Doppler shift that will be observed in light emitted from an atom in a gas at temperature T. Use the low-velocity approximation of Newtonian mechanics. Will this shift increase or decrease the observed frequency of the emitted light? This is one reason why a given spectral line from a gas excited in an electric discharge contains a narrow range of frequencies around a central frequency. The effect is called *Doppler broadening of spectral lines*.

84.* Photon energy shift due to recoil of emitter

(a) A free particle of initial rest mass m and initially at rest emits a photon of energy E. The particle (now of rest mass $\bar{m}$) recoils with velocity parameter θ (Fig. 113).
Formulate the conservation laws in a form that makes no reference to velocity or velocity parameter. Consider the case in which the fractional change in rest mass in the emission process is very small compared to unity. Show that the photon has an energy $E_0 = m - \bar{m}$. For the general case show that

$$E = E_0(1 - E_0/2m)$$

or

(123) $$\frac{E - E_0}{E_0} = \frac{\Delta E}{E_0} = -\frac{E_0}{2m}$$

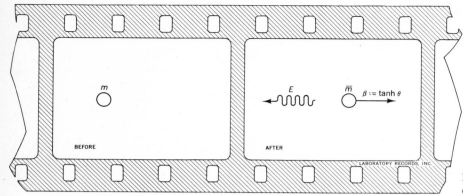

BEFORE

E

$\overline{m}$ $\beta := \tanh \theta$

AFTER

LABORATORY RECORDS, INC.

Fig. 113. Recoil of particle which emits a photon.

(b) Show that this shift in energy for *visible* light ($E_{0\ \mathrm{con}} \sim 3\ \mathrm{eV}$) emitted from *atoms* ($mc^2 \sim 10 \times 10^9\ \mathrm{eV}$) in a gas is very much less than the Doppler shift due to thermal motion (Ex. 83) even for temperatures as low as room temperature ($kT \sim (1/40)\ \mathrm{eV}$).

85.* The Mössbauer effect

(a) A free atom of iron Fe^{57}—formed in a so-called "excited state" by the radioactive decay of cobalt Co^{57}—emits from its nucleus a gamma ray (high-energy photon) of energy 14.4 keV and transforms to a "normal" Fe^{57} atom. By what fraction is the energy of the emitted ray shifted because of the recoil of the atom? The mass of the Fe^{57} atom is about equal to that of 57 protons,

(b) That *not all* emitted gamma rays experience this frequency shift was the important discovery made in 1958 by R. L. Mössbauer at the age of 29.† He showed theoretically on the basis of quantum mechanics—and demonstrated experimentally—that when iron atoms are embedded in a solid (as a consequence of the radioactive decay of parent cobalt atoms previously embedded in the same solid), then some significant fraction of these iron atoms *fail* to recoil as *free* atoms at the moment of emission. Instead they behave as if locked rigidly to the rest of the solid. The recoil in these cases is communicated to the solid as a whole. The solid being heavier than one atom by many powers of 10, these events are called *recoilless processes*. (Recoilless *emission* of photons from *nuclei* bound in a *solid* reminds one of Compton's finding that some photons *scattered* by electrons

†For a more detailed account of this discovery—for which the German scientist was awarded the Nobel prize in 1961—see S. DeBenedetti, "The Mössbauer Effect," *Scientific American*, **202**, 72 (April, 1960), available as Offprint 271 from W. H. Freeman and Company, San Francisco.

tightly bound in an *atom* have very little energy shift because the entire *atom* recoils as a unit—see Ex. 70.) For gamma rays emitted in recoilless processes, the m in Ex. 84 is the mass of the entire chunk in which the iron atoms are embedded. When this chunk has a mass of one gram, by what fraction is the frequency of the emitted ray shifted in "recoilless" processes?

(c) The gamma rays emitted from excited Fe^{57} atoms are not all of exactly the same energy but are spread over a narrow energy range—or frequency range—or *natural line width*. In practice one may count off a thousand or more photons into classes. A given photon belongs in one class or another as its frequency lies in one or another of many narrow frequency intervals of equal width. The number of photons in each class is plotted as a function of frequency. A bell shaped curve results (Fig. 114). The full width of this curve at half maximum is denoted by $\Delta\nu$. The fractional ratio $\Delta\nu/\nu_0$ has the very small value 3×10^{-13} for the 14.4 keV gamma ray from Fe^{57}. How much is the natural line width, $\Delta\nu$, of

Fig. 114. Natural line width of photons emitted from Fe^{57}.

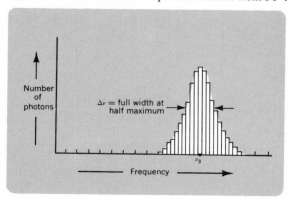

Number of photons

$\Delta\nu$ = full width at half maximum

ν_0

Frequency

Fe^{57} expressed in cycles per second? Compare the fractional natural line width with the fractional shift due to recoil of a free iron atom. And compare it with the fractional shift of a gamma ray from a recoilless process.

Mössbauer's discovery of recoilless processes thus put into one's hands a source of radiation sharp in frequency to the fantastic precision of 3 parts in 10^{13}. The next exercise (86) deals with the detection of this radiation. The subsequent problem (Ex. 87) uses motion (Doppler effect) as a means for producing controlled changes of a few parts in 10^{13}—or much larger changes—in the effective frequency of source or detector or both. To what uses can radiation of precisely defined frequency be put? There are many uses. For instance the Mössbauer effect is the basis of an important new technique in solid state physics, molecular physics, and biophysics. One can detect the change in the natural frequency of radiation from Fe^{57} atoms caused by other atoms in the neighborhood—and by external magnetic fields—and in this way analyze the interaction between the iron atom and the surrounding crystal (example: frequency difference between Fe^{57} atoms in solid iron and in an iron carbide crystal lattice) or the interaction between the iron atom and the surrounding molecule (example: frequency shift of Fe^{57} atom bound in hemoglobin molecule).

86.** Resonant scattering

The nucleus of *normal* Fe^{57} will *absorb* gamma rays at the resonant energy of 14.4 keV much more strongly than it will absorb gamma rays of any nearby energy. The energy absorbed in this way is converted to internal energy of the nucleus and transmutes the Fe^{57} to the "excited state." After a time this excited nucleus will re-emit the absorbed gamma ray in a random direction and transform back to the "normal state." Thus the gamma rays absorbed from a beam incident in one direction will be re-emitted in all directions. Therefore the number of gamma rays transmitted through a thin sheet containing Fe^{57} will be less at the 14.4 keV resonance energy than at any nearby energy. This process is called *resonant scattering*. Show that when a gamma ray of the resonant energy E_0 is incident on a *free* iron atom initially at rest then the free nucleus cannot absorb the gamma ray *at its resonant energy* because the process cannot satisfy both the law of conservation of momentum and the law of conser-

vation of energy. Show that both conservation laws are satisfied when an iron atom embedded in a 1-gram crystal absorbs such a gamma ray by a recoilless process, in which the entire crystal absorbs the momentum of the incident gamma ray. ("Satisfied"? For momentum, yes; for energy, no. However, the fractional discrepancy in energy—equivalent to fractional discrepancy in frequency—is less than three parts in 10^{13}, and therefore small enough so that the iron nucleus is "unable to notice" the discrepancy and therefore absorbs the gamma ray.)

87.** Measurement of Doppler shift by resonant scattering

In the experimental arrangement shown in Fig. 115 a source containing excited Fe^{57} nuclei emits (among other radiations) gamma rays of energy E_0 by a recoilless process. An absorber containing Fe^{57} nuclei in the normal state absorbs some of these gamma rays by another recoilless process and re-emits them in all directions. Thus the counting rate on a gamma ray counter placed as shown is *less* for an absorber containing normal Fe^{57} than for an equivalent absorber without normal Fe^{57}. Now the source is moved toward the absorber with speed β. What must this velocity be if the gamma rays are to arrive at the absorber shifted in frequency by 3 parts in 10^{13}—corresponding to one resonance line width? Express your answer in centimeters per second. Will the counting rate of the counter *increase* or *decrease* under these circumstances? What will happen to this counting rate if the source is moved *away* from the absorber with the same speed? Make a rough plot of counting rate of the counter as a function of the source velocity. Does this method allow one to measure the *absolute* velocity of the source, in violation of the principle of relativity?

88.** Mössbauer test of the gravitational red shift

A 14.4 keV gamma ray emitted from Fe^{57} without recoil travels vertically upward in a uniform gravitational field. By what fraction will the energy of this photon be reduced in rising to a height z (Ex. 73)? An

Fig. 115. Resonant scattering of photons.

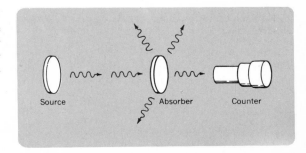

Fe^{57} absorber located at this height must move with what speed and in what direction in order to scatter such gamma rays by recoilless processes? Calculate this velocity when the height is 22.5 meters. Plot the counting rate as a function of absorber velocity as expected if (a) the gravitational red shift exists, and (b) there is no gravitational red shift. A frequency shift of $\Delta\nu/\nu_0 = (2.56 \pm 0.51) \times 10^{-15}$ was derived statistically from a very large number of photon counts in an experiment conducted by R. V. Pound and G. A. Rebka, Jr.[†]

89.** Mössbauer test of the clock paradox

For a twin Peter to leave his brother Paul behind in the laboratory, go away at high speed, return, and find himself younger than stay-at-home Paul is so contrary to everyday experience that it is astonishing to find that the experiment has already been done and the prediction has been upheld! Chalmers Sherwin has pointed out that the twins can be identical iron atoms just as well as living beings.[‡] Let one iron atom remain at rest. Let the other make one forth-and-back trip. Or many round trips. The *percentage* difference in aging of the twin atoms is the same after a million round trips as after one round trip—and is easier to measure. How does one get the second atom to make many round trips? He embeds it in a *hot* piece of iron, so that it vibrates back and forth about a position of equilibrium (thermal agitation!). How does one *measure* the difference in aging? In the case of Peter and Paul the number of birthday firecrackers that each had set off during their separation are counted. In the experiment with iron atoms one compares, not the number of flashes of firecrackers up to the time of meeting but the frequency of the photons emitted by recoilless processes, and thus—in effect—the number of ticks from two identical nuclear clocks, in the course of one laboratory second. In other words, one compares *the effective frequency of INTERNAL nuclear vibrations* (not to be confused with the back-and-forth vibration of the iron atom as a whole!) as observed in the laboratory for (a) an iron nucleus at rest and (b) an iron nucleus in a hot specimen.

It is difficult to obtain an iron nucleus at rest. Therefore the actual experiment compared the *effective* internal nuclear frequency, not for (a) and (b), but for (b) and (b'): two crystals of iron with a *difference*

[†]Physical Review Letters, **4**, 337 (1960).

[‡]Physical Review, **120**, 17 (1960).

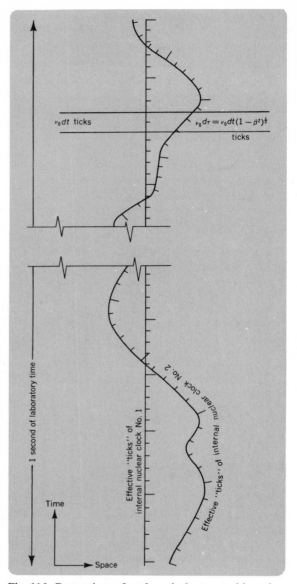

$\nu_0\,dt$ ticks

$\nu_0\,d\tau = \nu_0\,dt(1 - \beta^2)^{\frac{1}{2}}$
ticks

1 second of laboratory time

Time

Effective "ticks" of internal nuclear clock No. 1

Effective "ticks" of internal nuclear clock No. 2

Space

Fig. 116. Comparison of nuclear clock at rest with nuclear clock in thermal motion.

of temperature ΔT. R. V. Pound and G. A. Rebka, Jr.[†] measured that a sample warmed up by the amount $\Delta T = 1$ degree Kelvin underwent a fractional change in effective frequency of $\Delta\nu/\nu_0 = (-2.09 \pm 0.24) \times 10^{-15}$ (fewer vibrations; fewer clock ticks; fewer birthdays; more youthful!).

To simplify thinking about the experiment, go back to the idea that one iron atom is at rest and the other

[†]Physical Review Letters, **4**, 274 (1960).

is in thermal agitation at temperature T; *predict the fractional lowering in number of internal vibrations in the hot sample per laboratory second;* and compare with experiment.

Discussion: Figure 116 compares the effective "ticks" of the two "internal nuclear clocks" in the laboratory time dt. Note that the speed of thermal agitation is about 10^{-5} the speed of light. What algebraic approximation suggests itself for the discrepancy factor $1 - (1 - \beta^2)^{1/2}$? How much is the deficit in number of "ticks" (for hot atom versus atom at rest) in the lapse of laboratory time dt? Show that the cumulative deficit in number of "ticks" from the hot atom in one second is

$$\nu_0(\beta^2/2)_{Av}\,(1\ \text{sec})$$

where $(\beta^2)_{Av}$ means "the time average value of the square of the atomic speed" (relative to the speed of light). Note that the mean kinetic energy of thermal agitation of a hot iron atom (mass $m_{Fe} \approx 57\,m_{proton}$) is given by the classical kinetic theory of gases

$$1/2\,m_{Fe}(\beta^2)_{Av}c^2 = 3/2\,kT$$

Here k is Boltzmann's factor of conversion between two units of energy, degrees and joules (or degrees and ergs); $k = 1.38 \times 10^{-23}$ joule per degree Kelvin ($k = 1.38 \times 10^{-16}$ erg per degree Kelvin). How does the experimental result of Pound and Rebka compare with the result of your calculation?

E. COLLISIONS

90. Symmetric elastic collision

After a particle of mass m and kinetic energy T collides elastically with a particle of the same mass at rest and the two particles emerge with *unequal energies*, the directions of their velocities also make unequal *angles* with the continuation of the original direction. Nevertheless the angle α *between* the two final velocity vectors is predicted by Newtonian mechanics always to be 90 degrees. Not so in relativity mechanics! It predicts an angle *less* than 90 degrees (Ex. 40). Question: *How much less* than 90 degrees is the angle α in the simplest case, that of a *symmetric elastic collision*, where the two particles separate with equal energies and at equal angles (Fig. 117)? Determine this angle using only the relativistic form of the laws of conservation of momentum and energy.

Discussion: How much is the *total* energy of the system before the collision? How much therefore is the total energy of *one* of the two particles after the collision? And, in consequence, how much is its momentum? (See the introduction to the exercises, page 139, for the relation between momentum and energy and the reason for avoiding any mention or use of *velocity* in a problem concerned only with *momentum* and *energy*.) How much was the original momentum of the system? Show that the angle is given by the expression

$$\cos^2(\alpha/2) = \frac{T + 2m}{T + 4m}$$

From the trigonometric identity

$$\cos^2(\alpha/2) = (1/2)(1 + \cos\alpha)$$

show that

(124) $$\cos\alpha = \frac{T}{T + 4m}$$

What is the total angle α (1) for a Newtonian elastic collision at low velocity and (2) for an extreme relativistic collision with *very* large T?

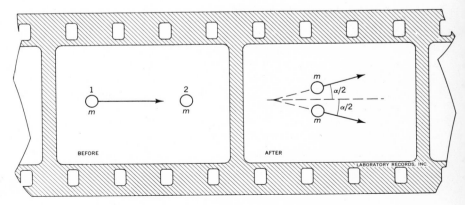

Fig. 117. Symmetric elastic collision between identical particles.

91. David and Goliath—a worked example

What is the smallest kinetic energy that an electron must have in order to be able to impart *half* of this kinetic energy to a proton—originally at rest—in an elastic head-on collision? Arrange your calculations so that you end up with a single equation that might be solved (and in fact can be solved!) to determine the single, dimensionless, unknown quantity T_e/m_p where T_e is the kinetic energy of the incoming electron and m_p is the rest mass of the proton. Find the value of $T_{e \, con}$ in MeV using the approximate value $m_p c^2 \approx$ 1000 MeV. (If you solve the equation by approximation, estimate the error in your answer.)

Solution: This problem is an exercise in algebraic manipulation—and how to avoid unnecessary algebraic manipulation! The collision is elastic, so the electron and proton are not annihilated by the collision and no radiation is given off. In this case the conservation of energy implies the *conservation of kinetic energy*. Let T_e be the kinetic energy of the incident electron. The problem says that after the collision the proton has *half* of the kinetic energy of the incoming electron: $\bar{T}_p = T_e/2$. Therefore the electron must carry away the other half of its original kinetic energy: $\bar{T}_e = T_e/2$.

The collision is head-on, so all motion is along the x axis, and momenta add like scalars with due regard for sign. The electron will rebound from the proton, so its momentum after the collision will be negative. The conservation of momentum implies

$$p_e = \bar{p}_p - \bar{p}_e$$

To relate momentum to energy we use the general formula

$$E^2 - p^2 = m^2$$

from which

$$
\begin{aligned}
p^2 &= E^2 - m^2 \\
&= (T + m)^2 - m^2 \\
&= T^2 + 2mT + \not{m}^2 - \not{m}^2 \\
&= T^2 + 2mT
\end{aligned}
$$

so that

$$p = (T^2 + 2mT)^{1/2}$$

Therefore the equation for conservation of momentum becomes

$$
(T_e^2 + 2m_e T_e)^{1/2} = (\bar{T}_p^2 + 2m'_p \bar{T}_p)^{1/2} - (\bar{T}_e^2 + 2m_e \bar{T}_e)^{1/2}
$$

Substitute the results of applying the law of the conservation of energy

$$\bar{T}_p = \bar{T}_e = T_e/2$$

to obtain

$$(T_e^2 + 2m_e T_e)^{1/2}$$

$$
= \left(\frac{T_e^2}{4} + m_p T_e\right)^{1/2} - \left(\frac{T_e^2}{4} + m_e T_e\right)^{1/2}
$$

Divide both sides of this equation by $T_e^{1/2} m_p^{1/2}$ to obtain

$$
\left(\frac{T_e}{m_p} + \frac{2m_e}{m_p}\right)^{1/2} = \left(\frac{T_e}{4m_p} + 1\right)^{1/2} - \left(\frac{T_e}{4m_p} + \frac{m_e}{m_p}\right)^{1/2}
$$

This equation contains the single unknown quantity T_e/m_p as requested in the statement of the problem. Solve it approximately, using the fact that the rest mass of the electron is approximately 2000 times smaller than the rest mass of the proton, so that $m_e/m_p \ll 1$. Neglect this fraction in the equation above.

$$
\left(\frac{T_e}{m_p}\right)^{1/2} \approx \left(\frac{T_e}{4m_p} + 1\right)^{1/2} - \frac{1}{2}\left(\frac{T_e}{m_p}\right)^{1/2}
$$

$$
\frac{3}{2}\left(\frac{T_e}{m_p}\right)^{1/2} \approx \left(\frac{T_e}{4m_p} + 1\right)^{1/2}
$$

Square both sides of this equation.

$$
\frac{9}{4}\left(\frac{T_e}{m_p}\right) \approx \frac{T_e}{4m_p} + 1
$$

$$
\frac{T_e}{m_p} \approx \frac{1}{2}
$$

The correct answer will differ from this one by some fraction or multiple of $m_e/m_p = 1/2000$. Multiply both sides of the equation by $m_p c^2$

$$
T_{e \, con} = T_e c^2 = \frac{m_p c^2}{2} = \frac{1000 \text{ MeV}}{2} = 500 \text{ MeV}
$$

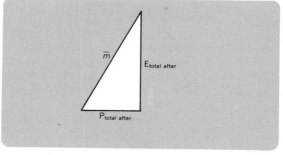

Fig. 118. Energy-momentum 4-vector of combined particle after perfectly inelastic collision.

92. Perfectly inelastic collision

A free particle of mass m_1 initially at rest is hit by a second particle of kinetic energy T and of *different* rest mass m_2. After the collision the two particles stick together. What is the rest mass $\bar{m}$ of the *combined* particle after the collision? Under what conditions will the rest mass of the combined particle reduce to the Newtonian result $\bar{m} = m_1 + m_2$? What do these conditions say about the maximum magnitude of the kinetic energy T of the incoming particle if a Newtonian analysis is to be approximately correct? Discussion: How much is the momentum of the system before the collision? After? Once this value is determined, what quantities in Fig. 118 are known and what is to be found? Does the Pythagorean rule apply to the "hypotenuse" of this "triangle"?

93.* Creation of particles by protons

One purpose of building high energy particle accelerators is to create in quantity for study some of the short-lived particles that ordinarily come through the laboratory only occasionally as cosmic-ray products. In the process of creation, some of the kinetic energy of a high-energy particle from an accelerator is converted into rest mass of the new particle. In 1955 Segré and collaborators at the University of California at Berkeley produced antiprotons (same mass as proton, negative charge) by bombarding a stationary target containing hydrogen (protons) with a beam of protons.† Various conservation laws of particle physics (conservation of charge, conservation of heavy particles) require that if an antiproton is created,

a proton must be created as well. So after the collision the incident and target protons will remain, plus a proton-antiproton pair. The question is: *What is the minimum kinetic energy of an incident proton that can cause pair production?* This mimimum kinetic energy is called the *threshold energy*.

(a) *A first—and incorrect—approach.* Analyze the collision in Fig. 119 in which *all* of the kinetic energy of the incident proton is converted into rest mass, leaving all four final particles at rest. Does this reaction satisfy both the law of conservation of energy and the law of conservation of momentum?

(b) *Second approach.* Find a frame of reference in which the final four particles *can* all be at rest and yet in which the collision satisfies the law of conservation of momentum. Discussion: A frame of reference in which the total momentum is zero is called a *center-of-momentum frame.* In the center-of-momentum frame the collision has the appearance of Fig. 120. The incoming protons need less total energy when the four final particles remain together than when the four particles fly apart. Why? (Consider the collision in this center-of-momentum frame. Disregard electric forces between the particles—they have negligible influence at the high energies of interest here.)

(c) *Third approach.* From the second approach we know that the greatest possible conversion of kinetic energy to rest mass consistent with conservation of momentum will occur when the resulting particles remain together. In the laboratory frame these particles will then all move with the same velocity (Fig. 121). Starting anew with this picture and employing only the laws of conservation of momentum and energy as expressed in the *laboratory* frame, find the threshold kinetic energy T_{th} for the production of proton-antiproton pairs. Express your answer both as a multiple of the rest energy of the proton and in GeV.

---

†O. Chamberlain, E. Segrè, C. Wiegand, and T. Ypsilantis, Physical Review, **100,** 947 (1955).

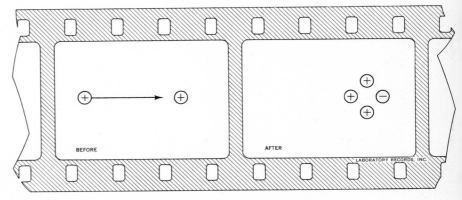

Fig. 119. Incorrect laboratory diagram of creation of proton-antiproton pair at threshold.

BEFORE　　　　AFTER

LABORATORY RECORDS, INC.

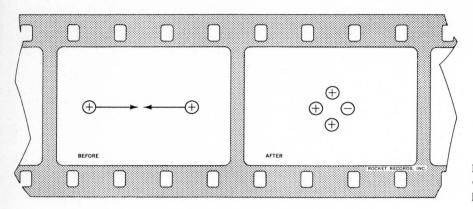

Fig. 120. Correct rocket diagram of creation of proton-antiproton pair at threshold.

(d) What is the energy of each particle after the collision?

(e) Show that the threshold energy calculated in part c can be derived from the answer of Ex. 92. Assume that *each* of the initial particles in that exercise has the mass of the proton and that the final mass $\overline{m}$ is equal to four times the mass of the proton.

(f) Why can proton-antiproton pairs be produced with a lower threshold energy of the incident proton when heavy nuclei are used in the target instead of hydrogen?

94.* Creation of particles by electrons

What is the threshold kinetic energy T_{th} of the incident electron for the process

electron (fast) + proton (at rest)

$$\longrightarrow \text{electron} + \text{antiproton} + \text{two protons}$$

95.* Photoproduction of a pair by a single photon

(a) A gamma ray (high-energy photon, zero rest mass) can carry an energy greater than the rest energy of an electron-positron pair. (Remember that a positron has the same mass as the electron but opposite charge.) Nevertheless the process

(energetic gamma ray) $\longrightarrow$ (electron) + (positron)

cannot occur in the absence of other matter or radiation. *Prove* that this process is incompatible with the laws of conservation of momentum and energy as employed in the laboratory frame of reference. Treat the most general case, in which the paths of the alleged positron and electron do *not* make equal angles with the extended path of the incoming gamma ray. Repeat the demonstration—which then becomes much more impressive—in the center-of-momentum frame

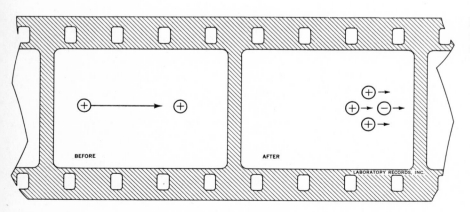

Fig. 121. Corrected laboratory diagram of creation of proton-antiproton pair at threshold.

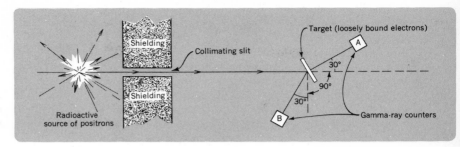

Fig. 122. Schematic diagram of experiment to test the principle of relativity.

of the alleged pair (the frame of reference in which the total momentum of the two resulting particles is zero).

(b) In the presence of other matter, a gamma ray *can* produce a positron-electron pair. What is the threshold energy T_{th} at which a gamma ray becomes capable of bringing about the often observed process

(gamma ray) + (electron at rest)

$$\longrightarrow \text{(positron)} + 2\text{(electrons)}$$

The rest energy of the electron—and of the positron—is about one-half MeV.

96.** Photoproduction of a pair by two photons

Two gamma rays of different energies collide in a vacuum and disappear, bringing into being an electron-positron pair. For what ranges of energies of the two gamma rays, and for what range of angles between their initial directions of propagation can this reaction occur?

97.** Positron-electron annihilation

A positron e^+ of kinetic energy T is annihilated on a target containing electrons e^- practically at rest in the laboratory frame:

$$e^+ \text{(fast)} + e^- \text{(at rest)} \longrightarrow \text{radiation}$$

(a) By considering the collision in the center-of-momentum frame (the frame of reference in which the total momentum of the initial particles is equal to zero) show that it is necessary for at least *two* gamma rays (rather than one) to result from the annihilation.

(b) Derive an expression for the energy of one of the gamma rays in the laboratory frame as a function of the angle between the direction of emergence of that gamma ray and the direction of travel of the positron before its annihilation. Let your derivation be free of any reference to velocity or velocity parameter—both are irrelevant in this problem.

(c) What are the maximum and minimum gamma ray energies possible in the laboratory frame?

(d) Using simple approximations, evaluate the answer to (c) in the limiting cases of (1) very small T and (2) very large T.

98.* Test of the principle of relativity

(a) In the apparatus of Fig. 122, the only events detected are those in which gamma-ray counters A and B, which are equidistant from the target, record gamma rays *simultaneously*—are "in coincidence." What are the energy and speed of the incoming positrons that are detected in this way?

(b) The principle of relativity (Section 3) states that the speed of light is the same in every inertial frame regardless of the motion of the source of the light. In contrast, W. Ritz long ago tried to argue that light emitted in the forward direction by a moving source travels faster than light emitted in the backward direction. If the coincidence between counters is no longer demanded in the apparatus above, how can the measurement of the time lapse between the arrival of the gamma rays at counters A and B be used to choose between these two hypotheses concerning the speed of light? For the results of such an experiment, see Fig. 123.†

99.* Identifying particles from bubble chamber tracks

Moving *charged* particles can leave visible tracks in cloud chambers, bubble chambers, and spark chambers because the charges on these particles interact at a distance with electrons in the atoms, creating ions. The ions are detected in different ways in the three kinds of chambers. Bubble chambers are filled with liquid hydrogen which is ready to boil ("superheated"). The ions created by passing high-energy charged particles act as starting points ("centers of nucleation") for bubbles. Figure 124 is a bubble

†D. Sadeh, *Physical Review Letters*, **10**, 271 (April 1963).

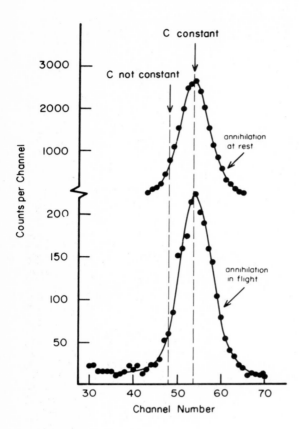

Fig. 123. Results of the experiment on the constancy of light velocity performed by D. Sadeh (reproduced here with his permission). Time lapse between counts by counters A and B was recorded for many such pairs of events. Different time lapses were sorted automatically into different "channels" of a multi-channel counter. Thus the horizontal axis of the graph (labeled "channel number") gives a relative measure of the time between gamma ray arrivals at counters A and B. The vertical axis represents number of times a pair of gamma rays with a given time lapse between them were recorded. The lower curve is the result for an experimental arrangement similar to that of Fig. 122 in which positrons of a given energy were annihilated in flight. The upper curve was obtained by moving counter A to a position 180° from counter B. In this case only those pairs of gamma rays are recorded in which the positron comes to rest before annihilation (laboratory frame is then the center-of-momentum frame in which gamma rays are given off in opposite directions!). Lower and upper curves have peaks at the same time lapse, showing that light (gamma ray) moves from target to counter A at the same velocity whether the emitting positron is in flight or at rest. The peak of the lower curve would have coincided with the dashed line on the left if the velocity of the gamma rays added on to the velocity of the positrons in flight.

chamber picture. Four different π^+ mesons are shown entering the chamber. All four *stop* in the liquid hydrogen. In a first reaction each π^+ meson decays into a μ^+ meson—whose track is shown—plus an uncharged particle, which leaves no track. In a subsequent reaction each μ^+ meson comes to rest and decays into a positive electron (e^+) plus a pair of neutral particles. The spiral track of one of the positive electrons in an externally applied magnetic field dominates the center of the picture.

Focus attention on the first reaction

$$\pi^+ \text{ (at rest)} \longrightarrow \mu^+ + x$$

where x is the unknown neutral particle. From the radius of curvature of the track of the μ^+ meson in the magnetic field one learns that its momentum is $p_\mu = 58.2\ m_e$ in units of the rest mass of the electron.

(a) Using the conservation laws, find the rest mass of the uncharged particle x. ($m_{\pi^+} = 273.2\ m_e$ and $m_\mu = 206.8\ m_e$).

(b) What *is* this uncharged particle? Discussion: The least massive known particle of nonzero rest mass is the electron. The approximate calculation in (a) leads one to suspect that particle x has zero rest mass. Is it a photon? This possibility is ruled out by another conservation law: the conservation of angular momentum. The initial π^+ meson has zero angular momentum. If angular momentum is to be conserved the angular momenta of the product particles must add up to zero. The product μ^+ meson has a spin angular momentum $1/2\ \hbar = 1/2\ (h/2\pi)$ where h is Planck's constant. In addition the photon is known to have a spin angular momentum of $\hbar$. There is no way that an angular momentum $1/2\hbar$ and an angular momentum $\hbar$ can be oriented to give zero total angular momentum. Therefore particle x cannot be a photon. What is the spin angular momentum of particle x? Particle x is called a neutrino. You have derived two of the fundamental properties of the neutrino without seeing a visible trace of it at all!

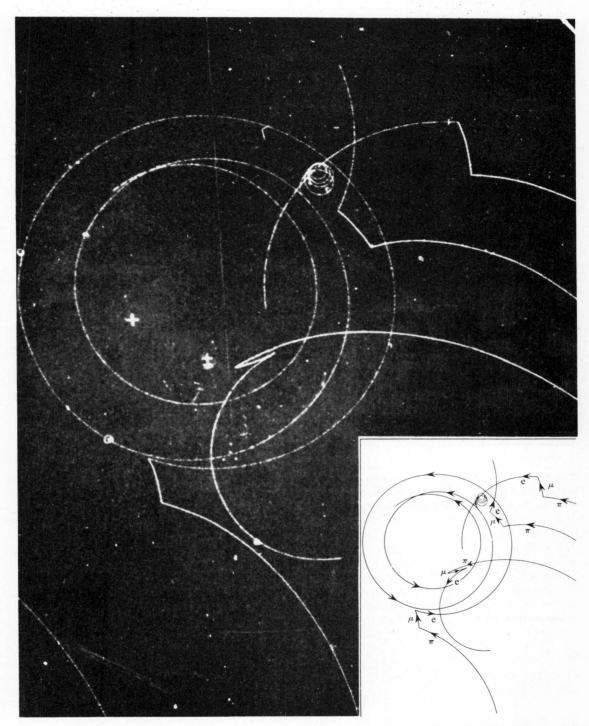

Fig. 124. Bubble chamber photograph showing the decays of four separate π^+-mesons. From R. D. Hill, *Tracking Down Particles* (W. A. Benjamin, New York, 1963).

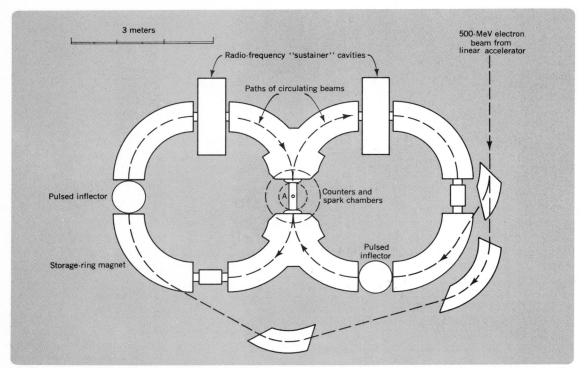

Fig. 125. Princeton-Stanford experiment on clashing electron beams. Electrons are injected into one ring for about 10 minutes. The second ring is then filled in the same way, after which the linear accelerator is switched off and data is taken for 30 minutes. The radio frequency "sustainer" cavities replace the energy that electrons radiate away as they accelerate in a circular path.

100.* Storage rings and clashing beams

How much more violent is a collision in which two electrons that are moving toward one another from opposite directions collide than one in which a moving electron collides with one at rest? *Discussion:* When a moving particle strikes a stationary one the energy available for the creation of new particles, for heating, and for other interactions—or, in brief, the *available interaction energy*—is less than the initial energy (the sum of the rest and kinetic energies of the initial two particles). See Ex. 93. Reason: The particles that are left over after the reaction have a net forward motion (law of conservation of momentum!), the kinetic energy of which is available neither for giving these particles velocity *relative* to each other nor for producing more particles. For this reason much of the particle energy produced in accelerators is not available for studying interactions because it is carried away in the kinetic energy of the products of the collision. However, in the *center-of-momentum frame* (defined as that reference frame in which the total momentum of the interacting particles is equal to zero) the total momentum is equal to zero both before and

after the collision. Therefore in the center-of-momentum frame the energy available for interaction is equal to the total energy of the incoming particles. Is there some way that the laboratory frame can be made also the center-of-momentum frame? One way is to build *two* particle accelerators and have the two beams collide head-on. If the energy and rest masses of the particles in each beam are respectively the same, then the laboratory frame *is* the center-of-momentum frame, and *all* the energy in each collision is available interaction energy. It is easier and cheaper to achieve the same efficiency by using a *single* accelerator, and storage rings in which particles are stored after they reach maximum energy (Fig. 125). A magnetic field keeps the particles (in this example, electrons) in their circular paths. The accelerator beam is injected in such a way that the direction of circulation is opposite in the two rings. Collisions between particles in the two beams takes place at point *A* where the two beams intersect (hence the name *clashing beams*). One advantage of the storage rings is that electrons that do not interact at one intersection are not wasted, but may interact on subsequent trips around the ring.

Electrons of kinetic energy 500 MeV are stored in

each ring. What is the total available interaction energy in the laboratory frame? What would have to be the kinetic energy of a moving electron incident on a stationary electron in order to provide the same available interaction energy? (At this writing the greatest electron energy available from a single ac-

celerator is 6 GeV.) *Protons* of what kinetic energy must be stored in storage rings in order to obtain an available reaction energy equivalent to 1000-GeV protons striking stationary protons? (At this writing the greatest proton energy available from a single accelerator is 35 GeV.)

F. ATOMIC PHYSICS

101.* de Broglie and Bohr

Show that the results of Ex. 72 yield the relation $p = h/(\lambda c)$ for the momentum of a photon in units of mass. Consider the following intuitive argument (based on the mystical derivation of de Broglie,† which is incomplete but of historical note, for it led to very fruitful investigations and ultimately to the correct derivation—and to the development of *quantum mechanics*). Suppose that a wavelength $\lambda = h/pc$ can be associated with a particle of *nonzero* rest mass: for instance, an electron. Suppose that this electron is revolving on a circular path around a fixed nucleus. In order for the wave that represents the electron to have a single value everywhere, it is necessary that the number of wavelengths λ around the circumference of the path be equal to some integral multiple n of this circumference $2\pi r$. From this requirement show that

$$(125) \qquad r\, p_{\text{con}} = \frac{nh}{2\pi} = n\hbar \qquad (n = 1, 2, 3, \ldots)$$

where p_{con} is the momentum of the electron in conventional units. What does this equation say about the *angular momentum* of the electron in such an orbit? For the low-velocity limit of Newtonian mechanics show that the radius of the orbit is given by the equation

$$(126)$$

$$r = \frac{(4\pi\epsilon_0)n^2h^2}{4\pi^2 Ze^2 m} \quad \left(\begin{array}{c} e \text{ in coulombs} \\ 4\pi\epsilon_0 = 1.113 \times 10^{-10} \\ (\text{coul sec})^2/(\text{kg m}^3) \\ h, m, r \text{ in kg m sec} \end{array} \right)$$

$$r = \frac{n^2\hbar^2}{Ze^2 m} \quad \left(\begin{array}{c} e \text{ in esu} \\ \hbar, m, r \text{ in g cm sec} \end{array} \right)$$

in which Z is the atomic number of (number of protons in) the nucleus, and m and e are the mass and charge of electron respectively. These are the Bohr orbits of an atom. Show that the speed β of the elec-

tron in its orbit is given (for low speeds) by

$$(127) \qquad \beta = \frac{\alpha Z}{n}$$

in which $\alpha = e^2/[(4\pi\epsilon_0)(h/2\pi)c] = 1/137$ is a dimensionless constant called the *fine structure constant*. (Formula valid for e in coulombs; $4\pi\epsilon_0 = 1.113 \times 10^{-10}$ (coul sec)^2/(kg m^3); h, c in kg m sec. When expressed in units of g cm sec, with e in esu or in g$^{1/2}$ cm$^{3/2}$/sec, then $\alpha = e^2/\hbar c = 1/137$.) This equation for β was used in Ex. 41.

102.* Seeing with electrons

It is a general principle of physical optics that no image can be formed of the details of an object that is smaller than about one wavelength of the light used to form the image. Assume that the same is true of the matter waves discussed in the last exercise. Through what voltage should electrons be accelerated that are to form an image of a bacterium (size, about one micron, or 10^{-6} meters) in an electron microscope? What energy in MeV should electrons have that are used to investigate the structure of protons and neutrons (diameter, about one fermi, or 10^{-15} meters)?

103.** Thomas precession

Picture the electron as a ball of negative charge spinning on its axis like a gyroscope. This crude classical model is incorrect, but is adequate for some purposes, such as the present one! Newtonian mechanics predicts that as an electron in an atom revolves in its orbit about the nucleus, it will maintain the direction of its spin axis with respect to an inertial frame, just as any gyroscope would when carried around in a circle.

On the other hand, according to a discovery of L. H. Thomas in 1927,† the theory of relativity makes the surprising prediction that an electron that revolves once around a nucleus will have its spin axis pointing in a *different* direction than when it started on the

---

†Academie des Sciences, Paris, Comptes Rendus, **177**, 507 (1923).

†L. H. Thomas, Philosophical Magazine, (7), **3**, 1 (1927).

orbit. This precession—called *Thomas precession*—has an observable effect on the emission lines of some atomic spectra. The explanation of this precession is related to the effect of the tilted meter stick of Ex. 52 and results from the *relativity of simultaneity. Analyze* the Thomas precession of the electron using the following outline or another method.

Why should the spin axis of the electron precess to a new angle as the electron moves in a circle? Motion in a circle involves *acceleration* of the electron toward the center of the circle. Unhappily, special relativity is not equipped to analyze the effects of *acceleration* on orientation. Therefore proceed as one so often does in physics: If one cannot solve the problem at hand, he finds a simpler but analogous problem that he *is* able to solve! In this case, approximate the circular path of the classical electron by a regular polygon of n sides. In moving once around this orbit the electron moves in straight-line paths interrupted by n sudden changes of direction, each through an

angle $\alpha = 2\pi/n$. *Plan of attack on the problem:* Study the change of spin orientation of the electron as it rounds *one* of these corners (parts a through c). Then let the number of sides n increase without limit—so that the angle α of *each* change of direction becomes very small—until the classical *circular* orbit is obtained as a limiting case (parts d and e).

(a) Figure 129 shows the electron before (A) and after (B) it has changed its direction of motion by an angle α. The heavy line across each electron represents the *projection* of the spin axis on the xy plane of the orbit. The figure shows the *special case* in which this projection lies in the x direction before the electron changes its direction of motion. *After* the change of direction of motion of the electron as a whole, its *orientation* will also have changed by some small angle $d\phi$—a change that is totally incomprehensible in terms of Newtonian mechanics! Why this change in orientation? The change results from the relativity of simultaneity.

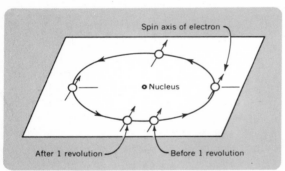

Fig. 126. Newtonian mechanics predicts no change in the spin orientation of the electron as it revolves about the nucleus.

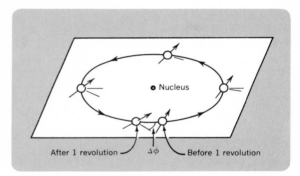

Fig. 127. The theory of relativity predicts that during one revolution the spin axis of the electron will *precess* through some angle, called $\Delta\phi$ in this figure.

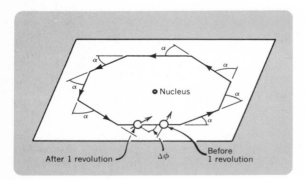

Fig. 128. Regular polygon as an approximation to the Newtonian circular path of the electron.

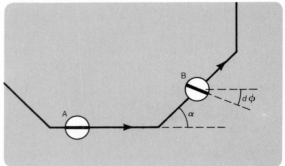

Fig. 129. Special case of the change of orientation of the electron as it changes its direction of motion.

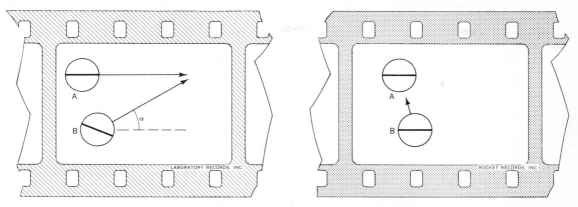

Fig. 130. Replace the single electron that rounds a corner with two electrons A and B that move on intersecting straight lines. Demand that orientation of A and B be the same in the rocket frame in which ball A is at rest.

Rounding the corner involves a large sudden acceleration of the electron. Happily we can treat balls A and B as separate balls, each traveling with the same speed along straight lines that make an angle α in the laboratory frame, as shows in Fig. 130. Neither ball accelerates, but as their paths cross, observers who ride on balls A and B can check to see that the spin axes of the two balls point in the same direction. The rocket frame figure shows this relative orientation of spins in a frame in which ball A is at rest. This is the rocket frame in which the observer on A will make his comparison of spin orientations. (Note: Will observer A or observer B make this comparison? In the case of a very small angle α, observers A and B will be *nearly at rest* with respect to one another, so in this limit *either* can make the comparison!) Since we are replacing the single ball which rounds a corner with the two balls A and B, we demand that *in the rocket frame* the spin projections of A and B are to be parallel to each other. The central point is that even though these projections are parallel in the *rocket* frame, they are *not* parallel in the *laboratory* frame. As a result, the orientation of the spin of the electron changes direction as it rounds the corner as observed in the laboratory.

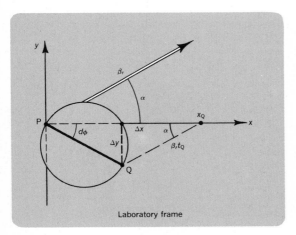

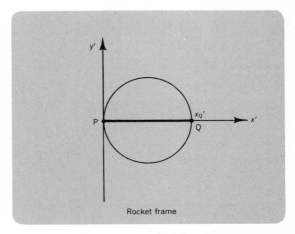

Fig. 131. Analysis of the orientation of ball B in laboratory and rocket frames—designed to answer the questions: Where and when does point Q cross the x axis? Where therefore is point Q at laboratory time $t = 0$?

Figure 131 is a larger picture of ball B. Label the two ends of the spin projection P and Q as shown. Choose the laboratory and rocket origins so that at $t = t' = 0$ both origins coincide with point P. Then in the rocket frame point Q will cross the x axis *at this same time* $t' = t_Q' = 0$. Not so in the laboratory frame! Figure 131 shows electron B at laboratory time $t = 0$. Let x_Q and t_Q be the *different* place and *later* time respectively in the laboratory frame at which point Q crosses the x axis. Use the Lorentz transformation equations with $t_Q' = 0$ to show that

(128)
$$x_Q = x_Q' \cosh \theta_r$$
$$t_Q = x_Q' \sinh \theta_r$$

Question: Where was point Q at *laboratory* time $t = 0$? In the time t_Q, point Q has moved a distance $\beta_r t_Q$ as shown in the figure. Using the figure, *show* that in this time the x and y coordinates of point Q have changed by an amount

(129)
$$\Delta x = \beta_r t_Q \cos \alpha = \beta_r x_Q' \sinh \theta_r \cos \alpha$$
$$\Delta y = \beta_r t_Q \sin \alpha = \beta_r x_Q' \sinh \theta_r \sin \alpha$$

where the last step makes use of Eqs. 128. This means that at laboratory time $t = 0$ point P was at the origin (by definition) and point Q was at the cordinates $x_Q - \Delta x$ and $-\Delta y$. Therefore the angle of inclination $(d\phi)$ of the line PQ calculated at laboratory time $t = 0$—the *change* in orientation as the electron rounds the corner—is given by the expression

(130)
$$\tan (d\phi) = \frac{-\Delta y}{x_Q - \Delta x}$$

Substitute into Eq. 130 from Eqs. 128 and 129 and simplify to obtain

$$\tan (d\phi) = \frac{-\beta_r^2 \sin \alpha}{1 - \beta_r^2 \cos \alpha}$$

For an atom $\beta_r \leq Z/137$ (Ex. 101), and for small Z, $\beta_r \ll 1$. Therefore

$$\tan (d\phi) \approx d\phi \approx -\beta_r^2 \sin \alpha$$

This is the angle by which the electron spin axis will precess when it rounds a corner of angle α in the *special case* in which the projection of this spin axis on the plane of the orbit lies along the initial direction of motion of the electron.

(b) Consider another special case, this time one in which the projection of the spin axis lies along the y axis of the xy plane of the orbit.

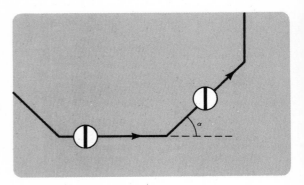

Fig. 132. Special case in which electron does *not* change orientation as it changes direction of motion.

Show that in this case there is no disagreement between laboratory and rocket observers that points P and Q cross the y axis simultaneously. Therefore—in this case—there is no rotation of the spin axis in the laboratory frame as the electron rounds the corner.

(c) As the electron moves around its orbit, the projection of its spin axis on the xy plane of the orbit (Fig. 127) will occasionally be *parallel* to its direction of motion (a), and occasionally *perpendicular* to its direction of motion (b). More generally it will have some angle ϕ to its direction of motion, which will change by $d\phi$ as it rounds a corner. What does one *expect* the magnitude of this change $d\phi$ to be? For $\phi = 0$ (a), the change $d\phi$ is $-\beta_r^2 \sin \alpha$. For $\phi = 90°$ (b) the change is zero. For a general angle ϕ one expects the change to have a value between zero and $-\beta_r^2 \sin \alpha$. Use Fig. 133 and the following outline to show that for small α and β_r^2 this change is in fact $-\beta_r^2 \sin \alpha \cos^2 \phi$. In addition to the indicial line PQ, draw its horizontal and vertical components PR and QR. From parts a and b we know that the vertical line QR will remain unrotated when the electron rounds the corner, whereas the horizontal line PR will rotate *clockwise* by an angle $\beta_r^2 \sin \alpha$. Show that for small angles α this has the effect of leaving the x component of PQ unchanged but reducing the y component by the value $(L \cos \phi)(\beta_r^2 \sin \alpha)$. Therefore the tangent of the new angle $\phi + d\phi$ is

(131)
$$\tan (\phi + d\phi) \approx \frac{L \sin \phi - (L \cos \phi)(\beta_r^2 \sin \alpha)}{L \cos \phi}$$
$$= \tan \phi - \beta_r^2 \sin \alpha$$

We wish to find $\tan (d\phi) \approx d\phi$. From Table 8

$$\tan (d\phi) = \tan [(\phi + d\phi) - \phi] = \frac{\tan (\phi + d\phi) - \tan \phi}{1 + \tan (\phi + d\phi) \tan \phi}$$

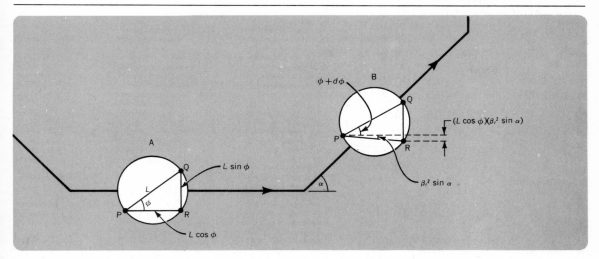

Fig. 133. General case of the change of orientation of electron as it changes its direction of motion.

Substitute from Eq. 131

$$\tan (d\phi) = \frac{\cancel{\tan \phi} - \beta_r{}^2 \sin \alpha - \cancel{\tan \phi}}{1 + (\tan \phi - \beta_r{}^2 \sin \alpha) \tan \phi}$$

$$= \frac{-\beta_r{}^2 \sin \alpha}{1 + \tan^2 \phi - \beta_r{}^2 \sin \alpha \tan \phi}$$

For very small α neglect the last term in the denominator. Then the denominator which remains is

$$1 + \tan^2 \phi = 1 + \frac{\sin^2 \phi}{\cos^2 \phi} = \frac{\cos^2 \phi + \sin^2 \phi}{\cos^2 \phi} = \frac{1}{\cos^2 \phi}$$

so that

(132) $\tan (d\phi) \approx d\phi \approx -\beta_r{}^2 \sin \alpha \cos^2 \phi$

This is the angle by which the electron spin axis will precess when it rounds a corner of angle α in the *general case* in which the projection of this spin axis on the plane of the orbit lies at an angle ϕ to the direction of motion of the electron.

(d) Equation 132 tells by what angle $d\phi$ the spin axis of the electron will precess when the electron rounds *one* corner of angle α. What will be the *total angle of precession* $\Delta\phi$ when the electron traverses *one complete orbit* (Figs. 127 and 128)? In one complete orbit there will be n changes of direction, each through an angle $\alpha = 2\pi/n$. For large n (small α) $\sin \alpha \approx \alpha$, so the total angle of precession for one orbit is

$$\Delta\phi \approx -\beta_r{}^2(n\alpha) \langle \cos^2 \phi \rangle_{\text{average}}$$
$$\approx -2\pi\beta_r{}^2 \langle \cos^2 \phi \rangle_{\text{average}}$$

What about the term $\langle \cos^2 \phi \rangle_{\text{average}}$? Assume that the total precession angle $\Delta\phi$ for one orbit is small (small β_r!). Then as the electron traverses its orbit the angle ϕ between the changing direction of motion and the projection of the spin axis on the plane of the orbit will take on all values between 0 and 2π. Show that in this case

$$\langle \cos^2 \phi \rangle_{\text{average}} = \frac{1}{2\pi} \int_0^{2\pi} \cos^2 \phi \, d\phi = \frac{1}{2}$$

Hence the total angle of precession of the electron spin in one complete orbit is

(133) $\Delta\phi = -\pi\beta_r{}^2$ (precession angle for one orbit)

(e) The electron moving with speed $\beta = \beta_r$ precesses through an angle $\Delta\phi = -\pi\beta_r{}^2 = -\pi\beta^2$ in one complete orbit. Show that it requires $2\pi/\Delta\phi = 2/\beta^2$ orbits for the electron to precess around once to its original orientation (through 2π radians). Now let ν_B be the *Bohr frequency* with which the electron orbits the nucleus. Show that the *Thomas precession frequency* ν_T—the frequency with which the electron spin precesses—can be expressed in terms of the Bohr frequency by the equation

(134) $\nu_T/\nu_B \approx 1/2 \, \beta^2$ (*Thomas precession frequency*)

Exercise 101 tells us that the speed of the electron in its orbit is, according to the simple Bohr theory,

$\beta = \dfrac{\alpha Z}{n} = \dfrac{Z}{137n}$. Here Z is the number of elementary charges on the nucleus and n is the energy level of the electron, with $n = 1$ for the lowest energy level. It follows that the frequency of the Thomas precession in an atom is given by the expression

(135) $\nu_T/\nu_B \approx 1/2 \left(\dfrac{Z}{137n}\right)^2$ (*Thomas precession frequency*)

(*Note:* In some atoms there is an additional precession of the electron spin due to the torque exerted on its magnetic moment by the magnetic field of the nucleus. For an electron in the inner orbit of the hydrogen atom this magnetic precession is in the *opposite* sense and has *twice* the magnitude of the Thomas precession. The net effect is thus *half* as great a frequency as would be predicted from magnetic interactions alone without using special relativity.)

G. INTERSTELLAR FLIGHT

104.* Difficulties of interstellar flight†

Throw all technological worries to the winds. *Evaluate the difficulties of interstellar space flight imposed by the theory of relativity alone.* A rocket engine is available (1984?) which has negligible mass. It draws in matter and antimatter in a controlled way from fuel tanks so as to produce only photons, and directs *all* of the resulting radiation out the back of the rocket. This engine powers a rocket whose structure and shielding have negligible mass. Contract specifications: Accelerate a payload to a speed such that the time dilation factor is ten, decelerate to visit the planets of a distant star (assumed to be at rest relative to our sun), and then return to earth using the same speed. The payload, including passengers, to be carried on the round trip is one hundred metric tons (100×10^3 kilograms).

(a) Use the results of Ex. 58 to find the total mass of fuel necessary for the round trip. (*Not* four times the mass necessary for a single acceleration from rest to the maximum speed of the rocket!)

(b) What is the distance (in light years) of the most distant star that can be visited in the lifetime of an astronaut (life expectancy in 1984: 100 years)? (For simplicity neglect the time during which the rocket engine is turned on compared to the much longer times of travel at uniform speed.) Approximately how much earth-time will elapse during such a trip?

(c) Assuming an interstellar density of one hydrogen atom per cubic centimeter, what is the kinetic energy of these atoms (in GeV) in the frame of the rocket moving at full speed? How does the number of these particles incident on a square meter of the forward surface of the rocket per second compare with the beam of a high-intensity proton accelerator (about 10^{12} protons per second, each with an energy of the order of 10 GeV)? To protect the workers at such an accelerator from over-irradiation a shield of ferroconcrete 3 or 4 meters thick is employed. Draw conclusions about space travel between stars!

---

†See Edward Purcell, in *Interstellar Communication*, edited by A. G. W. Cameron, (W. A. Benjamin, New York, 1963).

The Physics of Curved Spacetime

3

> *Only historical judgment liberates the spirit*
> *from the pressure of the past; it maintains its*
> *neutrality and seeks only to furnish light.*
> BENEDETTO CROCE

What spacetime physics means today can be seen in no way more clearly than by recalling how it was hammered out by workers of the past. The full course of the trial-by-combat evolution of the subject is a story too great to be compressed into these few pages; but a few great men and a few decisive turning points cannot be overlooked. By surveying this history we can hope to see, at least in broad outline, the relation between physics in a local Lorentz reference frame and physics in a larger region of spacetime, such as the space around the earth or the sun.

New features of physics in an extended region of spacetime

Galileo and Newton viewed motion as properly described with respect to a rigid Euclidean reference frame that extends through all space and endures for all time. This reference frame stands high above the battles of matter and energy. Within this ideal space of Galileo and Newton there acts a mysterious force of gravity, an interloper from the world of physics, a foreign influence, not described by geometry. In contrast, Einstein says there is no mysterious "gravitation," only the structure of spacetime itself. Climb into a space ship, he says, and see for yourself that there is no gravity there. Physics is locally gravity-free (Section 2 in Chapter 1). All free particles move in straight lines at uniform speed. In an inertial frame physics looks simple. But such frames are inertial only in a limited region of spacetime—a fact emphasized here by repeated use of the word *local* in describing inertial frames. Complications arise in describing the relation between the direction of motion of a particle in one local frame and the direction of motion of the same particle as observed from a nearby local frame. Any difference between the direction in one local frame and that in a nearby frame is described in terms of the "curvature of spacetime," Einstein tells us. The existence of this curvature destroys the possibility of describing motion with respect to a single ideal Euclidean reference frame that pervades all space. What is simple is only the geometry in a region small enough to look flat. In brief, Einstein makes use of many local regions in each of which the geometry is Lorentzian ("special relativity"); the laws of gravitation arise from the lack of ideality in the relation between one local region and the next (gravitation; spacetime curvature; "general relativity"). Newton has one global reference frame, but within this reference frame no satellite is ever gravity-free, and no particle ever moves in a straight line at constant speed.

Einstein versus Newton: many inertial frames, each local, versus one global frame

How did the views of Galileo, Newton, and Einstein develop? And what is the concrete substance of the strange phrase "curvature of spacetime?"

No disagreement is more widely known than that between Galileo's experiments on free fall and Aristotle's statement that "the downward movement of a mass of gold or lead, or of any other body endowed with weight, is quicker in proportion to its size." Some years before Galileo's experiments, Moletti of Padua had stated that lead and wood weights fall at the same rate, but his statement was not enough to prove Aristotle wrong. It took Galileo to demonstrate the point. Whether Galileo dropped lead and wood weights from the Leaning Tower of Pisa is uncertain. It is certain that he carried out more decisive experiments of higher potential accuracy than the Leaning Tower experiment.†

Who could pioneer the statement of the law of accelerated fall without being drawn into the consideration of projectiles? Studying the motion of a projectile, and struggling for the simplest way to describe it, Galileo was led to the idea of superposed motion: a vertical motion of uniform downward acceleration combined with a horizontal motion of uniform translation. From here it was but a step to the principle of relativity in its first known formulation. Listen to the characters in Galileo's book:‡

Galileo: First known formulation of principle of relativity

SALVATIUS: Shut yourself up with some friend in the main cabin below decks on some large ship, and have with you there some flies, butterflies, and other small flying animals. Have a large bowl of water with some fish in it; hang up a bottle that empties drop by drop into a wide vessel beneath it. With the ship standing still, observe carefully how the little animals fly with equal speed to all sides of the cabin. The fish swim indifferently in all directions; the drops fall into the vessel beneath; and, in throwing something to your friend, you need throw it no more strongly in one direction than another, the distances being equal; jumping with your feet together, you pass equal spaces in every direction. When you have observed all these things carefully (though there is no doubt that when the ship is standing still everything must happen in this way), have the ship proceed with any speed you like, so long as the motion is uniform and not fluctuating this way and that. You will discover not the least change in all the effects named, nor could you tell from any of them whether the ship was moving or standing still. In jumping, you will pass on the floor the same spaces as before, nor will you make larger jumps toward the stern than toward the prow even though the ship is moving quite rapidly, despite the fact that during the time that you are in the air the floor under you will be going in a direction opposite to your jump. In throwing something to your companion, you will need no more force to get it to him whether he is in the direction of the bow or the stern, with yourself situated opposite. The droplets will fall as before into the vessel beneath without dropping toward the stern, although while the drops are in the air the ship runs many spans. The fish in their water will swim toward the front of their bowl with no more effort than toward the back, and will go with equal ease to bait placed anywhere around the edges of the bowl. Finally the butterflies and flies will continue their flights indifferently toward every

†For details see Galileo Galilei, *Dialogues Concerning Two New Sciences*, originally published March 1638; one modern translation is by Henry Crew and Alfonso de Salvio (Northwestern University Press, Evanston, Illinois, 1950).

‡Galileo Galilei, *Dialogue Concerning the Two Chief World Systems—Ptolemaic and Copernican*, first published February 1632; the translation quoted here is by Stillman Drake (University of California Press, Berkeley, 1962), pages 186ff. Galileo's writings, along with those of Dante, by reason of their strength and aptness, are treasures of human thought, studied today in Italy by secondary school students as part of a great literary heritage.

GALILEO GALILEI

Pisa, February 14, 1564—Arcetri, near Florence, January 8, 1642

"My portrait is now finished, a very good likeness, by an excellent hand."—September 22, 1635

★   ★   ★

"If ever any persons might challenge to be signally distinguished for their intellect from other men, Ptolemy and Copernicus were they that had the honor to see farthest into and discourse most profoundly of the World's systems."

★   ★   ★

"My dear Kepler, what shall we make of all this? Shall we laugh, or shall we cry?"

★   ★   ★

"When shall I cease from wondering?"

side, nor will it ever happen that they are concentrated toward the stern, as if tired out from keeping up with the course of the ship, from which they will have been separated during long intervals by keeping themselves in the air. . . .

SAGREDUS: Although it did not occur to me to put these observations to the test when I was voyaging, I am sure that they would take place in the way you describe. In confirmation of this I remember having often found myself in my cabin wondering whether the ship was moving or standing still; and sometimes at a whim I have supposed it going one way when its motion was the opposite. . . .

The Galilean principle of relativity is simple in this early formulation, yet not as simple as it might be. In what way is it simple? Physics looks the same in a ship moving uniformly as in a ship at rest. Relative uniform motion of two ships does not affect the laws of motion as described in either ship. In either ship one sees a free body undergoing uniform horizontal translation and uniform vertical acceleration. A ball falling straight down onto one ship appears from the other ship to follow a parabolic course; a ball falling straight down onto that second ship also appears to follow a parabolic course when observed from the first ship. The simplicity of the Galilean principle of relativity lies in the equivalence of the two earthbound frames and the symmetry between them. In what way is this simplicity not as great as it might be?

Extension of Galileo's reasoning from ship to space ship

In Galileo's account the frames of reference are not yet inertial. To make them so requires only a small conceptual step: from two sea-going ships to two space ships. Then up and down, north and south, east and west, all become alike. A ball untouched by force undergoes no acceleration. Its motion with respect to one space ship is as uniform as it is with respect to the other. This identity of the law of free motion in all inertial reference frames is what one means today by the Galilean principle of relativity.

Galileo could not by any stretch of the imagination have asked his hearer to place himself in a space ship in the year 1632. Yet he could have described the greater simplicity of physics when viewed from such a vantage point. Bottles, drops of water, and all other test objects float at rest or move at uniform velocity. The zero acceleration of every nearby object relative to the space ship would have been intelligible to Galileo of all people. Who had established more clearly than he that relative to the earth all nearby objects have a common acceleration? And how could he be surprised that an astronaut would float in space near his space ship (Fig. 134)?

Other developments of recent times have further dramatized Galileo's principle of identical fall without changing it. Roll, Krotkov, and Dicke[†] have verified the identity of acceleration of aluminum and gold to three parts in 10^{11}.

"Conscience-guided" space ship. What guides the conscience?

Martin Schwarzschild has proposed a "conscience-guided" space ship designed to assure that the same motion will be maintained when thin air or solar wind resists the ship as when it moves through perfect emptiness. The "conscience" is a second satellite that floats inside the larger ship (Fig. 135). It undergoes no acceleration relative to the ship as long as the ship moves freely. When relative motion does occur, the error in the tracking must be due to the space ship. By small rockets the space ship gives itself a brief spurt of acceleration and comes back into step with the inner conscience. Though resistance is

---

[†]P. G. Roll, R. Krotkov, and R. H. Dicke, Annals of Physics, **26,** 442 (1964).

Fig. 134. Major Edward White does not experience any acceleration relative to the space ship carrying Major James McDivitt except when he spurts oxygen gas out of the jet he holds in his right hand. California is seen a hundred miles below. Gemini flight of June 3–7, 1965. (Photograph courtesy of the National Aeronautics and Space Administration.)

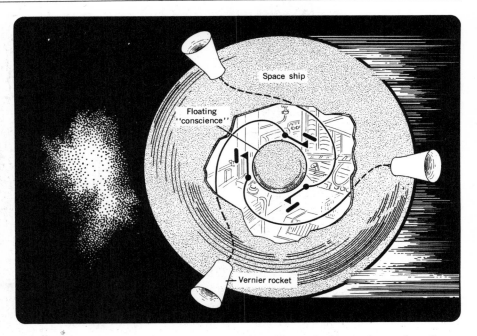

Fig. 135. "Conscience-guided" space ship. Any obstruction to its free motion, such as the gas cloud at the left, results in a velocity change. The floating "conscience"—a smaller satellite inside the space ship—is protected from impact on the gas cloud. It continues in its original state of motion. Observing this conscience through sensing devices (symbolized here by contact switches) the space ship becomes aware that it is not keeping up with the motion demanded by the inner satellite. The touched switch fires the opposite vernier rocket long enough to bring the space ship back into concord with its conscience.

present, the rocket power overcomes this resistance. The space ship takes the same course that it would have taken had both resistance and power been absent.

As space ship and conscience come to empty space, they fly through it in perfect step, without use of rockets or sensing devices. What a remarkable harmony they present! The inner satellite does not see outer space. It does not touch, feel, or see the ship that surrounds it on every side. Yet it follows faithfully the ship's route through spacetime. Moreover, the tracking is as perfect when the satellite is made of aluminum as when it is made of gold. How do consciences—of whatever atomic constitution and whatever construction—know enough to follow a standard track? Where does mass get its moving orders?

Locally, answers Einstein. From a distance, answers Newton.

Einstein says the satellite gets its information in the simplest way possible. It responds to the structure of spacetime in its immediate vicinity. It moves on a straight line in the local inertial frame. No simpler motion and no straighter motion could be imagined.

Newton says the satellite gets its information about how to move from a distance, via a "force of gravitation." Motion relative to what? Motion relative to an ideal God-given never-changing Euclidean reference frame that per-

ISAAC NEWTON

Woolsthorpe, December 25, 1642—Kensington (London), March 20, 1727

"The marble index of a mind forever
Voyaging through strange seas of thought, alone."—*Wordsworth*

★   ★   ★

"I do not know what I may appear to the world; but to myself I seem to have been only like a boy, playing on the sea-shore, and diverting myself, in now and then finding a smoother pebble or a prettier shell than ordinary, whilst the great ocean of truth lay all undiscovered before me."—*Newton*

★   ★   ★

"Why do I call him a magician? Because he looked on the whole universe and all that is in it as a *riddle*, as a secret which could be read by applying thought to certain evidence, certain mystic clues which God had laid about the world to allow a sort of philosopher's treasure hunt to the esoteric brotherhood. He believed that these clues were to be found partly in the evidence of the heavens and in the constitution of elements (and that is what gives the false suggestion of his being an experimental natural philosopher), but also partly in certain papers and traditions handed down by the brethren in an unbroken chain back to the original cryptic revelation in Babylonia. He regarded the universe as a cryptogram set by the Almighty—just as he himself wrapt the discovery of the calculus in a cryptogram when he communicated with Leibnitz. By pure thought, by concentration of mind, the riddle, he believed, would be revealed to the initiate."—*Keynes*†

†Reprinted by permission of the publisher, Horizon Press, from *Essays in Biography* by John Maynard Keynes. Copyright 1951.

vades all space and endures for all time. He tells us that the satellite would have moved along an ideal straight line in this global frame had not the earth deflected it. How can this ideal line be seen? How sad! There is nothing, absolutely nothing, that ever moves along this ideal line. It is an entirely imaginary line. But it nevertheless has a simple status, Newton tells us, in this respect: Every kind of satellite, going at whatever speed, is deflected away from this ideal line at the same acceleration (Fig. 136).

Physics is simple only when analyzed locally

Einstein says: Face it. There is no ideal background Euclidean reference frame that extends over all space. And why say there is, when even according to Newton no particle, not even a light ray, ever moves along a straight line in that ideal reference frame. Why say spacetime is Euclidean on a large scale when nothing directly evidences that hypothesis? To try to set up an all-encompassing Euclidean reference frame and attempt to refer motion to it is the wrong way to do physics. Don't try to describe motion relative to faraway objects. *Physics is simple only when analyzed locally.* And locally the world line that a satellite follows is already as straight as any world line can be. Forget all this talk about "deflection" and "force of gravitation." I'm inside a space ship. Or I'm floating outside and near it. Do I feel any "force of gravitation?" Not at all. Does the space ship "feel" such a force? No. Then why talk about it? Recognize that the space ship and I are traversing a region of spacetime free of all force. Acknowledge that the motion through that region is already ideally straight.

How can one display the straightness of the motion? Set up a local lattice of meter sticks and clocks, a local inertial reference frame—also called a Lorentz reference frame (Section 2). How does one know the frame is inertial? Watch every particle, check every light ray, test that they all move in straight lines at uniform speed relative to this frame. And having thus verified that the frame is inertial, note that the space ship too moves at a constant speed in a straight line—or remains at rest—relative to this local inertial frame. What could be simpler than the moving orders for mass: "Follow a straight line in the local inertial reference frame." Does a satellite have to know the location of the earth and the moon and the sun before it knows how to move? Not at

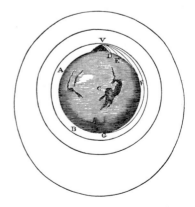

Fig. 136. In Newtonian mechanics different particles going at different speeds are all deflected away from the ideal straight line with equal acceleration. In this respect there is no difference in principle between the fall of a projectile and the motion of a satellite. In this picture of Newton's, published in 1686, cannon of successively greater power mounted on a mountaintop fire out their balls horizontally. The most powerful cannon launches a satellite. The outer two curves show other possible satellite orbits.†

†How Newton came only in stages to the solution of the problem of fall is told nowhere with such care for the fascinating documentation as in Alexander Koyré, "A Documentary History of the Problem of Fall from Kepler to Newton," Transactions of the American Philosophical Society, **45,** part 4, (1955). Picture from Newton's *Principia Philosophiae Naturalis Principia Mathematica*, Joseph Streater, London, July 5, 1686; Motte translation into English revised and edited by Florian Cajori and published in two paperback volumes (University of California Press, Berkeley, 1962).

all. Surrounded on all sides by the black walls of a space ship, it has only to sense the local structure of spacetime—right where it is—in order to follow the correct track.

Splendid! And also simple! But isn't Einstein's view of motion *too* simple? We started out interested in the motion of a space ship around the earth and in "gravitation." We seem to have ended up talking only about the motion of the space ship—or of a satellite—relative to a strictly local inertial reference frame, a trivially simple straight-line motion. Where is there any evidence of "gravitation" to be seen in that? None. This is the great lesson of Einstein: *Spacetime is always and everywhere locally Lorentzian.* No evidence of gravitation whatsoever is to be seen by following the motion of a single particle.

One has to observe the *relative* acceleration of *two* particles slightly separated from each other to have any proper measure of a gravitational effect. Separated by how much? That depends upon the sensitivity of the measuring equipment. Two ball bearings with a horizontal separation of 25 meters, dropped from a height of 250 meters with zero initial relative velocity, hit the ground 7 seconds later (21×10^8 meters of light-travel time) with a separation that has been reduced by 10^{-3} meter (Section 2 and Fig. 5; calculation in Ex. 32). Two ball bearings with a *vertical* separation of 25 meters, dropped from a height of 250 meters with zero initial relative velocity, in the same 7 seconds increase their separation by 2×10^{-3} meter (Fig. 6). To measuring equipment unable to detect such small relative displacements the ball bearings count as moving in one and the same inertial reference frame. No evidence for gravitation is to be seen. More sensitive apparatus detects the "tide-producing action" of gravity—the accelerating shortening of separations parallel to the earth's surface, the accelerating lengthening of vertical separations. Each tiny ball bearing still moves in a straight line in its own local inertial reference frame. But now—with the new precision—the region of validity of the one inertial reference frame does not reach out far enough to give a proper account of the motion of the other steel ball. The millimeter or two discrepancy is the way "gravity" manifests itself.

Here gravitation is displayed as a local phenomenon. No mention here of the distance of the steel balls from the center of the earth! No mention here of acceleration relative to that center! The only accelerations that come into consideration are those of nearby particles relative to each other ("tidal accelerations;" the same as the relative accelerations described on page 9). These relative accelerations are doubled when the separations are doubled. The true measure of the tide-producing effect has therefore the character of "an acceleration per unit of separation." Let the acceleration be measured in meters of distance per meter of light-travel time per meter of light-travel time; that is, in units m/m^2 or $1/m$. Then the measure of the tide-producing effect (different in different directions) has the units (acceleration/distance) or ($1/m^2$). In the example, in the horizontal directions (x and y) this quantity has the value $[-0.001 \ m/(21 \times 10^8 \ m)^2]/25 \ m = -9 \times 10^{-24} \ m^{-2}$ and in the vertical (z) direction twice the value, and the opposite sign: $+ 18 \times 10^{-24} \ m^{-2}$. The tide-producing effect is small but it is real and it is observable. More, it is a locally defined quantity. And Einstein tells us we must focus our attention on locally defined quantities if we want a simple description of nature.

Not one particle, but the relative motion of two particles, is appropriate indicator of gravitation

FIG. 5, PAGE 8

FIG. 6, PAGE 8

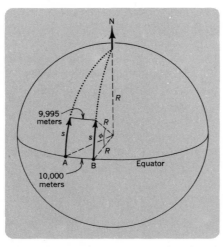

Fig. 137. Travelers A and B, starting out parallel, and deviating neither to the left nor to the right, nevertheless find themselves approaching each other after they have traveled some distance. Interpretation 1: Some mysterious force of "gravitation" is at work. Interpretation 2: They are traveling on a curved surface.

Einstein says more: that this "tide-producing effect" does not require for its explanation some mysterious force of gravitation, propagated through spacetime, and additional to the structure of spacetime. Instead, it can and should be described in terms of the geometry of spacetime itself: as the **curvature of spacetime**. Though Einstein speaks of four-dimensional spacetime, his concepts of curvature can be illustrated in terms of two-dimensional geometry on the surface of a sphere (Fig. 137).

The Parable of the Two Travelers

One traveler, A, stands at the equator, ready to travel straight north. A's companion B, standing against him shoulder-to-shoulder, wheels 90 degrees and marches straight east. He paces off $(\Delta x)_0 = 10$ kilometers along the equator. There he again turns a sharp 90 degrees and faces straight north. Both men now start north and travel 200 kilometers (Fig. 137). In the beginning their tracks are strictly parallel. Moreover, no travelers can be more conscientious than they are in continuing precisely in their original directions. They deviate neither to the right nor to the left. Yet an umpire sent out to measure their separation after their 200-kilometer treks finds it to be less than the original 10 kilometers. Why? We know perfectly well: because the surface of the globe is curved. Ultimately they will meet at the north pole. Let the latitude be called ϕ ($\phi = 0°$, $\cos \phi = 1$, at the equator; $\phi = 90°$, $\cos \phi = 0$ at the north pole). Then the separation of the travelers at any intermediate latitude is (10 kilometers) $\cos \phi$. For latitudes only a little above the equator the first two terms in the power series expansion of the cosine are adequate. They give for the separation the expression

$$\Delta x = (\Delta x)_0 (1 - \phi^2/2)$$

Moreover, the angle ϕ is given by the northbound arc distance s divided by the radius R of the globe, $\phi = s/R$. Thus the shrinkage of the original separation $(\Delta x)_0$ is given by the expression

$$(\Delta x)_0 - (\Delta x) = (\Delta x)_0 (\phi^2/2) = (\Delta x)_0 (s^2/2R^2)$$

With an original separation of $(\Delta x)_0 = 10$ kilometers, a trek of $s = 200$ kilometers, and a radius of $R = 6371$ kilometers, the shortening is calculated to be 0.005 kilometers, or 5 meters. This amount is impressive, not by reason of its magnitude (what significance have 5 meters in 10,000 meters?), but because there is any such discrepancy at all. There would be no discrepancy if the 10 kilometer $\times$ 200 kilometer region checked upon in this manner by the travelers were flat. The existence of the discrepancy is the most direct evidence that the geometry used to describe the two-dimensional surface of the globe must be the geometry of a curved surface.

What is the appropriate way to describe and to measure quantitatively this curvature? *Curvature measured by* How can one arrive at a number that is independent of the length of the trek and the *change in separation of* separation between the travelers—a number that describes the local curvature, not the *two originally parallel* travelers? Note first that the distance between A and B shortens at an accelerating pace. *ideal lines* Therefore the appropriate quantity to talk about is this acceleration. How can one evaluate it? Use the fact that relative acceleration is rate of change of relative velocity, and that relative velocity in turn is rate of change of separation. Start then by considering the separation

$$\Delta x = (\Delta x)_0 - (\Delta x)_0 (s^2/2R^2)$$

Travel a small additional distance, so that s increases to $s + ds$, where ds is very small compared with all other quantities that come to attention. In consequence of this additional movement the separation shortens to

$$\Delta x_{new} = (\Delta x)_0 - (\Delta x)_0 (s + ds)^2/2R^2$$

Evaluate this expression, recognizing that the square of the small quantity ds can be neglected:

$$\Delta x_{new} = (\Delta x)_0 - (\Delta x)_0 (s^2 + 2s\,ds)/2R^2$$

Take the difference between the new separation and the previous separation. Divide this difference by the supplementary distance, ds, and find the rate of change of the separation, or the "velocity of separation":

(136) $\left(\begin{array}{c}\text{"velocity of}\\ \text{separation"}\end{array}\right) = \dfrac{(\text{change of separation})}{(\text{supplementary distance of travel})}$

$$= \frac{(\Delta x)_{new} - (\Delta x)}{ds} = -(\Delta x)_0\, s/R^2$$

The velocity of separation is zero when A and B start off at the equator ($s = 0$) and this is so for a simple reason—the routes of A and B are then exactly parallel. But the farther they travel on their way—or the larger s is in Eq. 136—the more rapidly A and B find themselves approaching each other. The "acceleration of the separation" is measured by the ratio

(137) $\left(\begin{array}{c}\text{"acceleration of}\\ \text{separation"}\end{array}\right) = \dfrac{(\text{"velocity of separation"})}{\left(\begin{array}{c}\text{distance from place where}\\ \text{velocity of separation was zero}\end{array}\right)}$

$$= \frac{-(\Delta x)_0\, s/R^2}{s} = -(\Delta x)_0/R^2$$

If the two travelers had started with twice the original separation $(\Delta x)_0$, the "acceleration of the separation" would have been twice as great, according to Eq. 137. In other words, the true measure of the curvature of the globe is given, not by the "acceleration of the separation" itself, but by the "acceleration of the separation per unit of original separation":

$$\left(\begin{array}{c}\text{measure of}\\ \text{curvature}\end{array}\right) = \dfrac{\left(\begin{array}{c}\text{"acceleration of}\\ \text{separation"}\end{array}\right)}{(\text{original separation})} = \frac{-(\Delta x)_0/R^2}{(\Delta x)_0} = -1/R^2$$

*Tide-producing rela-
tive acceleration in
gravitational physics
understood as curva-
ture of spacetime
geometry*
This quantity has the small but detectable magnitude $-1/ (6.371 \times 10^5 \text{ meters})^2 =$ $2.5 = 10^{-14} \text{ m}^{-2}$. How close the analogy to the "tide-producing effect" of page 183! Even the units are the same! This parallelism between the geometrical concept of "curvature" and the gravitational concept of "tide-producing effect" foreshadows Einstein's geometrical interpretation of gravity.

The two travelers, who started out so conscientiously on parallel treks, and deviated neither to the left nor to the right, have been told by the umpire of distances that despite all precautions they are now slowly approaching each other. They blame this development on the existence of some mysterious "gravitational force," which deflects their paths. They explore the nature of this "gravitational force." Repeating the travel with bicycles, motorcycles, light cars, and heavy cars, they find always the same shortening of the original separation. They know Newton's equation

$$\text{(force)} = \text{(mass) (acceleration)}$$

They conclude from the identity of the relative acceleration for all kinds of vehicles that the force exerted by "gravity" must be directly proportional to the mass of the vehicle.

Others take up the discussion with the announced intention of being much more careful. They say that gravitational force should be written as the product

$$\text{(gravitational force)} = \left(\begin{array}{c} \text{gravitational mass of} \\ \text{the object acted upon} \end{array} \right) \left(\begin{array}{c} \text{gravitational} \\ \text{field strength} \end{array} \right)$$

They put this force into Newton's equation of motion, strongly emphasizing that the mass that appears there is the "inertial mass" of the object acted upon. They end up with the equation

$$\left(\begin{array}{c} \text{inertial mass of} \\ \text{object acted upon} \end{array} \right) \left(\text{acceleration} \right) = \left(\begin{array}{c} \text{gravitational mass of} \\ \text{object acted upon} \end{array} \right) \left(\begin{array}{c} \text{gravitational} \\ \text{field strength} \end{array} \right)$$

or

$$\text{acceleration} = \frac{\text{(gravitational mass)}}{\text{(inertial mass)}} \left(\begin{array}{c} \text{gravitational} \\ \text{field strength} \end{array} \right)$$

They say, "See here. You find the same acceleration for every vehicle you try. This means that the ratio of gravitational mass to inertial mass is the same for all sorts of objects. You have made a great discovery about mass."

All this time a space traveler has been looking down from on high. He has seen the many treks, watched the many measurements of distance shortening, and listened on his intercommunication system to these weighty discussions on "gravitation." He smiles. What is at issue—he knows—is not "gravitation" but the geometry of curved space. All this talk about the identity of "gravitational mass" and "inertial mass" completely obscures the truth. Curvature and nothing more is all that is required to describe the increasing rate at which A and B approach each other.

*Acceleration towards
earth understood as
totalized effect of rela-
tive accelerations, each
particle towards its
neighbor, in a chain of
test particles that
girdles the earth*
Einstein smiles, too. Curvature of spacetime and nothing more, he tells us, is all that is required to describe the millimeter or two change in separation of two ball bearings, originally 25 meters apart in space above the earth, and endowed at the start with zero relative velocity. Moreover, this curvature completely accounts for gravitation. "What a preposterous claim," is one's first reaction. "How can such minor—and slow—changes in the distance between one tiny ball and another offer any kind of understanding of the enormous velocity with which a falling mass hits the earth?" The answer is simple: many local reference frames, fitted together, make up the global structure of space-

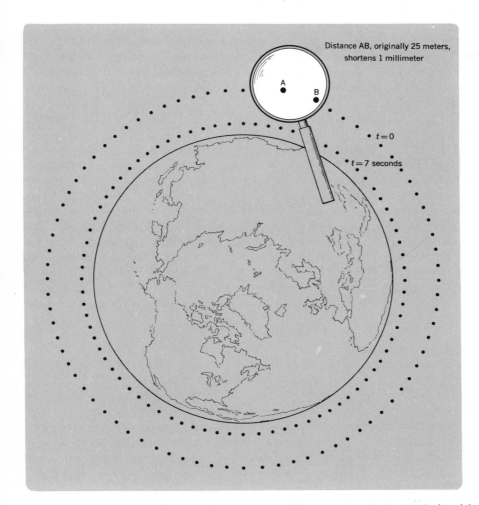

Fig. 138. Local curvature adding up to the appearance of long-range gravitation. In the inertial frame associated with ball bearing A, the second ball bearing B shortens its original separation (25 meters) by 1 millimeter in the course of 7 seconds (local curvature of geometry near AB). A similar shortening takes place between every other adjacent pair of tiny spheres. In consequence the entire circle shrinks in the course of 7 seconds by the fraction 1 millimeter/25 meters = 1/25,000 of its original value. The distance from the center of the earth drops by the same fraction; that is, by the amount (1/25,000)(6,371,000 meters) = 250 meters. This apparently large-scale effect is caused—in Einstein's picture—by the addition of a multitude of small-scale effects: the changes in the local dimensions associated with the curvature of geometry (failure of B to *remain* at rest as viewed in the inertial frame associated with A).

time. Each local Lorentz frame can be regarded as having one of the ball bearings at its origin. When these ball bearings all simultaneously approach their neighbors ("curvature"), then the global spacetime structure itself shrinks—and pulls nearer to the earth (Fig. 138). Thus the totalized effect of many local manifestations of curvature gives the appearance of gravitation originating at long range from the earth as a whole.

In brief, the geometry used to describe motion in any local inertial frame is the flat-space geometry of Lorentz ("special relativity"). Relative to such a local inertial frame every nearby electrically neutral test particle moves in a straight line with constant velocity. Slightly more remote particles are detected as slowly changing their velocities, or the directions of their world lines in spacetime. These changes are described as "tidal effects of gravitation." They are understood as originating in the local curvature of spacetime. From the point of view of the student of local physics, gravitation shows itself not at all in the motion of one test particle, but only in the change of separations of two or more nearby test particles. However, these local dimension changes add up to an effect on the global spacetime structure that one interprets as "gravitation" in its everyday manifestations.

Einstein: Every feature of gravitation arises from local effects exclusively—from local curvature of spacetime

In contrast, Newton supposed the existence of one ideal overall reference frame:

"Absolute space, in its own nature, without relation to anything external, remains always similar and immovable."

"Absolute, true, and mathematical time, of itself, and from its own nature, flows equably without relation to anything external . . ."†

The ball bearing or space ship is regarded by Newton as actually accelerated with respect to this ideal frame. The "force" that accelerates it acts mysteriously across space and is produced by distant objects. That the man in the spaceship finds no evidence either of the acceleration or the force is an accident of nature, according to the Newtonian view. One can interpret this accident of nature as the fortuitous equality of "gravitational mass" and "inertial mass" or in some other way.

Newton's courage and judgment: do the doable; put off deeper understanding to a future age

In conversations with one of the authors of this book at various times over the years, Einstein emphasized his great respect for Newton and, in particular, his admiration for Newton's courage. He stressed that Newton was even better aware than his 17th century critics of the difficulties with the ideas of absolute space and time. However, to postulate those ideas was the only practical way at that time to get on with the task of describing motion. In effect, Newton chopped the problem of motion into two parts: (1) space and time and their meaning: ideas that were puzzling but usable and that were destined to be clarified only 230 years later and (2) the laws of acceleration with respect to that idealized spacetime: laws that Newton gave the world.

> Nature and Nature's laws lay hid in night:
> God said, Let Newton be! and all was light.
> —*Pope*

---

†Sir Isaac Newton, *Mathematical Principles of Natural Philosophy and His System of the World,* translated by Andrew Motte in 1729, revised and annotated by Florian Cajori (University of California Press, Berkeley, 1947), Vol. 2, page 6.

Hal McIntosh.   Courtesy of the Saturday Review

ALBERT EINSTEIN

Ulm, Germany, March 14, 1879—Princeton, New Jersey, April 18, 1955

"Newton himself was better aware of the weaknesses inherent in his intellectual edifice than the generations which followed him. This fact has always roused my admiration."

★   ★   ★

"Only the genius of Riemann, solitary and uncomprehended, had already won its way by the middle of the last century to a new conception of space, in which space was deprived of its rigidity, and in which its power to take part in physical events was recognized as possible."

★   ★   ★

"All of these endeavors are based on the belief that existence should have a completely harmonious structure. Today we have less ground than ever before for allowing ourselves to be forced away from this wonderful belief."†

---

†These three quotations come from Albert Einstein, *Essays in Science*, Philosophical Library, New York, 1934.

*Einstein's long-term
vision: description of
the physical universe in
terms of geometry
alone*
Today we find that Einstein's insight on the nature of space and time gives new understanding of gravitation as a purely geometric phenomenon. Einstein has died, bequeathing to the world his long-term still-unproven vision—that not only gravitation, but all of the physical universe can be completely described in terms of geometry and nothing more. It may help cast some perspective on physics to ask in a final dialogue what parts of physics lend themselves to simple description in terms of spacetime geometry and what parts are still far removed from any such understanding.

Table 15

OUTLINE OF PHYSICS AS SEEN FROM THE SPACETIME VIEWPOINT

How does a free and electrically uncharged particle move?

It follows the straightest possible track through spacetime, or, in the language of geometry, a "geodesic" world line.

How many components are there of this particle's energy-momentum 4-vector?

Four.

Are these components independent?

No. They are connected by one relation:

$$E^2 - (p^x)^2 - (p^y)^2 - (p^z)^2 = m^2$$

What is the effect of an electromagnetic field of force on the motion of an electrically *charged* particle?

At any given point the *actual* world line of the particle systematically deviates, or curves away, from that ideal geodesic world line which passes through the same point with the same slope. In the language of everyday physics, the charged particle *accelerates* away from an ideal neutral test particle.

How can one measure quantitatively the electromagnetic field in a given region of spacetime?

From the curvature of the world line of any charged particle—going through the given region in any timelike direction—away from the ideal geodesic which goes through the same point with the same slope. The electromagnetic field can be measured in all details of directional properties and magnitude in a locality—it so happens—by measuring the curvature of three world lines of charged particles passing through that region.

What is the number of independent components of the electromagnetic field at a point?

Six. To an observer in a *given* inertial frame the electromagnetic field manifests itself as separate electric and magnetic fields (three components for each). When a charged particle is instantaneously at rest in a given inertial frame, then its acceleration is governed only by the *electric* field (as measured in that frame). When the particle is in motion, the *magnetic* field makes a contribution to its acceleration ("magnetic force").

What is the effect of a gravitational field on the motion of one particle? (Think of gravitational field as properly defined, in a local *inertial* frame of reference, and as distinguished from the everyday or apparent gravitational field sensed, for example, on the surface of the earth, which is *not* an inertial frame and is *not* in free fall.)

None—because the standard of reference is the world line of the particle itself! (or the world line of an ideal test particle, which will follow the same track through spacetime).

What is the effect of a gravitational field on the *relative* motion of *two* test particles? (Assume, for simplicity, that they start on world lines initially parallel and are separated by a small but non-zero interval.) This effect is better described by the phrase "tidal field" than by the ambiguous phrase "gravitational field": "tidal" because the *relative* acceleration of water particles on opposite sides of the earth, caused by the moon, shows itself in tides.

The *separation* of the two test particles systematically changes with time measured from the moment of initial parallelism ("geodesic deviation").

How can it possibly be justified to give more attention to the tidal force—nearly negligible in its effect, for example, on a satellite, or a swarm of satellites—than to the everyday or apparent gravitational field that holds a satellite in orbit?

Because the simple way to analyze physics has been found to be a local analysis, an analysis with respect to a local inertial frame. *Locally*—to the man on the satellite—*there is no apparent gravitational field*. What interests him is his distances from his neighbors in the other ships of the fleet. These distances gradually change because of tidal forces in his neighborhood (forces produced at that location by the earth and—in lesser measure—by the moon and the sun).

How can one measure quantitatively the tidal field in a given vicinity of spacetime—or, in the language of the curved-space geometry of Riemann (1854) or of the general theory of relativity of Einstein (1916), the "curvature of spacetime" in that vicinity?

From the geodesic deviation between two world lines. The tidal field—or curvature—can be measured in all details of directional properties and magnitude in a given region by measuring the geodesic deviations between world lines of a suitable number of test particles passing through that region.

Why all this mention of "curvature of spacetime?" Why not merely record the *facts* about the tidal effects and forego this geometric interpretation?

Why—in everyday mensuration—should a geometrical explanation be given for the 90 degree angle in a 3:4:5 triangle? Why not simply record millions of assorted facts about all kinds of measurements? Answer (both to these questions and to the original questions at the left): Because a geometrical interpretation gives economy and insight in keeping track of the facts. And—in the case of gravitation—one has a simple interpretation for observations in terms of the geometry of curved spacetime. One no longer has to assume that the world is built of spacetime plus some mysterious magical "physical" force of gravitation, foreign to and added to spacetime.

Perhaps the geometrical description of *gravitation* does have a justification. But what about *electromagnetism?* After all, this familiar field is different in character from gravitation. Moreover, in accounting for gravitation has not geometry exhausted its possibilities? Must not electromagnetism now be interpreted as something nongeometrical, that is, as something foreign and mysterious and "physical" *added to* spacetime? And if one field (the electromagnetic field) is described as nongeometrical, then why make such a point about describing gravitation physics in terms of pure geometry?

For many everyday purposes it *is* convenient to think of electromagnetism as a foreign and "physical" field undergoing its own characteristic dynamical evolution in the arena of an ideal flat spacetime. Even in the everyday analysis of gravitational effects (slowly accelerated and not too massive bodies) one often simplifies and speaks as if gravitation were a "physical" field acting through—and immersed in—a flat spacetime background. However, as far as concerns questions of principle, it has long been known that *both* the electromagnetic field *and* the gravitational field—or better, the tidal field—*may be understood as aspects of the curvature of spacetime.* The tidal field at a point—in this description of nature—is only another name for the *curvature* of spacetime at that point. The *electromagnetic* field at a point is correlated with the variation of this curvature in the neighborhood of that point.

What has been the focus of attention in the analysis up to this point?

The effect of *field* on *particle* (or on the motion of *any* localized collection of mass-energy, such as a cloud of radiation).

What other aspect is required for a complete account of field physics?

The effect of a *particle* (or any localized collection of mass-energy) on the *field*.

Are there alternative and essentially equivalent ways to describe this effect of particle on field?

Yes. Description 1: Particle affects the field—that is, it alters the structure of spacetime—only in its own locality. This influence is propagated from place to place in the surrounding spacetime. Description 2: Disregard the details of this propagation process and simply note how much effect is produced at a distance by a particle that suddenly here and now undergoes a change of velocity ("action-at-a-distance point of view").

What are the effects produced in a given frame of reference by a particle *at rest* in that frame?

An electric field proportional to charge and inversely proportional to the square of the distance; no magnetic field; a tidal field proportional to mass and inversely proportional to the cube of the distance; no other components of the tidal field.

What are the effects produced in a given frame of reference by a particle *in uniform motion* in that frame?

Not only an electric field but also a magnetic field; not only the tidal field of a particle at rest but also additional tidal fields.

What are the effects produced by a momentarily *accelerated* particle at a distance that is great in comparison with the time (in meters!) during which the acceleration takes place?

Electric and magnetic fields proportional to the charge *and* the acceleration, and inversely proportional to the *first* power of the distance ("electromagnetic wave"). Propagated to that distance with the standard speed (light!). Tidal fields whose magnitudes are proportional to the mass *and* the acceleration, and inversely proportional to the *first* power of the distance. Propagated to that distance with the speed of light ("gravitational waves"; not yet detected; detectors now being constructed).

Is the *internal structure* of the elementary particles that produce these electromagnetic and gravitational effects at a distance understood?

There is no adequate description of the internal constitution of an elementary particle (electron, meson, proton, etc.). Understanding is lacking (1) despite the construction of accelerators of very high energy and the consequent steady accumulation of an enormous number of interesting and quantitative observations on the masses and transformations of "elementary" particles and (2) despite the discovery from time to time of striking and beautiful regularities in these data.

Not understanding the *structure* of elementary particles, how can one speak sensibly about their motions and interactions?

The *size* of these particles is very small compared to the *separation* of the particles in atoms, let alone compared to the distance from radio transmitter to radio receiver! Therefore, the details of internal structure are largely irrelevant—as the details of the internal structure of the earth are largely irrelevant for understanding the pull that it exerts on the moon.

Aware of this ignorance about the constitution of particles, how does one currently view them?

They are treated as strange and nongeometrical objects immersed in spacetime.

How can one possibly uphold the ideal of a purely geometrical description of nature when *particles* are foreign objects *immersed in* spacetime rather than objects *constructed out of* spacetime?

The best current thinking does not claim that particles are *not* built out of spacetime. Rather, it argues that one does not know enough even to discuss the issue intelligently. For the time being, as a means to get on with the world's work, and to deal with particles on a practical working basis, it makes sense to *treat* particles as if they are foreign objects. This working procedure does not exclude any longer-term possibility to account for a particle in terms of geometry—as one today accounts for the eye of a hurricane in terms of aerodynamics, and the throat of a whirlpool in terms of hydrodynamics.

To explain the world of everyday physics are any other basic concepts required in addition to those of particles (which may or may not be geometrical in constitution) and electromagnetic and gravitational fields (which one *does* know how to view in geometric terms)?

One more concept: the quantum principle, central to all of physics.

Is there any simple example of the kind of issue resolved by the quantum principle?

How a free particle (when it is in an essentially flat region of spacetime) moves from point A to point B along a straight line: (1) How this particle "smells out" the conceivable alternative routes that it might have followed. (2) The fuzzing out of the "straight" line that leads from A to B by reason of this process of "smelling out" that is continually going on. (3) How one defines more clearly—and measures—this kind of actual physical spread about the so-called "classical" or ideal route from A to B.

Do "quantum forces" hold an atom together? Do they bind one atom to another (chemistry!)? Are they responsible for the electrical conductivity and elasticity of solid bodies?

No! There is no such thing as a "quantum force." The only forces relevant to the structure of atoms, molecules, and solids are *electrical* forces. The existence of (1) these forces, (2) elementary particles, and (3) the *quantum principle*—which *governs the motion* of these *particles* under these *forces*—are all that is needed to account for the whole of everyday physics (excluding gravity).

Is there another example that illustrates fundamental processes illuminated by quantum physics?

An electron moving in a circular orbit about a proton, which is 1,836 times heavier, is held in orbit by the electrical attraction between the two particles: (1) How the *percentage* fuzzing out of this orbit is small when the orbit is large. (2) How the ability of the article to "smell out" the distance around the orbit makes it physically impossible for any orbit to exist except one in which a whole number of waves fit into the circuit ("quantum number," "quantum condition," see Ex. 101). (3) How great the percentage spread or *uncertainty* in position is for an orbit with a small quantum number. (4) The characteristic energy or "quantum level" associated with one of these "quantum states of motion." (5) The energy given out in the "transition" of an electron from one of these levels to another.

If all of physics is governed by the quantum principle (the exact formulation of which is not presented here), how can it make sense under *any* circumstances to speak of motion in the language of "classical" (nonquantum) physics? How can one analyze "position" and its change from "moment" to "moment" along the "world line" of a particle when there is an inescapable quantum spread or uncertainty in the route followed in spacetime?

The *fractional* spread in orbit dimensions is smaller and smaller for larger and larger orbits; that is, for orbits of large "quantum number." More generally, the predictions of quantum physics—though very different in *character* ("probabilities"; "quantum states") from those of classical physics ("when" and "where")—nevertheless in their practical *consequences* come closer and closer to those of classical mechanics in the limit of large quantum numbers (Niels Bohr's *principle of correspondence* between classical and quantum physics).

If one limits attention to conditions for which quantum uncertainties in position are of negligible importance, and for which *classical* (nonquantum) ideas are usable ("correspondence principle limit") is there really much physics that one can account for?

An enormous amount of physics! Mechanics of particles and of rigid bodies, planetary dynamics and gravitational phenomenology, dynamics of elastic media, aero- and hydrodynamics and sound, thermodynamics, electricity and magnetism, and geometrical and physical optics.

What additional areas of physics can one analyze successfully when one takes into account the *quantum principle* but still limits attention to electromagnetic and gravitational forces and to circumstances for which the *separations* between the particles are large compared to the sizes of the particles (no consideration of elementary-particle physics!)?

All of *atomic physics:* energy levels of all atoms; dimensions; emission of light in the transition of the atomic electrons from one state to another; effect on atom of bombardment with light or material particles. All the major features of *chemistry:* collisions between atoms; strength of binding of atoms into molecules; shape and dimension of molecules; normal and excited states of molecules; stiffness of molecules to deformation; mechanism of chemical reactions; mechanisms for the molecular storage and transfer of energy. All the major features of *solid state physics:* crystal structure; heat of formation; elasticity; thermal and electrical conductivity; superconductivity; coefficient of absorption of light; magnetic properties; dislocations and work-hardening; excitons, phonons, plasmons, magnons and other mechanisms for the storage and transfer of energy at the microscopic level in a solid. The *statistical mechanics* of thermal equilibrium in and among solids, liquids, gases, and their phases. Superfluidity. Rates of reaction.

What is a sample from the many topics in solid state physics that need further experimental and theoretical research?

An atom or molecule contained in the solid has been raised to an "excited energy state" as a consequence of absorbing light that came in from outside. What is the *mechanism* by which this concentration of *energy* is *degraded*, to diffuse outward through the solid in the form of heat or lattice vibrations ("phonons")?

Can one make any progress in analyzing systems where the separation between elementary particles is *not* very great compared to the size of a particle?

Yes: in *nuclear physics.* In a nucleus the separation between elementary particles is of the order of 10^{-13} centimeters compared to estimated effective dimensions of neutron and proton of the order of 10^{-14} centimeters. Enormous wealth of data on nuclear-energy levels, on nuclear dimensions, on the departure of atomic nuclei from sphericity, on nuclear radioactivity, on nuclear fission, and on nuclear transformations under bombardment. Many aspects of these effects are predictable with precision despite the fact that the nature of the principal forces at work is not known (they are neither electric nor gravitational but short-range "nucleonic forces" that fall off much faster than the inverse square of the distance). Other aspects of the observations are understood less well or not at all.

What is one of many topics in nuclear physics that appears ripe for further experimental and theoretical investigation at this time?

The mechanism of fission; in particular, the mechanism by which a helium nucleus or heavy hydrogen nucleus is occasionally given off simultaneously with the two much larger fragments resulting from the fission of a uranium or other heavy nucleus.

Is there any simple way to compare the relative importance of (1) the internal interactions responsible for elementary-particle structure, (2) nuclear, (3) electric, and (4) gravitational interactions in a given situation?

Yes! Evaluate the *energy* associated with each of these interactions!

What are the relative values of these four kinds of energy in a sphere of iron one meter in radius?

(1) Internal energy of elementary particles (as measured by the rest masses of the constituent neutrons and protons): 3.3×10^4 kilograms. (2) Nuclear energy (as measured by change of mass in combining neutrons and protons to make iron Fe^{56}): 3.1×10^2 kilograms. (3) Electric energy (as measured by the binding of the electrons to the iron nuclei plus the binding energy of the resulting iron atoms into the crystal lattice of solid iron—this energy then translated into mass units): about 2×10^{-2} kilogram. (4) Gravitational energy (energy required to take the iron atoms to infinite separation against the force of gravitation—this energy then translated into mass units): about 5×10^{-19} kilogram.

Which of these four kinds of energy increases most rapidly as the number of particles increases?

The gravitational energy—because each particle interacts gravitationally with every other particle.

Is there any circumstance under which the relative magnitudes of these four energies are radically altered?

Yes: in a sufficiently massive star (if cold, a star with mass of approximately the same magnitude as that of the sun, 2×10^{30} kilograms; if hot, of greater mass—being more dilute, so that the gravitational forces have to act over a greater distance).

In an astronomical object that is sufficiently massive or sufficiently compact or both, can gravitational forces of attraction overwhelm the forces responsible for the internal structure of elementary particles and cause the elementary particles to disappear from existence?

The answer is not known although this is a subject of great interest, now intensively investigated under the name of "gravitational collapse." Interest in this hypothetical mechanism was greatly stimulated by the discovery in January, 1963, of a so-called "quasistellar source"—part of a galaxy at a distance of 2×10^9 light years—that in the astronomically short time of about 10^6 years or less produced energy (about 10^{54} joules) equivalent to the amount that would be produced by the complete conversion into energy of the mass of about 10^7 suns. Many more quasistellar sources (name now shortened to "quasars") have now been, and continue to be, discovered.

Are there any other circumstances for which effects similar to those in gravitational collapse are expected—the disappearance of elementary particles—or the reverse process in which pressures are relieved and expansion occurs?

Conditions existing during early stages of the expansion of the universe and late stages of the subsequent recontraction of the universe.

What evidence is there for the expansion of the universe?

Galaxies receding, galaxies twice as far away receding twice as fast, etc., *as if* all had started from a common point with different velocities about 14×10^9 years ago.

What is the dominating force in the large-scale dynamics of the universe?

Gravitation (curvature of the structure of spacetime).

Index

Subentries are arranged according to the logic of development in the text, rather than alphabetically. Key concepts are set in **boldface**. Page numbers of topics covered in the exercises are preceded by the parenthesis (Ex).

Summary of Chapter 1 | COMPARISON BETWEEN EUCLIDEAN AND LORENTZ TRANSFORMATIONS

EUCLIDEAN GEOMETRY OF THREE DIMENSIONS	LORENTZ GEOMETRY OF FOUR DIMENSIONS

Problem: to find a relation between

the coordinates of a point in an unrotated coordinate system (unprimed coordinates!) and the coordinates of the same point in a rotated coordinate system (primed coordinates).	the coordinates (including time) of an event in the laboratory frame (unprimed coordinates!) and the coordinates of the same event in a rocket frame (primed coordinates).

Specializations accepted in order to simplify analysis

the origins coincide	the origins coincide at $t = t' = 0$ (reference event)
rotation in xy plane; y' axis inclined at angle θ_r to y axis (slope $S_r = \tan \theta_r$)	rocket frame moves in positive x direction with velocity parameter θ_r relative to laboratory (velocity $\beta_r = \tanh \theta_r$)
$z = z'$	$y = y'$, $\quad z = z'$
all coordinates measured in meters	all coordinates measured in meters (including time: "meters of light travel time")

The invariant that has the same value in both frames is

$(\text{length})^2 = L^2$ $= x^2 + y^2 + z^2$	$\left(\dfrac{\text{spacelike}}{\text{interval}}\right)^2 = \sigma^2 = -\left(\dfrac{\text{timelike}}{\text{interval}}\right)^2 = -\tau^2$ $= x^2 + y^2 + z^2 - t^2$
therefore	therefore
$x^2 + y^2 = x'^2 + y'^2$	$x^2 - t^2 = x'^2 - t'^2$

A way to satisfy this last condition uses the general relation

$\cos^2 \theta + \sin^2 \theta = 1$	$\cosh^2 \theta - \sinh^2 \theta = 1$
for circular functions	for hyperbolic functions

Transformation from primed to unprimed coordinates

$x = x' \cos \theta_r + y' \sin \theta_r$ $\quad = \dfrac{x' + S_r y'}{(1 + S_r^2)^{1/2}}$ $y = -x' \sin \theta_r + y' \cos \theta_r$ $\quad = \dfrac{-S_r x' + y'}{(1 + S_r^2)^{1/2}}$ (Euclidean transformation)	$x = x' \cosh \theta_r + t' \sinh \theta_r$ $\quad = \dfrac{x' + \beta_r t'}{(1 - \beta_r^2)^{1/2}}$ $t = x' \sinh \theta_r + t' \cosh \theta_r$ $\quad = \dfrac{\beta_r x' + t'}{(1 - \beta_r^2)^{1/2}}$ (Lorentz transformation)

Transformation from unprimed to primed coordinates

$x' = x \cos \theta_r - y \sin \theta_r$ $\quad = \dfrac{x - S_r y}{(1 + S_r^2)^{1/2}}$ $y' = x \sin \theta_r + y \cos \theta_r$ $\quad = \dfrac{S_r x + y}{(1 + S_r^2)^{1/2}}$	$x' = x \cosh \theta_r - t \sinh \theta_r$ $\quad = \dfrac{x - \beta_r t}{(1 - \beta_r^2)^{1/2}}$ $t' = -x \sinh \theta_r + t \cosh \theta_r$ $\quad = \dfrac{-\beta_r x + t}{(1 - \beta_r^2)^{1/2}}$

An important law of addition of

slopes: If a line makes an angle θ' with respect to the rotated y' axis, then the line will make an angle θ with respect to the unrotated y axis given by the expression $\theta = \theta' + \theta_r$ or, in terms of relative *slopes* $\tan \theta = \dfrac{\tan \theta' + \tan \theta_r}{1 - \tan \theta' \tan \theta_r}$ $S = \dfrac{S' + S_r}{1 - S' S_r}$	*velocities:* If a bullet moves in the x direction with a velocity parameter θ' with respect to the primed rocket frame, then the bullet will move with a velocity parameter θ with respect to the unprimed laboratory frame given by the expression $\theta = \theta' + \theta_r$ or, in terms of relative *velocities* $\tanh \theta = \dfrac{\tanh \theta' + \tanh \theta_r}{1 + \tanh \theta' \tanh \theta_r}$ $\beta = \dfrac{\beta' + \beta_r}{1 + \beta' \beta_r}$